T0090729

COLLAPSE II

First published in 2007 in an edition of 1000
comprising numbered copies 1–950
and 50 *hors-commerce* copies

Reissued Edition 2012

ISBN 978-0-9567750-4-7

Published by
Urbanomic Media Ltd.
The Old Lemonade Factory
Windsor Quarry
Falmouth
TR11 3EX
UK

Distributed by the MIT Press,
Cambridge, Massachusetts and London, England

All texts remain © of the respective authors.
Please address all queries to the editor at the above address.

www.urbanomic.com

COLLAPSE

Philosophical Research and Development

VOLUME II

Edited by
Robin Mackay

URBANOMIC

FALMOUTH

COLLAPSE II

March 2007
EDITOR: Robin Mackay
ASSOCIATE EDITORS: Damian Veal, Ray Brassier

Editorial Introduction

Robin Mackay

This volume comprises a selection of texts, some of which would not have existed, others of which may not have been published, and none of which would have ended up in such odd company, were it not for the underlying vision of **COLLAPSE**, which seeks to generate and to bring together philosophical writing from varying perspectives with work drawn from other fields, in order to challenge institutional and disciplinary orthodoxies and to set in motion new syntheses. This second volume has emerged, as did its predecessor, from the combination of this overall vision, a collaborative process with the authors, and a set of happy coincidences. The result is, we hope you will agree, a rich and rewarding set of conceptual conjunctions.

The first part of the volume coalesced into a 'dossier' centring on the work of QUENTIN MEILLASSOUX, whose recent book *After Finitude*[1] is a work designed to fundamentally disrupt that dubious consensus within continental philosophy which emphasises the primacy of the relation of consciousness to the world – however that may be construed – over any supposed objectivity of 'things themselves'. It may seem that, in the wake of Kant's Copernican Revolution, this 'correlationist' credo – the injunction that, unable to know things 'in themselves', philosophy must limit itself to the adumbration of 'conditions of experience' – is unassailable, something that only the most unsophisticated, 'pre-critical' thinker would seek to challenge. And yet, once this consensus is broken, the consequences are startling.

In 'The Enigma of Realism' RAY BRASSIER gives a lucid exposition of this transvaluation of the stakes of contemporary philosophical thought. However, questioning whether Meillassoux is right to single out the 'arche-fossil' as the privileged site of this contestation, Brassier ultimately suggests that the curse of correlationism runs deeper still, and intimates that an even more thoroughgoing 'decontamination' of the tools used to critique the current *doxa* might yet be necessary. Brassier's text already takes us beyond the scope of Meillassoux's book, identifying a number of serious problems which he identifies as issuing from a 'fundamental dilemma' relating to Meillassoux's proposal to reinstate some form of intellectual or mathematical intuition. Brassier's text almost tends toward a dialogic form, as Meillassoux responds to subsequent objections with further refinements of his own position.

---

1. *Après la Finitude: Essai sur la necessité de la contingence* (Paris: Seuil, 2006). English translation *After Finitude* (trans. R. Brassier) (London: Continuum, forthcoming 2008).

Editorial Introduction

Meillassoux's audacious countermanding of philosophy's historical abjuration of speculative rationalism proceeds via the positing of the 'necessity of contingency' indexed to an absolute time. In 'Potentiality and Virtuality' he sketches a route to this principle via a discussion of Hume's problem of causality. With admirable panache, Meillassoux rescues this perennially abandoned problem from its alleged epistemological dissolution and restores it to its most potent ontological form. This is a question of resisting the pragmatist referral of ontological problematics to heuristic solutions rooted in empirical consensus: the apparent necessity of a recourse to an empirical *genesis* of the law rather than a metaphysical *grounding* for it, Meillassoux suggests, results from supplementing the terms of the problem with a 'common-sense' judgement that is in turn rooted in an inappropriate application of probabilistic thinking. Conversely, a philosophical enterprise with the courage of its conviction in rationality would refuse to concede this 'defeat of reason', daring to affirm on the contrary that there is in fact no reason to postulate the constancy of natural laws.

Thus Meillassoux sketches the contours of a bold reclamation of rationalism issuing from the refusal of particular forms of (probabilistic) reasoning embedded in 'common-sense'. Rather than seeking a 'meta-law' to subtend the laws of reality, Meillassoux instead loosely binds reality within the singular rational principle of an 'absolute contingency'.

It is perhaps owing in part to his relative independence from the philosophical issues at stake here that our interview with theoretical cosmologist ROBERTO TROTTA serves in many ways as the centrepiece of this discussion. Following as it does upon the more abstractly philosophical discussions of the previous two papers, and yet circling around essentially the same issues, this interview serves to lend instructive insight into the transformation which ostensibly purely *a priori* philosophical problems undergo when transposed into the concrete contexts of scientific research programmes. It would be impossible here to provide more than the barest sense of the content of this lengthy conversation, which we feel sure will repay repeated reading. Fully confirming our faith in the potential of the interview as a (sadly under-exploited) form of contemporary intellectual engagement, this conversation provides an invaluable perspective upon the problems surrounding the determination of 'ancestral phenomena' (Meillassoux's 'arche-fossil') from the privileged 'insider' vantage-point of someone immersed in their empirical study and scientific interpretation on a daily basis. Touching as it does upon everything from the evidence for and ontological status of 'dark matter' through string theory, anthropic reasoning, inflationary cosmology and the meaning of concepts of time and space in cosmological contexts, this interview not only lends a much-needed sense of concreteness and specificity to the problems introduced by Brassier and Meillassoux, but also provides a helpful and readable introduction to the most up-to-date problems and findings of contemporary cosmology.

If Meillassoux's neo-rationalism draws upon the resources of transfinite mathematics and set-theory in order to precisely locate the fundamental parameters of rational thought itself, GRAHAM HARMAN's contribution aims at a

Editorial Introduction

different kind of precision, one which perhaps has more
affinity with Bergson's critique of dialectical concepts as
being 'too large', 'not tailored to the measurements of the
reality in which we live'[2] – 'baggy clothes'[3] which, covering
everything, reveal little and stifle movement. If Harman,
no less than Meillassoux, seeks to escape the prevailing
doxa which would see in the relation between consciousness and world the primary hinge of any philosophy
worthy of the name, and if both thinkers are equally intent
on resuscitating a 'speculative realism' long-since left for
dead by the philosophical mainstream, it would yet be
difficult to find two more starkly contrasting styles of
philosophizing.

Harman's inquiry bears no less than Meillassoux's
upon the problem of 'correlationism', however. Against
Meillassoux's positive desertion of a philosophical demon-
stration of causality, in 'On Vicarious Causation' Harman
seeks to revive the problem of causation itself in all its
specificity, beyond the question of whether it can be
known or justified, and claims that the revival of this
problem entails the rejection of Kant's Copernican turn
'and its single lonely rift between people and everything
else'. Whereas for Meillassoux the problem is the apparent
facticity of the 'correlationist gap', Harman sets out to
generalise this gap, shattering the cosmos into absolutely
disjunct objects. Through his generalisation
of Heidegger's famous tool-analysis in *Being and
Time*, Harman attempts to maintain a recognisably
phenomenological commitment to the ontological

2. H. Bergson *Oeuvres* (*La Pensée et le Mouvant*) (Paris: PUF, 1963), 1/1254.

3. G. Deleuze *Bergsonism*, trans. H. Tomlinson & B. Habberjam (New York: Zone Books, 1991), 44.

7

anteriority of the 'manifest' over the 'scientific' image of the world whilst simultaneously acknowledging the chronic futility of anti-scientific philosophies of presence. If here philosophy engages 'the same world as the various sciences' but 'in a different manner', it is not through a meditation on the presencing and absencing of Being, but rather through a tracking of the 'grain' of the immediate phenomenon in which a new 'first philosophy' is announced in the guise of an aesthetics.

In blazing this trail Harman introduces a refreshingly novel philosophical language which is still a work in progress. It is already, however, a work that finally goes beyond those interminable mantras preparatory to phenomenology in which the Heideggerian corps has by now been drilled for decades. Harman sets out, with a hard-won philosophical innocence, to *do* phenomenology in an entirely new way, a way which conjoins the immediacy of the phenomenon with the affirmation of the reality of the object. The future of this enterprise deserves to be followed closely.

Neurophilosopher PAUL CHURCHLAND has no qualms about cleaving to the scientific image, and in our informal and wide-ranging interview makes it entirely clear that, at least in his own area of research, the sense of unfamiliarity that gives rise to its traditional description as 'cold and machinelike' (Harman's 'grey matrix') should not be yielded to. Part of what is most intriguing in Churchland's take on the theme of common-sense and science is that, rather than seeing the two in a relation of dramatic rupture, he proposes that as the work of science continues, the corpus of folk-theory will gradually absorb its *prima facie*

Editorial Introduction

paradoxical statements.

Much of our discussion with Churchland relates to the problem of so-called 'qualia' – the supposedly irreducible subjective components of experience which have been for many years a touchstone for the relation between philosophy and science – and it is instructive to observe that these putatively *sui generis* elements also raise their head in Meillassoux's contribution in this volume. Having criticised advocates of so-called 'anthropic reasoning' for championing a neo-finalism on the grounds of 'astonishment', and having castigated Goodman for justifying induction on the grounds of the 'absurdness' of the alternative, Meillassoux himself ratifies his radical retraction of the Lucretian principle that 'nothing can come from nothing' with an appeal to 'new situations, whose qualitative content is such that it seems impossible to detect, *without absurdity* [emphasis added], its anticipated presence in anterior situations', giving as an example the fact that 'a life endowed with sensibility' could not, 'short of sheer fantasy', emerge from matter as conceived by mathematical physics.

How not to see in this dedication to radical novelty the 'good sense' – however exalted – of a grand style in French philosophy which has ever striven to reconcile a rigourous engagement with modern science with the moral exigency of an absolute sovereignty and freedom of thought? As Brassier points out, correlationism runs deep, and it may be difficult to break its circle without also subverting this neo-Cartesianism. And the requisite lifting of the proscription on the 'objectivation of thought' would require that philosophy take seriously the research programmes of neuroscience and cognitive science, and hold in abeyance any decision as to thought's putative 'irreducibility'.[4]

Certainly, Churchland holds any such rash decision in suspense, arguing that a study of the history of science gives us every reason to bracket our local conditions and to say with him: 'I agree … it is *hard to imagine* … [b]ut I am unimpressed by this'. One cannot help but feel that Churchland thus modestly inherits the boldest speculative enterprise of philosophy in the twentieth century: to reconcile scientific realism with evolutionary epistemology; to capture the vagaries of 'our' access to things as a *datum* rather than exalting it as an insuperable 'condition'; to reverse the humanity-function so as to accede to an unconditioned knowledge of nature 'itself'.

The apparently pleonastic 'speculative realism' only makes sense when we realise that here the ouroborian figure philosophy has grappled with since the birth of Galileanism is negotiated not by asserting the 'primacy' of one part of the unbroken circle over another, nor by anticipating an eventual accomplishment and unification, but rather by focusing on the process of autophagy itself in action. The two moments of such a programme are, firstly, the account *as datum* of the real conditions of our experience (a technical task descended from Kant's 'transcendental philosophy' as 'the idea of a science')[5] and secondly their effective neutralisation within our self-image (a cultural process). In two different ways – in the resistance of nature to our scientific theorising, and in our

---

4. On these points, see also our interview with Alain Badiou in *Collapse* Vol. I.

5. *Critique of Pure Reason*, tr. N. K. Smith (London: MacMillan 1929), A13/B27.

Editorial Introduction

own intuitive resistance to the absorption of those theories – it is the recalcitrance of our cognitive constitution that poses a natural obstacle. But as Churchland insists, there is no reason to think this obstacle insuperable in principle.

Just as the philosophical contributors to this volume draw afresh upon the philosophical tradition, so CLÉMENTINE DUZER and LAURA GOZLAN in their film *Nevertheless Empire* have returned to the traditions of expressionism and *noir*, as well as to later enigmatic figures such as Tarkovski, in order to create a science fiction which – as an exemplary instance of the genre – is a speculative portrait of the present, an extrapolation of the twenty-first century amalgam of social dysfunction, generalised fear, and techno-medical monstrosity. As well as maintaining that cinema was itself a very particular way of thinking, Deleuze wrote that 'a book of philosophy should be in part [...] a kind of science-fiction.'[6] To present a film, in a volume of philosophy, as a series of stills, represents a further convolution of this complex relationship between thought and image. But this 'stuttering' finds its own consistency on the page, the momentary glimpses re-forming in new depths.

In his contribution 'Islamic Exotericism', as in Volume I's 'Militarization of Peace', REZA NEGARESTANI petitions for the adoption of the term 'affordance' into the philosophical vocabulary. Negarestani traces the asymmetry of the 'War on Terror''s landscape of fear, and the shifting apocalyptic narratives engendered by the situation, to the refusal of affordance implicit in Islamic theology.

6. G. Deleuze, *Difference and Repetition*, trans.Paul Patton (London: Athlone,1994),xx.

KRISTEN ALVANSON's photo/diagrammatic essay emphasises a concrete locus for this difference in the theological image of thought: the graveyard as a 'staging of ontology' betrays once again the patterns of affordance, the exigency of survival inherent to Western thinking even in death. Alvanson's inquiry thus forms a concrete counterpart to Negarestani's theological disquisition.

According to Negarestani, through its spatial and temporal approaches to God and Apocalypse, Islamic theology formulates a methodology for the construction of a politically profound tool capable of turning theology itself into heresy. Where Meillassoux uses a rationality unbounded by real necessity to absolutize its own limits, 'touching' itself in a movement of intellectual intuition, Negarestani shows how theology can be reinvented as an epistemological tool for confronting a pure externality, without reducing it to ontological possibilities or to an object of 'affordance'. One might then say that the insubordinable externality Negarestani describes is cognate with the absolute time proposed by Meillassoux – a beyond of chronology, from which irrupt events in principle unpredictable by statistical or economical reason. This is perhaps the most surprising of the many subterranean connections linking the various contributions to this volume of **COLLAPSE**: Do a desacralized thinking of the infinite subtracted from the expectation of mystical union and a proper place for man, and a hyper-rationalism which refuses to bend to real necessity, deliver us to this Now of eternal externality, from which nothing may be expected? Does the conversion of god into a heresy invoke the divine inexistence?

Editorial Introduction

Obviously, it has only been possible in this brief intro-duction to give a very selective and superficial survey of a volume which suggests so many rich vectors of philosoph-ical thought and so many fascinating possibilities. But we hope to have lightly sketched a portrait here of the underlying conviction, expressed forcefully in so many different voices – and in an age where institutions and pub-lications seem to take pride in cleaving to narrow specialisms – that philosophy, in gloriously unqualified form, is still possible.

In concluding, we would like offer our thanks to our contributors for their generous collaboration on this volume, and to our readers for their enthusiastic response to Volume I. This reception encourages us in our belief that our experiment constitutes a necessary eccentricity in relation to the mainstream – and that in some way it helps set free some of the latent force of philosophical thought – once more 'to resume the offensive'.[7]

Robin Mackay,
Oxford, February 2007.

7. G. Harman, present volume, 174.

The Enigma of Realism: On Quentin Meillassoux's *After Finitude*[1]

Ray Brassier

1. THE ARCHE-FOSSIL

Quentin Meillassoux has recently proposed a compelling diagnosis of what is most problematic in post-Kantian philosophy's relationship to the natural sciences.[2] The former founders on the enigma of the 'arche-fossil'. A fossil is a material bearing the traces of pre-historic life, but an 'arche-fossil' is a material indicating traces of 'ancestral' phenomena anterior even to the emergence of life. It provides the material basis for experiments yielding estimates of ancestral phenomena – such as, for instance, the radioactive isotope whose rate of decay provides an index of the age of rock samples, or the starlight whose luminescence provides an index of the age of distant stars. Natural science produces ancestral statements, such as, for example, that the universe is roughly 13.7 billion years old, that the earth formed roughly 4.5 billion years ago, that life

1. This is a heavily edited version of a chapter from the author's *Nihil Unbound: Enlightenment and Extinction* (Basingstoke: Palgrave Macmillan, forthcoming 2007).

2. *Après la Finitude: Essai sur la nécessité de la contingence* (Paris: Seuil, 2006). English translation *After Finitude* (trans. R. Brassier) (London: Continuum, forthcoming 2008).

developed on earth approximately 3.5 billion years ago, and that the earliest ancestors of the genus *Homo* emerged about 2 million years ago.[3] Yet it is also generating an ever increasing number of 'descendent' statements, such as that the Milky Way will collide with the Andromeda galaxy in 3 billion years, or that the earth will be incinerated by the sun 4 billions years hence, or that all the stars in the universe will stop shining in 100 trillion years, or that eventually, one trillion, trillion, trillion years from now, all matter in the cosmos will disintegrate into unbound elementary particles. Philosophers should be more astonished by such statements than they seem to be, for they present a serious problem for post-Kantian philosophy. Yet strangely, the latter seems to remain entirely oblivious to it. The claim that these statements are philosophically enigmatic has nothing to do with qualms about the methods of measurement involved, or with issues of empirical accuracy, or any other misgivings about scientific methodology. They are enigmatic because of the startling philosophical implications harboured by their literal meaning. For the latter seems to point to something which violates the basic conditions of conceptual intelligibility stipulated by post-Kantian philosophy. In order to understand why this is so, we need to try to sketch the latter.

For all their various differences, post-Kantian philosophers can be said to share one fundamental conviction: that the idea of a world-in-itself, subsisting

---

3. 'Billion' and 'trillion' will be used throughout following their now internationally accepted US usage, as meaning a thousand million and a million million respectively.

independently of our relation to it, is an absurdity. Objective reality must be transcendentally guaranteed, whether by pure consciousness, intersubjective consensus, or a community of rational agents; without such guarantors, it is a metaphysical chimera. Or for those who scorn what they mockingly dismiss as the 'antiquated' Cartesian vocabulary of 'representationalism', 'subject/ object dualism', and epistemology more generally, it is our pre-theoretical relation to the world, whether characterized as *Dasein* or 'Life', which provides the ontological precondition for the intelligibility of the scientific claims listed above. No wonder, then, that post-Kantian philosophers routinely patronize these and other scientific assertions about the world as impoverished abstractions whose meaning supervenes on this more fundamental sub-representational or pre-theoretical relation to phenomena. For these philosophers, it is this relation to the world – *Dasein*, Existence, Life – which provides the originary condition of manifestation for all phenomena, including those ancestral phenomena featured in the statements above. Thus if the idea of a world-in-itself, of a realm of phenomena subsisting independently of our relation to it, is intelligible at all, it can only be intelligible as something in-itself or independent 'for-us'. This is the reigning *doxa* of post-metaphysical philosophy: what is fundamental is neither a hypostasized substance, nor the reified subject, but rather the relation between un-objectifiable thinking and un-representable being, the primordial reciprocity or 'co-propriation' of *logos* and *physis* which at once unites and distinguishes the terms which it relates. This premium on relationality in post-metaphysical philosophy – whose telling symptom is the preoccupation with 'difference' – has become an orthodoxy which is all the more insidious for being constantly touted as a profound innovation.[4]

Meillassoux has given it a name: 'correlationism'. Correlationism affirms the indissoluble primacy of the relation between thought and its correlate over the metaphysical hypostatization or representationalist reification of either term of the relation. Correlationism is subtle: it never denies that our thoughts or utterances *aim at* or *intend* mind-independent or language-independent realities; it merely stipulates that this apparently independent dimension remains internally related to thought and language. Thus contemporary correlationism dismisses the problematic of scepticism, and of epistemology more generally, as an antiquated Cartesian hang-up: there is supposedly no problem about how we are able to adequately represent reality, since we are 'always already' outside ourselves and immersed in or engaging with the world (and indeed, this particular platitude is constantly touted as the great Heideggerian–Wittgensteinian insight).

---

4. Graham Harman has elaborated a profound critique of this tendency in contemporary philosophy, seeing in it an avatar of a generalized anti-realism. Whether the relation in question is the epistemological relation between mind and world, the phenomenological relation between noesis and noema, the ekstatic relation between *Sein* and *Dasein*, the prehensive relation between event-objects, or the processual relation between matter and memory, Harman argues that this premium on relationality occludes the discontinuous reality of objects in favour of their reciprocal idealizations. Harman's startlingly original interpretation of Heidegger provides the point of departure for his complete re-orientation of phenomenology away from the primacy of the human relation to things and toward things themselves considered independently of their relation to humans or each other. Accordingly, the fundamental task for this 'object-oriented philosophy' consists in explaining how autonomous objects can ever interact with each other, and to that end Harman has developed a particularly ingenious theory of 'vicarious causation' – See Harman's contribution to the present volume, 171-205.

Note that correlationism need not privilege 'thinking' or 'consciousness' as the key relation – it can just as easily replace it with 'being-in-the-world', 'perception', 'sensibility', 'intuition', 'affect', or even 'flesh'. Indeed, all of these terms have featured in the specifically phenomenological varieties of correlationism.[5]

But the arche-fossil presents a quandary for the correlationist. For how is the correlationist to make sense of science's ancestral claims? Correlationism insists that there can be no cognizable reality independently of our relation to reality; no phenomena without some transcendental operator – such as life or consciousness or *Dasein* – generating the conditions of manifestation through which phenomena manifest themselves. In the absence of this originary relation and these transcendental conditions of manifestation, nothing can be manifest, apprehended, thought or known. Thus, the correlationist will continue, not even the phenomena described by the sciences are

5. The writings of Husserl and Heidegger are littered with paradigmatic expressions of the correlationist credo. Here are just two examples:

The existence of Nature *cannot* be the condition for the existence of consciousness, since Nature itself turns out to be a correlate of consciousness: Nature *is* only as being constituted in regular concatenations of consciousness. (Edmund Husserl, *Ideas Pertaining to a Pure Phenomenology and to a Phenomenological Philosophy. Book One*. Tr. F. Kersten, Dordrecht, The Netherlands: Kluwer, 1982: 116).

[S]trictly speaking we cannot say: there was a time when there were no human beings. At every *time*, there were and are and will be human beings, because time temporalizes itself only as long as there are human beings. There is no time in which there were no human beings, not because there are human beings from all eternity, but because time is not eternity, and time always temporalizes itself only at one time, as human, historical Dasein. (Martin Heidegger, *Introduction to Metaphysics*, tr. G. Fried and R. Polt, New Haven and London: Yale University Press, 2000: 88-9).

possible independently of the relation through which phenomena become manifest. Moreover, the correlationist will add, it is precisely the transcendental nature of the correlation as *sine qua non* for cognition that obviates the possibility of empirical idealism. Thus, *contra* Berkeley, Kant maintains that known things are not dependent upon being perceived precisely because known things are representations and representations are generated via transcendental syntheses of categorial form and sensible material. Synthesis is rooted in pure apperception, which yields the transcendental form of the object as its necessary correlate and guarantor of objectivity. The transcendental object is not cognizable, since it provides the form of objectivity which subsumes all cognizable objects; all of which must be linked to one another within the chains of causation encompassed by the unity of possible experience and circumscribed by the reciprocal poles of transcendental subject and transcendental object. Yet the arche-fossil indexes a reality which does not fall between these poles and which refuses to be integrated into the web of possible experience linking all cognizable objects to one another, because it occurred in a time *anterior to the possibility of experience*. Thus the arche-fossil points to a cognizable reality which is not given in the transcendental object of possible experience. This is a possibility which Kant explicitly denies:

> Thus we can say that the real things of past time are given in the transcendental object of experience; but they are objects for me and real in past time only in so far as I represent to myself (either by the light of history or by the guiding clues of a series of causes and effects) that a

regressive series of possible perceptions in accordance with empirical laws, in a word, that the course of the world, conducts us to a past time-series as the condition of the present time – a series which, however, can be represented as actual not in itself but only in the connection of a possible experience. *Accordingly, all events which have taken place in the immense periods that have preceded my own existence really mean nothing but the possibility of extending the chain of experience from the present perception back to the conditions which determine this perception in respect of time.*[6]

For Kant, then, the ancestral time of the arche-fossil cannot be represented as existing in itself but only as connected to a possible experience. But we cannot represent to ourselves any regressive series of possible perceptions in accordance with empirical laws capable of conducting us from our present perceptions to the ancestral time indexed by the arche-fossil. It is strictly impossible to prolong the chain of experience from our contemporary perception of the radioactive isotope to the time of the accretion of the earth indexed by its radiation, because the totality of the temporal series coextensive with possible experience itself emerged out of that geological time wherein there simply was no perception. We cannot extend the chain of possible perceptions back prior to the emergence of nervous systems, which provide the material conditions for the possibility of perceptual experience.

Thus it is precisely the necessity of an originary correlation, whether between knower and known, or *Sein* and *Dasein*, that science's ancestral statements flatly

6. *Critique of Pure Reason*, tr. N. K. Smith (London: MacMillan 1929), A495; emphasis added.

contradict. For in flagrant disregard of those transcendental conditions which are supposed to be necessary for every manifestation, they describe occurrences anterior to the emergence of life, and objects existing independently of any relation to thought. Similarly, science's descendent statements refer to events occurring after the extinction of life and the annihilation of thought. But how can such statements be true if correlationism is sound? For not only do they designate events occurring quite independently of the existence of life and thought; they inscribe the transcendental conditions of manifestation themselves within a merely empirical timeline. How can the relation to reality embodied in life or thought be characterized as transcendentally necessary (*sine qua non*) for the possibility of spatiotemporal manifestation when science unequivocally states that life and thought, and hence this fundamental relation, have a determinate beginning and end in spacetime? Don't science's ancestral and descendent statements strongly imply that those ontologically generative conditions of spatiotemporal manifestation privileged by correlationists – *Dasein*, life, consciousness, and so on – are themselves merely spatiotemporal occurrences like any other?

2. The Correlationist Response

Confronted by Meillassoux's argument from the archefossil, partisans of correlationism have not been slow in mounting a counter-offensive. In a supplement to the forthcoming English translation of *Après la finitude*, Meillassoux recapitulates the two most frequently voiced objections and responds to both. The correlationist defence is two-tiered. In the first stage, Meillassoux is accused of inflating an un-observed phenomenon into a negation of correlation, when in fact it is merely a lacuna in correlation. In the second stage, Meillassoux is deemed guilty of naively conflating the empirical and the transcendental. We will consider each of these objections, as well as Meillassoux's responses to them, in turn.

In the first stage, the correlationist contends that, far from being novel and challenging, the argument from the arche-fossil is merely a restatement of a hackneyed and rather feeble objection to transcendental idealism. Thus, the correlationist continues, the arche-fossil is simply an example of a phenomenon which went un-perceived. But un-perceived phenomena occur all the time and it is excessively naive to think they suffice to undermine the transcendental status of the correlation. In this regard, the temporal distance which separates us from the ancestral phenomenon is no different in kind from the spatial distance which separates us from contemporaneous but unobserved events occurring elsewhere in the universe. Thus the fact that there was no-one around 4.5 billion years ago to perceive the accretion of the earth is no more significant than the fact that there is currently no-one 25 million, million miles away perceiving events on the surface of Alpha Centauri. Moreover, the notion of 'distance' is an inherently ambiguous and unreliable indicator of the limits of perception: technology allows us to perceive objects extraordinarily far away in space and time, while myriad occurrences close at hand routinely go unperceived. In this regard, instances of spatiotemporal extremity are no different in kind from other banal instances of un-witnessed or un-perceived phenomena, such as the fact that we are never aware of everything going on inside our own bodies. Thus the arche-fossil is just another example of an un-perceived phenomenon and, as with all other examples of un-perceived phenomena, it merely exemplifies the inherently *lacunary* nature of manifestation – the fact that no phenomenon is ever exhaustively or absolutely apprehended by perception or consciousness. Far from denying this, both Kant and Husserl emphasized the intrinsically limited and finite nature of human cognition. Thus for Kant sensible intuition is incapable of exhaustively apprehending the infinite complexity of a datum of sensation. Similarly for Husserl, intentionality proceeds by adumbrations which never exhaust all the dimensions of the phenomenon. But the fact that every phenomenon harbours an un-apprehended remainder in no way undermines the constitutive status of transcendental consciousness. All that it shows is that manifestation is inherently lacunary and that the non-manifest inheres in every manifestation. A counterfactual suffices to establish the persistence of transcendental constitution even in cases of lacunary manifestation such as the arche-fossil. Thus the contingent fact that no-one was there to witness the accretion of the earth is ultimately of no importance; for *had there been* a witness, they *would have* perceived the phenomenon of accretion unfolding in conformity with the laws of geology and physics which are transcendentally guaranteed by the correlation. Ultimately, the correlationist concludes, the argument from the arche-fossil fails to challenge correlationism because it has simply confused a contingent lacuna in manifestation with the necessary absence of manifestation.

Against this initial line of defence, Meillassoux insists that the arche-fossil cannot be reduced to an example of the un-perceived because the temporal anteriority involved in the notion of ancestrality remains irreducible to any notion of temporal 'distance' concomitant with correlational manifestation. To reduce the arche-fossil to an un-witnessed or un-perceived occurrence is to beg the question because it is to continue to assume that there is always a correlation in terms of which to measure gaps or lacunae within manifestation. But the arche-fossil is not merely a non-manifest gap or lacuna *in* manifestation; it is the lacuna *of* manifestation *tout court*. For the anteriority indexed by the ancestral phenomenon does not point to an earlier time *within* manifestation; it indexes a time *anterior to the time of manifestation in its entirety*; and it does so according to a sense of 'anteriority' which cannot be reduced to the past of manifestation because it indicates a time wherein manifestation – along with its past, present, and future dimensions – originally emerged. Thus, Meillassoux contends, the 'ancestral' cannot be reduced to the 'ancient'. There are always greater or lesser degrees of 'ancientness' depending on whatever temporal metric one happens to choose. 'Ancientness' remains a function of a relation between past and present which is entirely circumscribed by the conditions of manifestation and in this sense any past, no matter how 'ancient', remains synchronous with the correlational present. In equating temporal remove with spatial distance, the correlationist objection outlined above continues to assume this underlying synchronicity. But ancestrality indexes a radical 'diachronicity' which cannot be correlated with the present because it belongs to the time wherein the conditions of correlation between past, present, and future passed from inexistence into existence. Accordingly, ancestrality harbours a temporal diachronicity which remains incommensurable with any chronological measure that would ensure a reciprocity between the past, present, and future dimensions of the correlation.

Meillassoux detects in this initial correlationist response a subterfuge which consists in substituting a lacuna *in* and *for* manifestation – a lacuna that is contemporaneous with constituting consciousness, as is always the case with the un-perceived – for a lacuna *of* manifestation as such; one which cannot be synchronized with constituting consciousness (or whatever other transcendental operator happens to be invoked). The correlationist's sleight-of-hand here consists in reducing the arche-fossil – which is non-manifest insofar as it occurs prior to the emergence of conditions of manifestation – to the un-perceived, which is merely a measurable gap or absence within the extant conditions of manifestation. However, Meillassoux insists, the arche-fossil is neither a lacunary manifestation nor a temporal reality internal to manifestation (internal to the correlation); for it points to the temporal reality in which manifestation itself first came into existence, and wherein it will ultimately sink back into inexistence. Consequently, Meillassoux concludes, it is a serious misunderstanding to think that a counterfactual suffices to reintegrate the arche-fossil within the correlation, for the diachronicity it indexes cannot be synchronized with any correlational present.

Having failed to rebuff the argument from the arche-fossil with this initial line of defence, the correlationist adopts a second strategy. This consists in contesting the claim that ancestrality indexes a temporal dimension within which correlational temporality itself passes into and out of being. For such an assertion betrays a fundamental confusion between the *transcendental* level at which the conditions of correlation obtain and the *empirical* level at which the organisms and/or material entities which support those conditions exist. The latter are indeed spatiotemporal objects like any other, emerging and perishing within physical space-time; but the former provide the conditions of objectivation without which scientific knowledge of spatiotemporal objects – and hence of the arche-fossil itself – would not be possible. Though these conditions are physically instantiated by specific material objects – *i.e.* human organisms – they cannot be said to exist in the same manner, and hence they cannot be said to pass into or out of existence on pain of paralogism. Thus, the correlationist continues, the claim that the conditions of objectivation emerged in space-time is an absurd paralogism because it treats transcendental conditions as though they were objects alongside other objects. But the transcendental conditions of spatiotemporal objectivation do not exist spatiotemporally. This is not to say that they are eternal, for this would be to hypostatize them once again and to attribute another kind of objective existence to them, albeit in a transcendent or supernatural register. They are neither transcendent nor supernatural – they are the logical preconditions for ascriptions of existence, rather than objectively existing entities. As conditions for the scientific cognition of empirical reality – of which the arche-fossil is a prime example – they cannot themselves be scientifically objectified without engendering absurd paradoxes. The claim that ancestral time encompasses the birth and death of transcendental subjectivity is precisely such a paradox, but one which dissolves once the confusion from which it has arisen has been diagnosed.

Yet for Meillassoux, the initial plausibility of this response masks its underlying inadequacy, for it relies on an unacknowledged equivocation. We are told that transcendental subjectivity cannot be objectified, and hence that it neither emerges nor perishes in space-time; but also that it is neither immortal nor eternal, in the manner of a transcendent metaphysical principle. Indeed this is precisely what distinguishes transcendental subjectivity in its purported finitude from any metaphysical hypostatization of the principle of subjectivity which would render it equivalent to an infinitely enduring substance. But as finite, transcendental subjectivity is indissociable from the determinate set of material conditions which provide its empirical support. Thus Husserl insists on the necessary parallelism which renders the transcendental indissociable from the empirical. Indeed, it is this necessary parallelism which distinguishes transcendental subjectivity from its metaphysical substantialization. Accordingly, though transcendental subjectivity is merely instantiated in the minds of physical organisms, it cannot subsist independently of those minds and the organisms which support them. Although it does not exist in space and time, it has no other kind of existence apart from the spatiotemporal existence of the physical bodies in which it is instantiated. And it is precisely insofar as it is anchored in the finite minds of bounded physical organisms with limited sensory and intellectual capacities that human reason is not infinite. But if transcendental subjectivity is necessarily instantiated in the spatiotemporal existence of physical organisms, then it is not quite accurate to claim that it can be entirely divorced from objectively existing bodies. Indeed, in the wake of Heidegger's critique of the 'worldless' or disembodied subject of classical transcendentalism, post-Heideggerean philosophy can be said to have engaged in an increasing 'corporealization' of the transcendental. Merleau-Ponty is probably the most prominent (though certainly not the only) advocate of the quasi-transcendental status of embodiment. Accordingly, although transcendental subjectivity may not be reducible to objectively existing bodies, neither can it be divorced from them, for the existence of bodies – and *a fortiori* of language, society, history, culture, etc. – provides the conditions of instantiation for the transcendental (i.e. the 'always already'). Thus, Meillassoux concludes, while it is perfectly plausible to insist that the correlation provides the transcendental condition for knowledge of spatiotemporal existence, it is also necessary to point out that the time in which the bodies that provide the conditions of instantiation for the correlation emerge and perish is also the time which determines the conditions of instantiation of the transcendental. But the ancestral time which determines the conditions of instantiation of the transcendental cannot be encompassed within the time that is co-extensive with the correlation, because it is the time within which those corporeal conditions upon which the correlation depends pass into and out of existence. Where such conditions of instantiation are absent, so is the correlation. Thus the ancestral time indexed by the arche-fossil is simply the time of the inexistence of the correlation. This ancestral time is indexed by objective phenomena such as the arche-fossil; but its existence does not depend upon those conditions of objectivation upon which knowledge of the arche-fossil depends, because it determines those conditions of instantiation which determine conditions of objectivation.

3. Ancestrality and Chronology

Meillassoux's responses to his correlationist critics are as trenchant as they are resourceful and they undoubtedly constitute a significant addition to his already weighty case against correlationism. However, they also invite a number of critical observations. First, it is not at all clear how Meillassoux's distinction between ancestrality and spatiotemporal distance can be squared with what twentieth-century physics has taught us concerning the fundamental indissociability of time and space, as enshrined in the Einstein-Minkowski conception of four-dimensional space-time. 'Anteriority' and 'posteriority' are inherently relational terms which can only be rendered intelligible from within a spatiotemporal frame of reference. In this regard, Meillassoux's insistence on the irreconcilable disjunction between a lacuna *in* manifestation and the lacuna *of* manifestation continues to rely on an appeal to the scalar incommensurability between the anthropomorphic time privileged by correlationism and the cosmological time within which the former is nested. This incommensurability is attributed to the fundamental asymmetry between cosmological and anthropomorphic time: whereas the former is presumed to encompass the beginning and end of the latter, the reverse is assumed not to be the case. However, Meillassoux conducts his case against correlationism in a logical rather than empirical register – indeed, we shall see below how this leads him to reiterate the dualism of thought and extension – yet the asymmetry to which he appeals here is precisely a function of empirical fact, and as Meillassoux himself acknowledges,[7] there is no *a priori* reason why the existence of mind, and hence of the correlation, could not happen to be coextensive with the existence of the universe. Indeed, this is precisely the claim of Hegelianism, which construes mind or *Geist* as a self-relating negativity already inherent in material reality. Accordingly, the transcendence which Meillassoux ascribes to ancestral time as that which exists independently of correlation continues to rely upon an appeal to chronology: it is the (empirical) fact that cosmological time *preceded* anthropomorphic time and will presumably *succeed* it which is invoked in the account of the asymmetry between the two. In light of this implicit appeal to chronology in Meillassoux's claim that the arche-fossil indexes the absence of manifestation, rather than any hiatus within it, it is difficult to see how the temporal anteriority which he ascribes to the ancestral realm could ever be understood wholly independently of the spatiotemporal framework in terms of which cosmology coordinates relations between past, present, and future events. A simple change in the framework which determines chronology would suffice to dissolve the alleged incommensurability between ancestral and anthropomorphic

7. *Cf. Après la finitude*, 161.

time, thereby bridging the conceptual abyss which is supposed to separate anteriority from spatiotemporal distance.

The conclusion to be drawn is the following: as long as the autonomy of the in-itself is construed in terms of a merely chronological discrepancy between cosmological and anthropomorphic time, it will always be possible for the correlationist to convert the supposedly absolute anteriority attributed to the ancestral realm into an anteriority which is merely 'for us', not 'in itself'. By tethering his challenge to correlationism to the spatiotemporal framework favoured by contemporary cosmology, Meillassoux mortgages the autonomy of the in-itself to chronology. The only hope for securing the unequivocal independence of the '*an sich*' must lie in prizing it free from chronology as well as phenomenology. This would entail a conception of objectivity which excludes chronological relationality as much as phenomenological intentionality. Spatiotemporal relations should be construed as a function of objective reality; rather than objective reality construed as a function of spatiotemporal relations. By insisting on driving a wedge between ancestral time and spatiotemporal distance, Meillassoux inadvertently reiterates the privileging of time over space which is so symptomatic of idealism and unwittingly endorses his opponents' claim that all non-ancestral reality can be un-problematically accounted for by the correlation. Thus the trenchancy of Meillassoux's rejoinders above actually masks a significant concession to correlationism. For surely it is not just ancestral phenomena which challenge the latter, but simply the reality described by the modern natural sciences *tout court.* According to the latter, we are surrounded by processes going on quite independently of any relationship we may happen to have to them: thus plate tectonics, thermonuclear fusion, and galactic expansion (not to mention undiscovered oil reserves or unknown insect species) are as much autonomous, human-independent realities as the accretion of the earth. The fact that these processes are contemporaneous with the existence of consciousness, while the accretion of the earth preceded it, is quite irrelevant. To maintain the contrary, and insist that it is only the ancestral dimension that transcends correlational constitution, is to imply that the emergence of consciousness marks some sort of fundamental ontological rupture, shattering the autonomy and consistency of reality, such that once consciousness has emerged on the scene, nothing can pursue an independent existence any more. The danger is that in privileging the arche-fossil as sole paradigm of a mind-independent reality, Meillassoux is ceding too much ground to the correlationism he wishes to destroy.[8]

3. THE PRINCIPLE OF FACTUALITY

Meillassoux distinguishes between two varieties of correlationism: weak correlationism, which claims that we can *think* noumena even though we cannot *know* them, and strong correlationism, which claims that we cannot even think them. Weak correlationism, exemplified by Kant, insists on the finitude of reason and the conditional nature of our access to being. The conditions for knowledge (the

8. I am indebted to Graham Harman, Robin Mackay, and Damian Veal for all these critical points.

categories and forms of intuition) apply only to the phenomenal realm, not to things in-themselves. Thus the cognitive structures governing the phenomenal realm are not necessary features of things-in-themselves. We cannot know why space and time are the only two forms of intuition or why there are twelve rather than eleven or thirteen categories. There is no sufficient reason capable of accounting for such a fact. In this sense, and this sense alone, these transcendental structures are contingent. But Hegel will point out that Kant has already overstepped the boundary between the knowable and the unknowable in presuming to know that the structure of things-in-themselves differs from the structure of phenomena. Accordingly, Hegel will proceed to re-inject that which is transcendentally constitutive of the 'for us' back into the 'in-itself'. Thus in Hegel's absolute idealism thinking grounds its own access to being once more and rediscovers its intrinsic infinitude. Where Kant's weak correlationism emphasises the uncircumventable contingency inherent in the correlation between thinking and being, Hegelianism absolutizes the correlation and thereby insists on the necessary isomorphy between the structure of thinking and that of being. In this regard, strong correlationism, which encompasses everything from phenomenology to pragmatism, can be understood as a critical rejoinder to the Hegelian absolutization of correlation. Though strong cor-relationism also jettisons the thing-in-itself, it retains the Kantian premium on the ineluctable contingency of the correlation, which Heidegger famously radicalizes in the notion of 'facticity'. Thus strong correlationism, as exemplified by figures such as Heidegger and Foucault, insists – contra Hegel – that the contingency of correlation cannot be rationalised or grounded in reason. This is the anti-metaphysical import of Heidegger's epochal 'history of being' or of Foucault's 'archaeologies of knowledge'. Accordingly, if we are to break with correlationism, we must re-legitimate the possibility of thinking the thing-in-itself, yet do so without either absolutizing correlation or resorting to the Principle of Sufficient Reason.

In a remarkable *tour de force*, Meillassoux shows how what is most powerful in strong correlationism can be used to overcome it from within. And what is most powerful in it is precisely its insistence on the facticity of correlation. For on what basis does strong correlationism reject the Hegelian rehabilitation of the Principle of Sufficient Reason – the claim that contradiction is the ground of being – and the ensuing isomorphy between thinking and being? It does so by insisting on the facticity or non-necessity of correlation against its Hegelian absolutization – thought's access to being is extrinsically conditioned by non-conceptual factors, which cannot be rationalised or reincorporated within the concept, not even in the form of dialectical contradiction. Thus, in order to emphasize the primacy of facticity against the speculative temptation to absolutize correlation, strong correlationism must insist that everything is without reason – even correlation itself. Against Hegel's speculative idealism, which seeks to show how the correlation can demonstrate its own necessity by grounding itself, thereby becoming absolutely necessary or *causa sui*, strong correlationism must maintain that such self-grounding is impossible by demonstrating that the correlation cannot know itself to be necessary. For though we can claim that an empirical phenomenon is necessary or contingent in conformity with the transcendental principles governing the possibility of knowledge, we cannot know whether these principles themselves are either necessary or contingent, for we have nothing to compare them to. This argument proceeds on the basis of a distinction between contingency, which is under the jurisdiction of knowledge, and facticity, which is not. Contingency is empirical and pertains to phenomena: a phenomenon is contingent if it can come into or out of existence without violating the principles of cognition that govern phenomena. Facticity is transcendental and pertains to our cognitive relation to phenomena, and hence to the principles of knowledge themselves, concerning which it makes no sense to say either that they are necessary or that they are contingent, since we have no other principles to compare them to. Against absolute idealism then, strong correlationism insists that to affirm the necessity of the correlation is to contravene the norms of knowledge. Yet in so doing, it violates its own stricture: for in order to claim that the correlation is not necessary, it has no choice but to affirm its contingency.

Accordingly, strong correlationism is obliged to contravene its own distinction between what is knowable and what is unknowable in order to protect it; it must assert the contingency of correlation in order to contradict the idealist's assertion of its necessity. But to affirm the contingency of correlation is also to assert the necessity of facticity and hence to overstep the boundary between what can be known – contingency – and what cannot be known – facticity – in the very movement that is supposed to reassert its inviolability. For in order to maintain the contingency of correlation and stave off absolute idealism, strong correlationism must insist on the necessity of its facticity – but it cannot do so without knowing something which, by its own lights, it is not supposed to know. Thus it finds itself confronted with the following dilemma: it cannot de-absolutize facticity without absolutizing the correlation; yet it cannot de-absolutize the correlation without absolutizing facticity. But to absolutize facticity is to assert the unconditional necessity of its contingency and hence to assert that it is possible to think something that exists independently of thought's relation to it: contingency as such. In absolutizing facticity, correlationism subverts the empirical-transcendental divide separating knowable contingency from unknowable facticity even as it strives to maintain it; but it is thereby forced to acknowledge that what it took to be a negative characteristic of our relation to things – *viz.*, that we cannot know whether the principles of cognition are necessary or contingent – is in fact a positive characteristic of things-in-themselves.

It is worthwhile pausing here to underline the decisive distinction between the idealist and realist variants of the speculative overcoming of correlationism. Speculative idealism claims that the in-itself is not some transcendent object standing 'outside' the correlation, but is rather nothing other than the correlation as such. Thus it converts relationality *per se* into a thing-in-itself or absolute: the dialectician claims that we overcome the metaphysical reification of the in-itself when we realize that what we took to be merely for-us is in fact in-itself. Correlation is absolutized when it becomes in-itself for-itself. But this involves transforming correlation into a metaphysically necessary entity or *causa sui*. By way of contrast, Meillassoux's speculative materialism asserts that the only way to preserve the in-itself from its idealist incorporation into the for-us without reifying it metaphysically is by realizing that what is in-itself is the *contingency* of the for-us, not its necessity. Thus, when facticity is absolutized, it is the contingency or groundlessness of the for-us (the correlation) which becomes in-itself or necessary precisely insofar as its contingency is not something which is merely for-us. Speculative materialism asserts that, in order to maintain our ignorance of the necessity of correlation, we have to know that its contingency is necessary. In other words, if we can never know the necessity of anything, this is not because necessity is unknowable but because we know that only contingency necessarily exists. What is absolute is the fact that everything is necessarily contingent or 'without-reason'.

Consequently, when forced to pursue the ultimate consequences of its own premises, correlationism is obliged to turn our ignorance concerning the necessity or contingency of our knowledge of phenomena into a thinkable property of things-in-themselves. The result, as Meillassoux puts it, is that '[t]he absolute is the absolute impossibility of a necessary being'.[9] This is Meillassoux's 'principle of factuality' and though it might seem exceedingly slight, its implications are far from trivial. For it imposes significant constraints upon thought. If a necessary being is conceptually impossible then the only

---

9 *Après la finitude*, 82.

absolute is the real possibility of the completely arbitrary and radically unpredictable transformation of all things from one moment to the next. It is important not to confuse this with familiar Heraclitean or Nietzschean paeans to absolute becoming, for the latter merely substitutes the metaphysical necessity of perpetual differentiation for the metaphysical necessity of perpetual identity. To affirm the metaphysical primacy of becoming is to claim that it is impossible for things not to change; impossible for things to stay the same; and *ergo* to claim that it is necessary for things to keep changing. The flux of ceaseless becoming is thereby conceived as ineluctable and metaphysically necessary as unchanging stasis. But metaphysical necessity, whether it be that of perpetual flux or of permanent fixity, is precisely what the principle of absolute contingency rules out. The necessity of contingency, Meillassoux maintains, implies an 'absolute time' which can interrupt the flux of becoming with the same arbitrary capriciousness as it can scramble the fixity of being. Absolute time is tantamount to a 'hyper-chaos' for which nothing is impossible, unless it be the production of a necessary being. It is a contingency which usurps every possible order, including the order of disorder or the constancy of inconstancy. It is all-powerful; but an absolute power which is 'without norms, blind, and devoid of all the other divine perfections [...] It is a power possessing neither goodness nor wisdom [...] a time capable of destroying becoming itself by bringing forth, perhaps forever, fixity, stasis, and death'.[10]

---

10. *Ibid.*, 88.

4. The Paradox of Absolute Contingency

In a move that effectively sidesteps the entire problematic of representation, Meillassoux boldly declares his intention to reinstate intellectual intuition:

> [W]e must project unreason into the thing itself, and discover in our grasp of facticity the veritable intellectual intuition of the absolute. 'Intuition', since it is well and truly in [à même] *what is* that we discover a contingency with no bounds other than itself; 'intellectual', since this contingency is nothing visible, nothing perceptible in the thing: only thought can access it as it accesses the Chaos which underlies the apparent continuities of phenomena.[11]

The deployment of this presumably non-metaphysical variety of intellectual intuition circumvents Kant's critical distinction between knowable phenomena and unknowable things-in-themselves – between reality as we relate to it through representation and reality as it is independently of our representational relation to it – and rehabilitates the distinction between primary and secondary qualities; the former being mathematically intuitable features of things-in-themselves; the latter being phenomenological features of our relation to things.[12] This reinstatement of intellectual intuition is of a piece with Meillassoux's overturning of Kant's critical delimitation of the possibilities of reason. Intellectual intuition now provides us with direct access to a realm of pure possibility coextensive with absolute time. Kant displaced the metaphysical hypostatization of logical possibility by

11. *Ibid.*, 111.
12. *Ibid.*, 28.

subordinating the latter to a domain of real possibility circumscribed by reason's relation to sensibility. Time *qua* form of transcendental synthesis grounds the structure of possibility.[13] But Meillassoux's absolutization of contingency effectively absolutizes the *a priori* realm of pure logical possibility and untethers the domain of mathematical intelligibility from sensibility. This severing of the possible from the sensible is underwritten by the chaotic structure of absolute time. Where the bounds of real possibility remain circumscribed by the correlational *a priori*, intellectual intuition uncovers a realm of absolute possibility whose only constraint is non-contradiction. Moreover, where real possibility is subsumed by time as form of transcendental subjectivity, absolute possibility indexes a time no longer anchored in the coherence of a subjective relation to reality or in the correlation between thinking and being. Thus the intellectual intuition of absolute possibility underwrites the 'diachronicity' of thinking and being; a diachronicity which for Meillassoux is implicit in the ancestral dimension of being uncovered by modern science. In ratifying the diachronicity of thinking and being, modern science exposes thought's contingency for being: although thought needs being, being does not need thought.

The question, then, is whether Meillassoux's reinstatement of intellectual intuition may not compromise the very asymmetry which he takes to be science's speculative import. Similarly, it may be that the Galilean hypothesis harbours ramifications concerning the

13. This is the upshot of Heidegger's reinterpretation of Kant in *Kant and the Problem of Metaphysics*, tr. R. Taft (Indianapolis: Indiana University Press, 1990).

mathematization of thinking which also vitiate Meillassoux's appeal to intellectual intuition. To consider these questions, we must examine the distinction which Meillassoux invokes in order to stave off idealism. This is the distinction between the reality of the ancestral phenomenon and the *ideality* of the ancestral statement. It is on the basis of this distinction that Meillassoux, like Badiou, seeks to distance himself from the Pythagorean thesis according to which being is mathematical:

> [W]e will maintain that, for their part, the statements bearing on the ancestral phenomenon which can be mathematically formulated designate effective properties of the event in question (its date, its duration, its extension), even though no observer was present to experience it directly. Accordingly, we will maintain a Cartesian thesis about matter, but not, let us underline this, a Pythagorean one: we shall not claim that the being of the ancestral phenomenon is intrinsically mathematical, or that the numbers and equations deployed in ancestral statements exist in themselves. For it would then be necessary to maintain that the ancestral phenomenon is a reality every bit as ideal as that of a number or an equation. Generally speaking, statements are ideal insofar as they possess a signifying reality; but their eventual referents are not necessarily ideal (the cat on the mat is real, though the statement 'The cat is on the mat' is ideal.) In this regard, we will say that the referents of ancestral statements bearing on dates, volumes, etc. existed 4.56 billion years ago as described by these statements – but not these statements themselves, which are contemporaneous with us.[14]

---

14. *Après la finitude*, 28-9.

This distinction between the reality of the ancestral phenomenon and the ideality of the ancestral statement is necessary in order to maintain the ontological disjunction between the correlational present and the ancestral past – precisely the diachronicity which correlationism cannot countenance. Nevertheless, if Meillassoux evokes such a distinction, he cannot sequester it on the side of being alone, for it must pertain to thinking as well as to being. Thus this secondary disjunction between real and ideal subdivides both poles of the primary disjunction between thinking and being: thought possesses a real and an ideal aspect, just as being possesses real and ideal features. Clearly, the diachronicity harboured by the arche-fossil can only be indexed by a disjunction between the ideality of the ancestral statement and the reality of the ancestral phenomenon which promises to prove irreducible to the neighbouring distinctions between the real and ideal aspect of thought and the real and ideal features of being, for both of these remain entirely encompassed by the correlation between thinking and being. For the point of Meillassoux's distinction between physical reality and discursive ideality is to discount the idealist claim that the reality of the phenomenon is exhausted by its mathematical idealization in the statement. Although the reality of the ancestral phenomenon can be mathematically encoded, it must transcend this mathematical inscription, otherwise Meillassoux finds himself endorsing Pythagoreanism. And as Meillassoux well knows, the latter provides no bulwark against correlationism, since it effectively renders being isomorphic with mathematical ideality. The point seems to be that the reality of the ancestral phenomenon must be independent of its mathematical intellection – being does not depend upon the existence of mathematics. But Meillassoux's problem consists in identifying a speculative guarantor for this disjunction between reality and ideality which would be entirely independent of the evidence provided by the mathematical idealization of the ancestral phenomenon in the ancestral statement. To rely upon the latter would be to render this speculative disjunction supervenient upon the procedures of post-critical epistemology and thus to find oneself confronted by the injunction to verify or otherwise justify it within the ambit of the correlationist circle.

Thus the question confronting Meillassoux's speculative materialism is: under what conditions would this secondary disjunction between the real and the ideal be intellectually intuitable without reinstating a correlation at the level of the primary disjunction between thinking and being? To render the distinction between the reality of the phenomenon and the ideality of the statement dependent upon intellectual intuition is to leave it entirely encompassed by one pole of the primary disjunction, *i.e.* thought, and hence to recapitulate the correlationist circle. For just as we cannot maintain that this primary disjunction is intellectually intuitable without reinscribing being within the ideal pole of the secondary disjunction, similarly, we cannot maintain that the secondary disjunction is encoded in the ancestral statement without reincorporating the real within the noetic pole of the primary disjunction. How, then, are we to guarantee the disjunction between real and ideal independently of the intelligible ideality of science's ancestral claims? For the ideality of the latter cannot be a guarantor of the reality of the former. Moreover, intellectual intuition subsumes both poles of the secondary disjunction within one pole of the primary disjunction.

Consequently, Meillassoux is forced into the difficult position of attempting to reconcile the claim that being is not inherently mathematical with the claim that being is intrinsically accessible to intellectual intuition. He cannot maintain that being is mathematical without lapsing into Pythagorean idealism; but this relapse into Pythagoreanism is precluded only at the cost of the idealism which renders being the correlate of intellectual intuition. The problem lies in trying to square the Galilean-Cartesian hypothesis that being is mathematizable with an insistence on the speculative disjunction whereby being is held to subsist independently of its mathematical intuitability. Part of the difficulty resides in the fact that although Meillassoux presumably discounts metaphysical and phenomenological conceptions of being, whether as necessary substance or eidetic presence, since both are encompassed within the correlationist circle, he has not provided us with a non-metaphysical and non-phenomenological alternative – such as we find, for example, in Badiou's subtractive conception of the void.[15] Like Badiou, Meillassoux recuses the Kantian formulation of the problematic of access while striving to uphold the authority of scientific rationality. However, unlike Badiou, he does not characterize ontology as a situation within which the presentation of being is subtractively inscribed in such a way as to obviate any straightforwardly metaphysical or phenomenological

15. *Cf. Being and Event*, tr. O. Feltham (London: Continuum, 2006).

correlation between thought and being.

But as a result he must explain why – given that science teaches us that intellection is in no way an inelim- inable feature of reality but merely a contingent by-product of evolutionary history, and given that for Meillassoux himself reality can be neither inherently mathematical nor *necessarily* intelligible – being should be susceptible to intel- lectual intuition. In this regard, it is worth noting that one of the more significant ramifications of the Galilean- Cartesian hypothesis about the mathematizability of nature consists in the recent endeavour to deploy the resources of mathematical modelization in order to develop a science of cognition. Admittedly, the latter is still in its infancy; nev- ertheless, its maturation promises to obviate the Cartesian dualism of thought and extension – and perhaps also the residues of the latter which subsist in Meillassoux's own brand of speculative materialism – while conceding nothing to correlationism. The diachronic disjunction between thinking and being is not the only speculative implication harboured by modern science; the development of a science of cognition implies that we, unlike Descartes and Kant, can no longer presume to exempt thought from the reality to which it provides access, or continue to attribute an exceptional status to it.

If thought can no longer be presumed to exempt itself from the reality which it thinks, and if the real can no longer be directly mapped onto being, or the ideal directly mapped onto thought, then thinking itself must be reinte- grated into any speculative enquiry into the nature of reality. Thus the central question raised by Meillassoux's speculative materialism becomes: Does the principle of factuality, which states that 'everything that exists is necessarily contingent', *include itself* in its designation of 'everything'? Like Badiou, Meillassoux sees Cantor as having definitively pulverized the concept of 'totality', so that the latter is now devoid of ontological pertinence. But we do not have to assume a spurious totalization of existence to enquire whether the thought that everything is necessarily contingent is itself necessarily contingent. On the contrary, all that we assume is that thinking is just a contingent fact like any other. What we should refuse, however, is the claim that it is necessary to exempt the thought that 'everything is necessarily contingent' from the existential 'fact' that everything is contingent on the grounds that a transcendental abyss separates thinking from being. Once the recourse to this transcendental divide has been ruled out, we are obliged to consider what follows if the principle refers to itself. More precisely, we must consider whether the truth of the principle, and *a fortiori* Meillassoux's speculative overcoming of correlation-ism, entails its self-reference. Here we have to distinguish between the contingency of the existence of the thought, which does *not* generate paradox, and the contingency of the truth of the thought, which does. Two distinct possibil-ities can be envisaged depending on whether the thought does or does not refer to itself. First let us consider what follows if it does refer to itself. Then if the thought exists, it must be contingent. But if it is contingent then its negation could equally exist: 'Not everything is necessarily contingent'. But in order for the thought to exclude the possibility of the truth of its negation, then its truth must be necessary, which means that the thought must exist

47

necessarily. But if it exists necessarily then not everything that exists is necessarily contingent; there is at least one thing which is not, *i.e.* the thought itself. Thus if the thought refers to itself it necessitates the existence of its own negation; but in order to deny the possible truth of its negation it has to affirm its own necessary truth, and hence contradict itself once more. What if the thought does not refer to itself? Then there is something which is necessary, but which is not included under the rubric of existence. Reality is 'not-all' because the thought that 'everything is necessarily contingent' is an ideality which exempts itself from the reality which it designates. But then not only does this very exemption become necessary for the intelligible ideality of the thought that 'everything is necessarily contingent', but the intelligibility of reality understood as the necessary existence of contingency becomes dependent upon the coherence of a thought whose exemption from reality is necessary in order for reality to be thought as necessarily contingent. Thus the attempt to exempt the ideal from the real threatens to re-instantiate the correlationist circle once more. Lastly, let us consider the possibility that the necessary contingency of existence does not depend on the truth of the thought 'everything is necessarily contingent'. If everything is necessarily contingent regardless of the truth of the thought 'everything is necessarily contingent', then everything could be necessarily contingent even if we had no way of thinking the truth of that thought coherently. But this is to re-introduce the possibility of a radical discrepancy between the coherence of thinking and the way the world is in-itself – any irrational hypothesis about the latter become possible and strong correlationism looms once again.

Whatever the shortcomings attendant upon their lack of formal stringency, these conjectures seem to point to a fundamental dilemma confronting Meillassoux's project. If he accepts – as we believe he must – that thinking is part of being as the second fundamental speculative implication of scientific rationality after that of diachronicity, then the universal scope of the principle of factuality generates a paradox whereby it seems to contradict itself: the claim that everything is necessarily contingent is only true if this thought exists necessarily. Alternatively, if Meillassoux decides to uphold the exceptional status of thinking vis-à-vis being then he seems to compromise his insistence on diachronicity, for the intelligible reality of contingent being is rendered dependent upon the ideal coherence of the principle of factuality. Indeed, the appeal to intellectual intuition in the formulation of the principle already seems to assume some sort of reciprocity between thinking and being

As one might expect, both these criticisms – *viz.*, that intellectual intuition reestablishes a correlation between thought and being and that the principle of factuality engenders a paradox – have elicited typically acute responses from Meillassoux. In a personal communication, Meillassoux has explained why he believes he can parry both objections. For Meillassoux, the principle of factuality is designed to satisfy two requirements. First, the fundamental *rationalist* requirement that reality be perfectly amenable to conceptual comprehension. This is a rebuttal of the prototypical religious notion that existence harbors some sort of transcendent mystery forever refractory to intellection. Second, the basic *materialist* requirement that being, though perfectly intelligible, remain irreducible to thought. Meillassoux insists that the claim that everything that is is necessarily contingent satisfies both criteria. In his own words:

> Being is thought without-remainder insofar as it is without-reason; and the being that is thought in this way is conceived as exceeding thought on all sides because it shows itself to be capable of producing and destroying thought as well as every other sort of entity. As a factual act produced by an equally factual thinking being, the intellectual intuition of facticity is perfectly susceptible to destruction, but not that which, albeit only for an instant, it will have thought as the eternal truth which legitimates its name, *viz.*, that it is itself perishable just like everything else that exists. [...] Thus, it is on account of its capacity for a-rational emergence that being exceeds on all sides whatever thought is able to describe of its factual production; nevertheless, it contains nothing unfathomable for thought because being's excess over thought just indicates that reason is forever absent from being, not some eternally enigmatic power.[16]

These remarks already prefigure Meillassoux's recusal of the second objection, *viz.*, that if applied to itself, the principle of factuality becomes contradictory. Meillassoux maintains that the paradox can be averted by carefully distinguishing the referent of the principle from its (factual) existence. Thus, though the latter is indeed contingent, and hence as liable to be as not to be, the former is strictly

16. Personal Communication, 9/8/2006.

necessary, and indeed it is the eternal necessity of the principle's referent that guarantees the perpetual contingency of the principle's existence:

> One may then say that the principle as something that is *thought* in reality is factual, and hence contingent. But what is not contingent is the referent of this principle; *viz.*, facticity as such insofar as it is necessary. And it is because this facticity is necessary that the principle, insofar as it is – in fact – proffered and insofar as it will be or will have been thought by some singular entity – no matter when or under what circumstances – it is for this reason that the principle will always be true the moment it is posited or thought. What is contingent is that the principle, as a meaningful statement, is actually thought; but what is not contingent is that it is true insofar as it is – as a matter of fact – thought in a time and place – no matter when or where. Consequently there is no paradox so long as the principle's domain of application is precisely restricted to entities in their being.[17]

The crucial operative distinction here is that between the necessity of contingency *qua* referent of thought and the contingency of the (factual) existence of the thought that everything is necessarily contingent. The question then is: How does Meillassoux propose to account for this separation between the contingent existence of thought and the necessary existence of its referent? Clearly, this separation is intended to safeguard the coherence of the principle, as well as the materialist primacy of the real over the ideal, by ensuring a strict differentiation between thought and reality. But given that, for Meillassoux,

17. *Ibid.*

thought's purchase on reality is guaranteed by intellectual intuition, it follows that it must also be the latter which accounts for this distinction between thought and referent. Accordingly, it would seem that it is in and through the intellectual intuition of absolute contingency that the contingency of the thought is separated from the necessity of its referent. Everything then hinges on how Meillassoux understands the term 'intellectual intuition'.

Clearly, he cannot be using the term in its Kantian acceptation, since, for Kant, intellectual intuition actively create its own object, unlike sensible intuition, which passively receives an independently existing object. According to Kant, only the intuitive understanding of an 'archetypical' intellect (*intellectus archetypus*) unburdened by sensibility – such as God's – possesses this power to produce its object; for our discursive understanding, mediated as it is by sensibility, it is the synthesis of concept and intuition which yields the cognitive relation between thought and its object. Meillassoux clearly rejects Kant's representationalist account of the relation between mind and world, just as he must refuse phenomenology's appeal to an intentional correlation between thought and referent. Yet it is far from evident what plausible theory of intellectual intuition could simultaneously ensure the scission between the contingency of thought and the necessity of its referent – which Meillassoux takes to be sufficient to stave off contradiction – while circumventing representational and intentional correlation as well as abjuring the archetypical intellect's production of its object (since the claim that intellection creates its object is clearly incompatible with any commitment to materialism). Though Meillassoux insists that the paradox of absolute contingency can be obviated by restricting the principle's domain of reference to 'entities in their being', he does not explain how he proposes to enforce this rigid demarcation between the principle's contingently effectuated *intension* and what he deems to be its 'eternally' necessary *extension*.

'Reference', of course, is intimately related to 'truth', but though Meillassoux claims that the truth of the principle is guaranteed by its ontological referent, this connection is anything but semantically transparent, since the extension of the expression 'absolute contingency' is no more perspicuous than that of the term 'being'. The customary prerequisite for realist conceptions of truth is an extra-theoretical account of the relation between intension and extension, but Meillassoux's attempt to construe the latter in terms of intellectual intuition makes it exceedingly difficult to see how it could ever be anything other than intra-theoretical.[18] Indeed, it is unclear how the referent 'absolute contingency' could ever be rendered intelligible in anything other than a purely conceptual register. Consequently, Meillassoux presents us with a case in which the determination of extension, or 'truth', remains entirely dependent upon a conceptually stipulated intension, or 'sense' – the referent 'absolute contingency' is exclusively determined by the sense of the contingently existing thought 'everything that is, is absolutely contingent'. But if the only way to ensure the separation between the (contingently existing) ideality of meaning and the (necessarily existing) reality of the referent is by

---

18. *Cf.* Hilary Putnam, 'The Meaning of "Meaning"' in *Mind, Language, and Reality: Philosophical Papers* Volume 2 (Cambridge: Cambridge University Press, 1975), 236.

making conceptuality constitutive of objectivity, then the absolutization of the non-correlational referent is won at the price of an absolutization of conceptual sense which violates the materialist requirement that being not be reducible to thought. Far from reconciling rationalism with materialism, the principle of factuality, at least in this version, continues to subordinate extra-conceptual reality to a concept of absolute contingency.

Although Meillassoux's speculative overcoming of correlationism strives to deploy the latter's strongest weapons against it – as we saw with the principle of factuality itself – the distinction between the real and the ideal is part of the correlationist legacy which cannot be mobilized against it without first undergoing decontamination. For correlationism secures the transcendental divide between the real and the ideal only at the cost of turning being into the correlate of thought. Meillassoux is right to insist that it is necessary to pass through correlationism in order to overcome it, and in this regard we should follow his recommendation and find a way of deploying the distinction between real and ideal against correlationism itself. But precisely here a fundamental speculative problem reveals itself, namely: Can we think the diachronic disjunction between real and ideal while obviating any recourse to a transcendental divide between thinking and being?

Potentiality and Virtuality[1]

Quentin Meillassoux

1. A DISSOLVED ONTOLOGICAL PROBLEM

'Hume's problem', that is to say, the problem of the grounding of causal connection, has known the fate of most ontological problems: a progressive abandonment, legitimated by the persistent failure that various attempts at resolving it have met with. Thus Nelson Goodman, in a famous article[2] can affirm without hesitation the 'dissolution of the old problem of induction'. This dissolution, as laid out by Goodman, concerns the ontological character of Hume's problem, which obliges whoever accepts its terms to accept the necessity of a principle of the uniformity of nature, a principle the proof of whose existence will then be attempted. The argument

1. Originally published as 'Potentialité et virtualité' in *Failles* no. 2 (Spring 2006).

2. N. Goodman, N, *Fact, Fiction and Forecast* (Camb., MA: Harvard University Press, 1983 [4th. Ed.]), Ch. 3.

which, in Goodman, concludes with the dissolution of the 'old problem of induction' is as follows:

• The problem of induction as formulated by Hume consists fundamentally in asking how we can justify that the future should resemble the past.

• Goodman, following Hume, fully affirms that we simply cannot do so: this justification is impossible by rational means.

• We must therefore abandon this undecidable problem, in order to pose it under another form, in which it will once again become amenable to treatment, namely: which rule, or set of rules, do we apply when we – and above all, when scientists – make inductive inferences? The question therefore no longer consists in proving the resemblance of the future and the past, but in describing an existing practice (induction) so as to try to extract its implicit rules. The dissolution of the ontological problem is thus accompanied by its methodological and epistemological reformulation: instead of vainly trying to prove the necessity of observable constants, we must set ourselves the task of describing the precise rules which scientists apply, usually implicitly, when they present us with inductive inferences. Thus Goodman can consider Hume's solution of his own problem – that our belief in induction derives from habit and not from consequent reasoning – correct in principle, however partial it might be: because in passing from the insoluble problem of the justification of an ontological principle to that of an effective genesis in the mind, Hume had already registered the intuition that the only adequate treatment of such a problem would consist in describing the effective process by which we draw inductions, not in seeking a metaphysical foundation for it. Consequently, Goodman proposes to follow such a path, forsaking however the psychological description of the spontaneous behaviour of individuals to which Hume confined himself (*viz.*, that we believe in our inductive inferences because of our faculty of believing more and more intensely in recurrent phenomena) in favour of a description of the practices and procedures of the scientific community.

In short, the dissolution of the problem of induction comprises two phases:

• A negative phase of abandonment of the supposedly insoluble problem.

• A phase of recomposition or reformulation of the problem, which consists in passing from an ontological question – is there something like a necessary connection between events? – to a question which evacuates all ontological problems, applying itself instead to the description of effective practices by which scientific inductions are carried out.

2. PRECIPITATION OF THE PROBLEM

My proposal is as follows: to contest the dissolution of Hume's problem, that is to say the abandonment of the ontological formulation of the problem, by maintaining that the latter can be resolved in a way which has, so it would seem, been hitherto neglected. I will intervene, then, only in the first stage of dissolutory reasoning – which is presupposed by the second (the recomposition of new problems): the proposition that the ontological problem of induction must be abandoned, since it is insoluble.

To open anew the ontological problem of the necessity of laws, we must distinguish this problem from that posed by Hume, which is in fact a *particular, already oriented,* formulation of this problem taken in its full generality.

Hume's formulation of the problem is as follows: Can we prove the effective necessity of the connections observed between successive events? The presupposition made both by Hume and by Goodman is that, if we cannot, then *any* ontological treatment of what is called real necessity (that is to say, of the necessity of laws, as opposed to so-called logical necessity) is consigned to failure, and consequently must be abandoned. I believe that it is possible at once to accept the Hume-Goodman verdict of failure, and yet to dispute that it follows that every ontological approach to the problem is thereby disqualified. For the ontological question of real necessity, formulated in its full generality, is not married to the Humean formulation, but rather can be formulated as follows: Can a conclusive argument be made for the necessity *or the absence of necessity* of observable constants? Or, once again: is there any way to justify either the claim that the future must resemble the past, *or* the claim that the future might *not* resemble the past? In the latter case, it is a question of establishing, not that the observable laws must change in the future, but that it is contingent that they should remain identical. This perspective must be distinguished from any thesis affirming the necessity of the changing of laws – for such a thesis would be a variant of the solution envisaged by Hume: this changing of laws, precisely in so far as it is necessary, would suppose yet another law, in a higher sense – a law, itself immutable, regulating the future changes of current constants. Thus it would lead straight back to the idea of a uniformity of nature, simply pushing it back one level.

On the contrary, the ontological approach I speak of would consist in affirming that it is possible rationally to envisage that the constants could effectively change *for no reason whatsoever*, and thus with no necessity whatsoever; which, as I will insist, leads us to envisage a contingency so radical that it would incorporate all conceivable futures of the present laws, *including that consisting in the absence of their modification*. It is thus a question of justifying the effective existence of a radical contingency not only of events submitted to laws, but of laws themselves, reduced to factical constants, themselves submitted to the eventuality of an ultimately chaotic becoming – that is to say, a becoming governed by no necessity whatsoever.

Let us be sure to grasp the significance of such a position, and what it involves. The problem of induction, as soon as it is formulated as the problem of the effective necessity of laws, issues in an avowal of the defeat of reason, because nothing contradictory can be detected in the contrary hypothesis of a changing of constants. For reason does not seem to be capable of prohibiting *a priori* that which goes against the purely logical necessity of non-contradiction. But in that case, a world governed by the imperatives of reason, would be governed only by such logical imperatives. Now, this would mean that anything non-contradictory *could* (but not *must*) come to pass, implying precisely the *refusal* of all causal necessity: for causality, on the contrary, asserts that amongst different, equally conceivable events certain of them must come to pass rather than others. This being so, we would indeed have to agree that *in a rational world everything would be devoid of any reason to be as it is.* A world which was entirely governed by logic, would in fact be governed *only* by logic, and consequently would be a world where nothing has a reason to be as it is rather than otherwise, since nothing contradictory can be perceived in the possibility of such a being-otherwise. Every determination in this world would therefore be susceptible to modification: but no ultimate reason could be given for such modifications, since in that case a prior cause would have to be supposed, which it would not be possible to legitimate in preference to another, equally thinkable. But what would such a world be? To speak in Leibnizian terms, it would be world *emancipated from the Principle of Sufficient Reason* – a world discharged of that principle according to which everything must have a reason to be as it is rather than otherwise: a world in which the logical exigency of consistency would remain, but not the metaphysical exigency of persistence.

Hume's discovery, according to our account, is thus that *an entirely rational world would be by that very token entirely chaotic*: such a world is one from which the irrational belief in the necessity of laws has been extirpated, since the latter is opposed in its very content to what constitutes the essence of rationality. If, contrary to our hypothesis, one were to *supplement* logical necessity with real necessity, if one were to doubly limit the possible both by non-contradiction and by actual constants, one would then

60

create an artificial riddle irresoluble by reason, since such an hypothesis would amount to the explicit, wholesale fabrication of a necessity foreign to all logic. *The Principle of Sufficient Reason is thus another name for the irrational* – and the refusal of this principle, far from being a way of doing away with reason, is in my opinion the very condition of its philosophical reactualisation. The refusal of the Principle of Sufficient Reason is not the refusal of reason, but the discovery of the power of chaos harboured by its fundamental principle (non-contradiction), as soon as the latter is no longer supplemented by anything else – the very expression 'rational chaos' from that moment on becoming a pleonasm.

But such a point of view also provides us with a new understanding of the 'end of metaphysics'. If metaphysics is essentially linked to the postulation – whether explicit or not – of the Principle of Sufficient Reason, the former cannot be understood, in Heideggerian fashion, as the final accomplishment of reason, but as the final accomplishment of real necessity, or again of what I call the reification of rational necessity. From this point of view, I understand by metaphysics, any postulation of a real necessity: so that it would constitute a metaphysical postulation that all or certain given determinate situations in this world are necessary (a determination being definable as a trait capable of differentiating one situation from another, equally thinkable situation). A metaphysics would thus affirm that it is possible, and moreover that it is the very task of reason, to establish why things must be thus rather than otherwise (why some particular individuals, law(s), God(s), *etc.*, rather than other individuals, laws, etc.)

3. ONTOLOGICAL REFORMULATION

The question now is as follows: in accepting the possibility of a change in natural constants, have we not suppressed the problem of induction itself? In other words: once the idea of a necessary constancy of laws is refused, can Hume's question still be posed in the form of a *problem* to be resolved, and more precisely as an ontological problem? It certainly can.

I would affirm that, indeed, there is no reason for phenomenal constants to be constant. I maintain, then, that these laws could change. One thereby circumvents what, in induction, usually gives rise to the problem: the proof, on the basis of past experience, of the future constancy of laws. But one encounters another difficulty, which appears at least as redoubtable: if laws have no reason to be constant, *why do they not change at each and every instant?* If a law is what it is purely contingently, it could change at any moment. The persistence of the laws of the universe seems consequently to break all laws of probability: for if the laws are effectively contingent, it seems that they must frequently manifest such contingency. If the duration of laws does not rest upon any necessity, it must be a function of successive 'dice rolls', falling each time in favour of their continuation or their abolition. From this point of view, their manifest perenniality becomes a probabilistic aberration – and it is precisely because we never observe such modifications that such an hypothesis has seemed, to those who tackled the problem of induction, too absurd to be seriously envisaged.

Consequently, the strategy of the reactualisation of the ontological problem of induction will be as follows:

Meillassoux – Potentiality & Virtuality

1) We affirm that there exists an ontological path which has not been seriously explored: that consisting in establishing, not the uniformity of nature, but the contrary possibility of every constant being submitted to change in the same way as any factual event in this world – and this without any superior reason presiding over such changes.

2) We maintain that the refusal to envisage such an option for the resolution of the problem is based on an implicit probabilistic argument consisting in affirming that every contingency of laws must manifest itself in experience; which amounts to identifying the contingency of laws with their frequent modification.

3) Thereby, we have at our disposal the means to reformulate Hume's problem without abandoning the ontological perspective in favour of the epistemic perspective largely dominant today. Beginning to resolve the problem of induction comes down to *delegitimating the probabilistic reasoning at the origin of the refusal of the contingency of laws.* More precisely, it is a matter of showing what is fallacious in the inference from the contingency of laws to the frequency (and thus the observability) of their changing. This amounts to refusing the application of probability to the contingency of laws, thereby producing *a valuable conceptual distinction* between contingency understood in this radical sense and the usual concept of contingency conceived as chance subject to the laws of probability. Given such a distinction, it is no longer legitimate to maintain that the phenomenal stability of laws compels us to suppose their necessity. This permits us to demonstrate that, without serious consequence, real necessity can be left behind, and with it the various

supposedly insoluble enigmas it occasioned.

In short, *Hume's problem becomes the problem of the difference between chance and contingency.*

4. PRINCIPLE OF THE DISTINCTION CHANCE/CONTINGENCY

To demonstrate why laws, if they can change, have not done so frequently, thus comes down to disqualifying the legitimacy of probabilistic reasoning when the latter is applied to the laws of nature themselves, rather than to events subject to those laws. Here is how such a distinction can, in my opinion, be effectively made: to apply a probabilistic chain of reasoning to a particular phenomenon supposes as given the universe of possible cases in which the numerical calculation can take place. Such a set of cases, for example, is given to a supposedly symmetrical and homogeneous object, a die or a coin. If the die or the coin to which such a calculative procedure is applied always falls on the same face, one concludes by affirming that it has become highly improbable that this phenomenon is truly contingent: the coin or die is most likely loaded, that is to say, it obeys a law – for example the law of gravitation applied to the ball of lead hidden within. And an analogous chain of reasoning is applied in favour of the necessity of laws: identifying the laws with the different faces of a universal Die – faces representing the set of possible worlds – it is said, as in the precedent case, that if these laws are contingent, we would have been present at the frequent changing of the 'face'; that is to say, the physical world would have changed frequently. Since the 'result' is, on the contrary, always the same, the result must be 'loaded' by the presence of some hidden necessity, at the origin of the constancy of observable laws. In short, we begin by giving ourselves a set of possible cases, each one representing a conceivable world having as much chance as the others of being chosen in the end, and conclude from this that it is infinitely improbable that our own universe should constantly be drawn by chance from such a set, unless a hidden necessity presided secretly over the result.[3]

Now, if this reasoning cannot be justified, it is because there does not truly exist any means to construct a set of possible universes within which the notion of probability could still be employed. The only two means for determining a universe of cases are recourse to experience, or recourse to a mathematical construction capable of justifying unaided the cardinality (the 'size') of the set of possible worlds. Now, both of these paths are equally blocked here. As for the empirical approach, obviously no-one – unless perhaps Leibniz's God – has ever been at leisure to survey the entire set of possible worlds. But the theoretical approach is equally impossible: for what would be attempted here would be to affirm that there is an infinity of possible worlds, that is to say of logically

3. It was through reading Jean-René Vernes' *Critique de la raison aléatoire* (Paris: Aubier 1981) that I first grasped the probabilistic nature of the belief in the necessity of laws. Vernes proposes to prove by such an argument the existence of a reality external to the representations of the Cogito, since it alone would be capable of giving a reason for a continuity of experience which cannot be established through thought alone.

As I have remarked elsewhere, I believe that an equally *mathematical* – more specifically, probabilistic – argument underlies the Kantian transcendental deduction of the categories in the *Critique of Pure Reason*. Kant's argument – as elaborate as it might be in its detail – seems to me to be in perfect continuity with what we might call the argument of 'good sense' against the contingency of natural laws. I argue that Kant's deduction consists simply in exacerbating the

thinkable worlds, which could only reinforce the conviction that the constancy of just one of them is extraordinarily improbable. But it is precisely on this point that the unacceptable postulate of our 'probabilist sophism' hinges, for I ask then: of which infinity are we speaking here? We know, since Cantor, that infinities are multiple, that is to say, are of different cardinalities – more or less 'large', like the discrete and continuous infinities – and above all that these infinities constitute a multiplicity it is impossible to foreclose, since a set of all sets cannot be supposed without contradiction. The Cantorian revolution consists in having demonstrated that infinities can be differentiated, that is, that one can think the equality or inequality of two infinities: two infinite sets are equal when there exists between them a biunivocal correspondence, that is, a bijective function which makes each element of the first correspond with one, and only one, of the other. They are unequal if such a correspondence does not exist. Further still, it is possible to demonstrate that, whatever infinity is considered, *an infinity of superior cardinality* (a 'larger' infinity) *necessarily exists.* One need only construct (something that is always possible) the set of the parts of this infinity. From this perspective, it becomes impossible to think a last

'probabilistic sophism' critiqued in the present article, to the point where the following is argued: if laws were contingent, they would change so frequently, so frenetically, that we would never be able to grasp anything whatsoever, because none of the conditions for the stable representation of objects would ever obtain. In short, if causal connection were contingent, we would know it so well that we would no longer know anything. As can be seen, this argument can only pass from the notion of contingency to the notion of frequency given the presupposition that it is extraordinarily *improbable* that the laws should remain constant rather than being modified in every conceivable way at every moment. ('Temps et surgissement ex nihilo', presentation in the seminar series *Positions et arguments* at the École Normale Supérieure, April 2006. See http://www.diffusion.ens.fr/index.php?res=conf&idconf=701).

infinity that no other could exceed.[4]

But in that case, since there is no reason, whether empirical or theoretical, to choose one infinity rather than another, and since we can no longer rely on reason to constitute an absolute totality of all possible cases, and since we cannot give any particular reason upon which to ground the existence of such a universe of cases, we cannot legitimately construct any set within which the foregoing probabilistic reasoning could make sense. This then means that it is indeed incorrect to infer from the contingency of laws the necessary frequency of their changing. So it is not absurd to suppose that the current constants might remain the same whilst being devoid of necessity, since the notion of possible change – and even chaotic change, change devoid of all reason – can be separated from that of frequent change: *laws which are contingent, but stable beyond all probability, thereby become conceivable.*

We must add, however, that there are two possible versions of such a strategy of resolution:

4. The set of parts of a set is the set of subsets of that set, that is to say the set of all possible regroupings of its elements. Take, for example, the finite set comprising three elements: (1, 2, 3). The set of its parts comprises (apart from the empty set, which is a part of every set): (1), (2) and (3) (the 'minimal' parts composed from its elements alone), (1,2), (1,3), (2,3), and (1,2,3) – this last part (1,2,3) being considered as the maximal part of the set, identical to it. It is clear that this second set is larger (possesses more elements) than the first. It can be proved that this is always the case, the case of an infinite set included. It is thus possible, for every infinite set, to construct a set of superior cardinality: the infinity which comprises the set of its parts. But this construction can equally be carried out on this new infinity, and so on indefinitely. For a clear introduction to axiomatic set theory, see Laurent Schwarz, *Analyse* I (Paris:Hermann,1991). The reference work on the philosophical importance of set-theory remains for me Alain Badiou's *L'être et l'événement* (Paris: Seuil, 1988), translated by Oliver Feltham as *Being and Event* (London: Continuum, 2006).

• A 'weak version' – a critical version, let us say – that would consist in limiting the application of aleatory reasoning to cases already submitted to laws (to observable events governed by the constants determining the universe where the calculation is carried out) but not to the laws themselves. Thereby, one would not be able to demonstrate positively the absence of real necessity, but only that its presupposition is of no use in giving an account of the stability of the world. One would content oneself with emphasising the theoretical possibility of contingent but indefinitely stable laws, by disqualifying the probabilist reasoning which concludes that such an hypothesis is aberrant. The two terms of the alternative – real necessity, or the contingency of laws – being equally non-demonstrable, the heuristic advantage of choosing the second hypothesis is invoked, by showing that it would obviate certain classical speculative enigmas linked to the unchallenged belief in the uniformity of nature.

• A 'strong', that is to say, speculative, version of the response to Hume's problem, would consist in maintaining positively the contingency of laws. Such an approach would incorporate the assets of the argument from heuristics in the above approach to its profit, but would go further, claiming to effectuate the consequences of the Cantorian intotalisation.

My overall project is to not limit myself to the critico-heuristic path, but to reactivate a speculative path (claiming to speak for the things themselves, despite the critical proscription), without ever reactivating metaphysics (that is to say, the absolutisation of a real necessity). Since it is impossible to give the full details of such an approach here, I will content myself with isolating the principal aspects of the critico-heuristic path.[5]

5. ONTOLOGICAL CONSEQUENCES OF THE NON-ALL.

We will adopt the following perspective: we suppose the ontological effectivity of the intotalisation of cases, in order to draw the consequences of such an hypothesis upon the notion of becoming, and to envisage its speculative advantages over the inverse hypothesis of the pertinence of real necessity.

In order to do this, let us reconsider the notion of the contingency of laws by restricting the notion of law to what constitutes its minimal condition, if not its complete definition: namely a determinate set, finite or infinite, of possible cases – a law, deterministic or aleatory, always comes down to a specific set of indexed cases.[6] We will try to determine the sense of a becoming within which laws themselves would be contingent, by comparing such a conception with the traditional vision according to which

5. For further indications as to the exigency of this reactivation, see my *Après la Finitude: Essai sur la nécessité de la contingence* (Paris:Seuil, 2006). I lay out the possible principles of the speculative approach in a forthcoming paper to be published by Éditions Ellipses (proceedings of Francis Wolff's Nanterre 2001 seminar series *Positions et arguments*).

6. I obviously do not claim that a law can be reduced to a set of possible cases, but that a condition of every law consists in the supposition that a determinate set of possible 'reals' can be discriminated amongst mere logical possibilities. I am thus adopting an argument *a minima*: I challenge the idea that one can even consider that there exists a set such that it would permit make of laws themselves cases of a Universe of laws (of a set of possible worlds determined by different laws). Since even this minimal condition of every law which is the definition of a determinate set of cases is not respected, this disqualifies *a fortiori* every attempt to think such laws in the same way as an event submitted to a law. To review the most important contemporary discussions of the notion of law, *cf.* A. Barberousse, P. Ludwig, M. Kistler, *La Philosophie des sciences au XXe siècle* (Paris: Flammarion, 2000), Chs. 4 and 5.

becoming is only thinkable as governed by immutable laws.

Every postulation of a legality, whether determinist or aleatory, identifies the world with a universe of possible cases indexable in principle, that is to say, pre-existing their ultimate discovery, and thereby constituting the potentialities of that universe. Whether a supposed law is considered probabilistic or deterministic, it posits in any case a pre-given set of possible cases which no becoming is supposed to modify. The affirmation of a fundamental hazard governing becoming thus does not challenge, but on the contrary presupposes, the essential fixity of such a becoming, since chance can only operate on the presupposition of a universe of cases determined once and for all. Chance allows time the possibility of a 'caged freedom', that is to say the possibility of the advent without reason of one of those cases permitted by the initial universe; but not the freedom of extracting itself from such a universe to bring forth cases which do not belong to the set thus defined. One cannot, within the aleatory vision of the world, deduce in univocal fashion the succession of events permitted by the law, but one can in principle *index* these events in their totality – even if, in fact, their apparent infinity prohibits for all time the definitive foreclosure of their recollection. In our terminology, such a belief in the aleatory legality of the world would constitute a *metaphysics of chance*, in so far as chance supposes the postulation of a law which would prescribe the fixed set of events within which time finds itself free to oscillate without any determined order. The belief in chance is inevitably a metaphysical belief, since it incorporates the belief in the factual necessity of determinate probabilistic laws, which it is no longer possible to account for except via the necessity of supposed deterministic laws.

In the guise of a radical evolution, it seems that since the Greeks, one conception, and one only, of becoming, has always imposed itself upon us: time is only the actual-isation of an eternal set of possibles, the actualisation of Ideal Cases, themselves inaccessible to becoming – this latter's only 'power' (or rather 'impotence') being that of distributing them in a disordered manner. If modernity is traditionally envisaged, as in Koyré's expression, as the passage from the closed world to the infinite universe, it remains no less true that modernity does not break with Greek metaphysics on one essential point: finite or infinite, the world remains governed by the law – that is, by the All, whose essential signification consists in the subordination of time to a set of possibles which it can only effectuate, but not modify.

Now, it is such a decision, common to the Greeks and to the moderns, from which we believe to have extracted ourselves, *by detotalising the possible*, and as a result liberating time from all legal subordination. In supposing the ontological legitimacy of the Cantorian conception of the infinite, we distinguish the infinite from the All, since the infinity of the possible cannot be equated with its exhaustion (every infinite set has a determinate cardinality, which another infinity is capable of exceeding). From this decision results the possibility of clearly distinguishing between the notions of contingency and chance, and indeed between the notions of potentiality and virtuality. *Potentialities* are the non-actualised cases of an indexed set of possibilities under the condition of a given law (whether aleatory or not). *Chance* is every actualisation of a potentiality for which there is no univocal instance of determination on the basis of the initial given conditions. Therefore I will call *contingency* the property of an indexed set of cases (not of a case belonging to an indexed set) of not itself being a case of a set of sets of cases; and *virtuality* the property of every set of cases of emerging within a becoming which is not dominated by any pre-constituted totality of possibles.

In short: I posit that the law can be related to a universe of determinate cases; I posit that there is no Universe of universes of cases; I posit that time can bring forth any non-contradictory set of possibilities. As a result, I accord to time the capacity to bring forth new laws which were not 'potentially' contained in some fixed set of possibles; I accord to time the capacity to bring forth situations *which were not at all contained in precedent situations*: of creating new cases, rather than merely actualising potentialities that eternally pre-exist their fulguration. If we maintain that becoming is not only capable of bringing forth cases on the basis of a pre-given universe of cases, we must then understand that it follows that such cases irrupt, properly speaking, *from nothing*, since no structure contains them as eternal potentialities before their emergence: *we thus make irruption* ex nihilo *the very concept of a temporality delivered to its pure immanence*.

This merits further explanation. If one thinks becoming in the mode of a temporality which does not supervene upon any determinate law, that is to say, any fixed set of possibles, and if one makes of laws themselves temporal events, without subordinating the possible passage from one law to another to a higher-level law which would determine its modalities, time thus conceived is not governed by any non-temporal principle – it is delivered to the pure immanance of its chaos, its illegality. But this is just another way to emphasise – something Hume was the first to maintain – that from a determinate situation, one can never infer *a priori* the ensuing situation, an indefinite multiplicity of different futures being envisageable without contradiction. Grafting the Humean thesis onto that of Cantorian intotality, we see emerging a time capable of bringing forth, outside all necessity and all probability, situations which are not at all pre-contained in their precedents, since according to such a perspective, the present is never pregnant with the future. The paradigmatic example of such an emergence, to which we shall return, is obviously that of the appearance of a life furnished with sensibility directly from a matter within which one cannot, short of sheer fantasy, foresee the germs of this sensibility, an apparition which can only be thought as an supplement irreducible to the conditions of its advent.

As it emerges according to the model of intotality, time might either, for no reason, maintain a universe of cases, a configuration of natural laws, within which it is possible to index a determinate set of recurrent situations constituting its 'potentialities' – or might, equally without reason, cancel the old universe, or supplement it with a universe of cases which were not at all pre-contained in the precedents, nor in any other Substrate wherein the possibilities of being would be ranged for all eternity. We must thus grasp the fact that the inexistence of a pre-constituted All of possibles makes of the emergence of a possible anticipated

by nothing in the preceding situation, the very manifestation of a time underwritten by no superior order: every
emergence of a supplement irreducible to its premises, far
from manifesting the intervention of a transcendent order
in rational becoming, becomes the rigorous inverse: a manifestation of a becoming which nothing transcends.[7]

Thus, for 'potentialism' (the doctrine that sees in each
possibility only a potentiality), time can only be the
medium by which what was already a possible case,
becomes a real case. Time, then, is the throw with which
the die offers us one of its faces: but in order for the faces
to be presented to us, it must be the case that they pre-
existed the throw. The throw manifests the faces, but does
not engrave them. According to our perspective, on the
contrary, time is not the putting-in-movement of possibles,
as the throw is the putting-in-movement of the faces of the
die: time creates the possible at the very moment it makes
it come to pass, it brings forth the possible as it does the
real, it inserts itself in the very throw of the die, to bring
forth a seventh case, in principle unforeseeable, which
breaks with the fixity of potentialities. Time throws the die,
but only to shatter it, to multiply its faces, beyond any
calculus of possibilities. Actual events cease to be doubled
by phantomatic possibilities which prefigure them before

7. To be more precise, we must say that the distinction potentiality/virtuality is
gnoseological rather than ontological, in so far as it designates essentially a
difference in our cognitive relation with temporality. The perpetuation of a Universe
of already-known cases (the constancy of laws) itself also escapes all consideration in
terms of potentiality. For if one can determine potentialities within a determinate set
of possibles, the maintenance across time of a determinate law itself cannot be eval-
uated in tems of potentiality (one possible case in a set of others). Even if the case
which comes to pass is already indexed, it is only foreseen upon condition – an
unforeseeable and improbabilisable condition – of the maintenance of the old set of

they occur, to be conceived instead as pure emergences, which before being are nothing, or, once again, which do not pre-exist their existence.

In other words, the notion of virtuality, supported by the rationality of the Cantorian decision of intotalising the thinkable, makes of irruption *ex nihilo* the central concept of an immanent, non-metaphysical rationality. Immanent, in that irruption *ex nihilo* presupposes, against the usually religious vision of such a concept, that there is no principle (divine or otherwise) superior to the pure power of the chaos of becoming; non-metaphysical in that the radical rejection of all real necessity assures us of breaking with the inaugural decision of the Principle of Sufficient Reason.

The most effective way to grasp properly the sense of the thesis proposed here is perhaps, as mentioned, to subtract it from the heuristic interest. This separation can be carried out through a series of elucidations permitted by such a model – elucidations of problems generally held to be insoluble, and thus sterile.

Firstly, as we have already said, such a model permits us to dissociate the notion of the stability of the empirical world from that of real necessity. The reprise of the problem of induction sought to show that it is possible to abandon the idea of a necessary constancy of laws, without this abandonment leading to the opposite idea of a

possibles. Ultimately, the Universe can be identified with the factual re-emergence of the same Universe on the ground of non-totality. But the virtualising power of time, its insubordination to any superior order, lets itself be known, or is phenomenalised, when there emerges a novelty that defeats all continuity between the past and the present. *Every 'miracle' thus becomes the manifestation of the inexistence of God*, in so far as every radical rupture of the present in relation to the past becomes the manifestation of the absence of any order capable of overseeing the chaotic power of becoming.

necessarily disordered world. For the disqualification of the probabilist reasoning which implicitly founds the refusal of a contingency of laws suffices to demonstrate that the possible changing of constants of this world does not indicate their necessary continual upheaval: by affirming that the world could really submit its laws to its own becoming, one posits the concept of a contingency superior to all necessity, *one whose actualisation is therefore subject to no constraint* – and above all not that of a frequential law supposed to render more and more improbable the non-effectuation of certain possibilities. For to affirm that the changing of laws, if it *could* happen, *must* happen, is to subordinate anew the contingency of becoming to the necessity of a law, according to which every possible must eventually be actualised. An entirely chaotic world – submitting every law to the power of time – could thus in principle be phenomenally *indiscernible* from a world subject to necessary laws, since a world capable of everything must *also* be able *not* to effect all that it is capable of. Thus it becomes possible to justify the postulate of all natural science – namely the reproducibility of experimental procedures, supposing a general stability of phenomena – whilst assuming the effective absence of a principle of uniformity of nature, and by the same token abandoning the canonical enigmas linked to the hypothesis of a necessity of laws. But this abandonment does not proceed, as in Goodman, from a simple refusal to think the problem, a refusal justified by its supposed insolubility: it proceeds from the conviction that one can think the contingency of constants compatibly with their manifest stability.

The critique of the probabilistic sophism given above

can also be extended to its application in various analogous arguments, which generally seek to restore a certain form of finalism. I will content myself here with mentioning one example of such an extension of the critical analysis, that of anthropism.

The thesis of anthropism – more precisely, of what is known as the Strong Anthropic Principle – rests fundamentally upon the following hypothesis:[8] one imagines oneself able to vary in an arbitrary fashion the initial givens of a universe in expansion, such as the numbers which specify the fundamental laws of contemporary physics (that is to say the relations and constants involved in these laws). One is then in a position to determine the evolution of these artificial universes, and one notes, in almost all cases, that these latter are incapable of evolving towards the production of the components indispensable for the emergence of life and, *a fortiori*, of intelligence. This result, which emphasises the extreme rarity of universes capable of producing consciousness, is then presented *as deserving of astonishment* – astonishment before the remarkable coincidence of the contingent givens of our universe (contingent in so far as there is no means to deduce their determinations – they can only be observed within experience) with the extremely restrictive physical conditions presiding over the appearance of conscious life: how is it that our universe should be so precisely furnished with the necessary characteristics for our appearance, whereas these characteristics prove to be

8. For a definition of the various versions of the Anthropic Principle, See J.D.Barrow and F.J.Tipler, *The Anthropic Cosmological Principle* (Oxford: Oxford University Press, 1986), Introduction and Section 1.2.

of such rarity on the level of possible universes? *Such an astonishment thus rests upon reasoning that is clearly probabilistic,* relating the number of possible universes to the number of universes capable of life. The anthropist begins by being surprised by a coincidence too strong to be imputed to chance alone, and then infers the idea of an enigmatic finality having predetermined our universe to comprise the initial constants and givens which render possible the emergence of man. Anthropism thus reactivates a classical *topos* of finalist thought: the remarking of the existence of a highly-ordered reality (inherent to the organised and thinking being) whose cause cannot reasonably be imputed to chance alone, and which consequently imposes the hypothesis of a hidden finality.

Now, we can see in what way the critique of the probabilist sophism permits us to challenge such a *topos* in a new way. For such reasoning is only legitimate if we suppose the existence of a determinate set (whether finite or infinite) of possible universes, obtained through the antecedent variation of the givens and constants of the observable universe. Now, it appears that there are no legitimate means of constituting the universe of possibles within which such reasoning could make sense, since this means, once more, could be neither experimental nor simply theoretically: as soon as one frees oneself from the imperatives of experience, in the name of what principle can one limit, as the Anthropic Principle implicitly does, the set of possible worlds to those obtained solely by the linear variation of constants and variables found in the currently observable universe, and in whose name do we limit such a set of worlds to a determinate infinity? In truth, once the possible is envisaged in its generality, every totality becomes unthinkable, and with it the aleatory construction within which our astonishment finds its source. The rational attitude is not, in actual fact, to seek an explanation capable of responding to our astonishment, but to trace the inferential genealogy of the latter so as to show it to be the consequence of an application of probabilities outside the sole legitimate field of their application.

Finally, the abandonment of real necessity permits one last elucidation, this time concerning the emergence of new situations, whose qualitative content is such that it seems impossible to detect, without absurdity, its anticipated presence in anterior situations. So that the problem appears in all clarity, let us take the classical example of the emergence of life, understood here not merely as the fact of organisation but as subjective existence. From Diderot's hylozoism, to Hans Jonas' neo-finalism,[9] the same argumentative strategies are reproduced time and time again in philosophical polemics on the possibility of life emerging from inanimate matter. Since life manifestly supposes, at least at a certain degree of its evolution, the existence of a set of affective and perceptive contents, either one decides that matter already contained such subjectivity in some manner, in too weak a degree for it to be detected, or that these affections of the living being did not pre-exist in any way within matter, thus finding oneself constrained to admit their irruption *ex nihilo* from that matter – which seems to lead to the acceptance of an intervention transcending the power of nature. Either a 'continuism', a

9. See for example H. Jonas, *The Imperative of Responsibility* (Chicago: University of Chicago, 1985), chap. 3, 4, 3b: 'The Monist Theory of Emergence'.

philosophy of immanence – a variant of hylozoism – which would have it that *all* matter is alive to some degree; or the belief in a transcendence exceeding the rational comprehension of natural processes. But such a division of positions can once more be called into question once irruption *ex nihilo* becomes thinkable within the very framework of an immanent temporality. We can then challenge both the necessity of the preformation of life within matter itself, and the irrationalism that typically accompanies the affirmation of a novelty irreducible to the elements of the situation within which it occurs, since such an emergence becomes, on the contrary, the correlate of the rational unthinkability of the All. The notion of virtuality permits us, then, to *reverse the signs*, making of every radical irruption the manifestation, not of a transcendent principle of becoming (a miracle, the sign of a Creator), but of a time that nothing subtends (an emergence, the sign of the non-All). We can then grasp what is signified by the impossibility of tracing a genealogy of novelties directly to a time before their emergence: not the incapacity of reason to discern hidden potentialities, but, quite on the contrary, the capacity of reason to accede to the ineffectivity of an All of potentialities which would pre-exist their emergence. In every radical novelty, time makes manifest that it does not actualise a germ of the past, but that it brings forth a virtuality which did not pre-exist in any way, in any totality inaccessible to time, its own advent.[10]

We thus glimpse if all-too-briefly, the outlines of a philosophy emancipated from the Principle of Sufficient Reason, and endeavouring, in this very recommencement, to maintain the double exigency inherent to the classical form of rationalism: the ontology of that which is given to experience, and the critique of representation.

10. It might be objected that in the preceding arguments I tend to conflate potential-ism – which makes of every possible a potentiality – and a continuism which claims to discern for every present novelty a past situation wherein all the elements of such a novelty already existed, if at a lesser degree. It will be objected that one might at once claim that the world is subject to immutable laws, and refuse the actualism of preformationism, which sees the world as a set of Russian dolls where everything is already effective before being manifest. I respond that I certainly do not conflate the two theses, but that potentialism and preformationism, having in common the refusal of virtuality, are equally incapable of thinking a pure novelty: potentialism, in particular, if it claims that sensation is a potentiality of matter which was not actu-alised by it before its emergence in the living, would accumulate disadvantages, since it would be constrained to combine the mystery of real necessity (matter is ruled by laws which give birth to sensitive contents under determinate conditions) and that of irruption *ex nihilo* (these contents are in no way contained in the conditions that make them emerge).

Dark Matter: Probing the Arche-Fossil

Interview with Roberto Trotta

Dr. Roberto Trotta[1] *coordinates* Oxford University's Dark Sector Initiative,[2] *an enterprise dedicated to elucidating the nature of 'dark matter' and 'dark energy'. The cross-disciplinary nature of this project – described as an intense collaborative work involving mathematics, theoretical physics, phenomenology and statistics – anticipates the problematic status of its objects. Trotta's work as a theoretical cosmologist takes place at the intersection of cosmology (the attempt to construct a coherent model and narrative of the origin and evolution of the universe), astrophysics (the description in physical terms of the objects observed in the universe), and theoretical physics (positing models of the elementary constituents of matter and their interactions). Observations of astrophysical entities are interpreted in cosmology within the framework of theoretical physics, drawing upon powerful statistical techniques to derive probabilistic inferences on the fundamental phenomena under scrutiny, even in cases where the astrophysical objects themselves are poorly understood. Equally, some of the most advanced and speculative theoretical physics finds its best (and sometimes unique) testing-ground in models of the early universe.*

1. See http://www-astro.physics.ox.ac.uk/~rxt/

2. See http://www-astro.physics.ox.ac.uk/darksector/

COLLAPSE II

Collapse interviewed Trotta at the Beecroft Institute for Particle Astrophysics and Cosmology (BIPAC) with a view to understanding how the process of determination of this field of research on the 'outer edge' of science, bounded equally by technological, probabilistic and logical constraints, brings to light the process of scientific thought, and problematises its very conceptual foundations, thus emphasising its continuities with traditionally 'philosophical' concerns.

COLLAPSE: We would like to investigate with you the general question of the status of the objects of your research. Could you describe to us how empirical observation, theoretical postulation, and the aspiration towards a coherent cosmological model interact to create this problematic object of study – 'dark matter' – and compel scientists to posit its reality?

ROBERTO TROTTA: We are interested in this 'dark matter', or 'dark sector' of the universe primarily because it enters, in an unexpected way, into our observations. Many different fundamental explanations for dark energy have been advanced, but the need for its postulation was brought forward primarily by empirical evidence; indirect, sometimes, but still empirical evidence, interpreted within the framework of a certain cosmological model.

According to the current paradigm, about 5 percent of the matter-energy of the universe is visible, and of this 5 percent only a fraction goes to form stars or planets or other heavenly bodies – the largest part is in the form of gas. 95 percent of the universe is 'dark', in one way or another: about 25 percent dark matter, 75 percent what we call dark energy.

The existence of dark matter is both predicted by fundamental models of theoretical physics, such as super-symmetry, and required by cosmological observations highlighting the problem of the 'missing mass' of the universe. In fact, many pieces of evidence strongly suggest that there is much more mass in the universe than the visible counterpart in the form of galaxies and clusters we can see. It is postulated that the missing mass does not interact with light, and this would explain why it is dark. But its existence is revealed by its gravitational effect on other massive bodies, for instance the distribution of galaxies in the universe, or the overall gravitational dynamics of the cosmos. This is how dark matter enters the cosmological model.

C: And what about 'dark energy'?

RT: The case for dark energy is even more puzzling: obser-vations of stellar explosions called supernovae indicated that the expansion of the universe is accelerating, rather than slowing down as it should under the influence of gravity if its content were in the form of ordinary matter (both visible and dark) and radiation. The accelerated expansion thus requires the presence of a new 'substance' with negative pressure, which would act as an 'anti-gravity' of sorts on cosmological scales: this is what has been dubbed 'dark energy'. In contrast to dark matter, at the moment we do not have many fundamentally motivated models for dark energy, except perhaps Einstein's cosmological constant – which, however, has to be inserted by hand into Einstein's equations to explain the present-day acceleration of the universe. But cosmologists are an inventive lot, and people were quick to introduce into the game new, *ad hoc* forms of energy to explain the accelerated expansion, perhaps in the form of so-called scalar fields. Fittingly, such models have been christened 'quintessence', since dark energy would be a fifth substance in the universe on top of the known four, *i.e.* photons, neutrinos, baryons (*i.e.* visible matter) and dark matter.

It's a very unsatisfactory state of things, thinking that after all this work in cosmology, forty years after cosmology was born with Penzias and Wilson, eighty years after Hubble discovered the expansion of the universe, we are stuck with this most incredible situation: that 95 percent of the universe is 'dark'. But we do believe that we have good reasons – empirical reasons – to have to go out and explain this missing mass and energy.

And so, the research programme is cross-disciplinary in the sense that it is really a field where you have the empirical observations – which I'll describe in more detail – of dark matter and dark energy. You have theoretical modelling, which is used both to interpret the observations cosmologically, and to try to give us a framework to predict further phenomena, or to explain phenomena. Then you have statistics, which is used to govern the data, to interpret them in a statistically sound way. And you have mathematics, since all these formulations, all these theories, are heavily mathematical, and we're trying to use them to derive the logical consequences of our observations. But it's really all interrelated. You can jump into this cycle at any point. You can start the cycle from, say, observations;

this gives you evidence for unexplained phenomena. At this point, you get the observation right, then you gather the statistical evidence for the phenomenon you are interested in; then you model it within a certain theoretical framework, which gives you predictions which in turn can be tested against new observations. So it's a connected chain of reasoning.

C: Historically, which observations first suggested the need to postulate dark matter?

RT: One of the first pieces of evidence for the need for dark matter goes back to the 30s and has been confirmed ever since. It's something called the 'flat rotational curves' of galaxies, and it can be explained like this. If you have a galaxy, with the visible mass of that galaxy you see there is a bulge in the middle, and then it declines – so, if it's a spiral galaxy, you have less stars in the spiral arms. Now, the further out you go in respect to the centre of the galaxy, you'd expect the velocity of the stars orbiting this galaxy to be reduced, simply because – in rather the same way as, say, Neptune goes more slowly around the Sun than the Earth does, because it's further out in the solar system – if all the gravity comes from the visible part of the galaxy, then stars which are further out should circle the galaxy more slowly than the stars that are in the centre. But observations of these velocities actually show that the velocity is constant with radius – which means either that our theory of gravity is wrong, and Newtonian-Einsteinian gravity doesn't hold on galactic scales; or that we need more matter than the visible part to keep those stars on track.

C: Evidently, in defining research programmes, a certain decision is called for: which elements of the current theoretical paradigm to preserve, and which to relinquish. For instance, in the context of physics a century ago, a decision had to be made between abandoning the Maxwellian equations regarding the constancy of the speed of light, or abandoning the Newtonian postulate of absolute simultaneity and the aether. The correct decision seems obvious to us now – perhaps it was even obvious to Einstein at the time, who seems not to have been significantly influenced by the negative outcome of the Michelson-Morley experiment. But nevertheless, it constituted a real decision, a kind of branching-point for science. Now, since you have just described the issue of these empirical observations as pressing us into a decision, let us ask: is it a straightforward matter to know which part to jettison? In the case of dark matter, why is it more cogent to hypothesise missing mass rather than a correction to the fundamental laws? Since, up to this point – despite its reassuringly substantial-sounding name – 'dark matter' has remained the name for a particular *gap* in our systematic account of the universe, then, as you say, the possibility remains that it may be, for instance, the result of a shortcoming in our understanding of gravity rather than evidence of 'missing mass'. Are both possibilities pursued in a research environment?

RT: They are pursued in parallel, to a certain extent, even though the majority of scientists would say that the dark matter hypothesis in this case would be preferred to a change in the fundamental laws of gravity, for two reasons. One reason is that we are extremely reluctant to change a theory as successful as general relativity [GR], because it accounts for phenomena on all sorts of scales, and is an extremely successful theory that has been tested to a high degree of precision. So it would seem strange – you would really have to have a compelling reason – to abandon it. That's one reason. The second reason, more from the empirical point of view, is that recent observations of the collision of clusters of galaxies – as recently as August 2006, in fact – have shown that even within the paradigm of a modified gravity, you wouldn't be able to explain these kinds of observations. So there are both reasons of theoretical prejudice – we don't want to abandon GR unless we need to; and empirical reasons – empirical facts don't seem to fit with current brands of modified gravity.

C: The flat rotational curves were the first piece of evidence, then, but others followed.

RT: Yes, we have this indirect observation from the flat rotational curves which, admittedly, relies on the fact that we have a certain model for how things spin around, certain laws of gravity – this is one piece of evidence. Then we have gravitational lensing, which is the bending of light through a gravitational field, which again, gives spectacular results, and is actually a way of highlighting the distribution of matter in the universe no matter whether it is visible or dark. This again cannot be accounted for: in the so-called 'strong' gravitational lensing, we see these beautiful arcs, light from background galaxies being deflected and distorted by foreground masses, and the degree of deflection cannot be accounted for merely by invoking the visible part of the foreground mass. That's another piece of evidence. Then we've got this 'fossil' of the cosmic microwave background radiation [CMBR]. Let's go back to the discovery of CMBR by Penzias and Wilson in 1965. Those two guys had a radio telescope set up somewhere in New Jersey, they were not looking for the background radiation, they just happened to find it. For two years they pointed their telescope to the skies, and they found the same noise everywhere, no matter where they pointed it. And they didn't know where this noise came from. They tried to clean the telescope, they tried to get rid of this noise, they couldn't – and eventually they got the Nobel prize for this discovery, because they'd just discovered CMBR, which is nothing else but the fact that the light emitted by the Big Bang, while travelling to us, was stretched by the expansion of the universe, and now it fills the whole universe, with a very low temperature of 3 Kelvin – so that's minus 269° C below zero. It's all around us. So those photons, those particles of light, come straight from the Big Bang. And they found it no matter where they looked, no matter where they pointed their telescope, which was an indication of its cosmological origin – it was not some type of local stuff, coming from a galaxy, it was really everywhere at the same time.

The CMBR leads us to attribute a global geometrical

property of flatness to the universe: we have measured this huge triangle – a 'cosmic triangle' – that is spanned by temperature differences in the CMBR thirteen billion light years away from us. So we have this cosmic triangle: we sit at one of the vertexes, with the other two vertexes being separated by the distance between fluctuations in the temperature of the CMBR, 13 billion light years away from us. Now we have measured the angle subtended by the distant side of the triangle, *i.e.* we have measured the angle between tiny temperature differences in the CMBR on the sky. This measurement tells us that we're living in a three-dimensional space that is analogous to a flat piece of paper, rather than a closed sphere. If I were stuck on a piece of paper like this, I would have Euclidean geometry on this piece of paper, the usual axioms of Euclidean geometry, say that parallel lines do not cross, and things like that. And that piece of paper would be a flat universe, flat, a two-dimensional universe. If we take a sphere, for instance, instead, that's a closed universe, we've got the great circles which intersect, we've got the angles of triangles on the sphere that do not add up to 180 degrees, but rather the sum has to be larger than 180 degrees, and so that's a closed geometry. We can measure the angles in this cosmic triangle, and they add up to 180 degrees with an accuracy better than 1 percent.

Now, if the CMBR tells us that the universe's spatial geometry must be flat, this means that we need something else to make up what's missing from the visible part; since the visible part, the dark matter, the dark energy, everything that's in the universe must add up to 1, in some appropriate units, if the universe is flat. And since in these units, the visible part is only 0.05, or 5 percent, we need another 0.95 to get up to 1, so that's another piece of evidence.

C: Again, an explanatory gap: the CMBR as a whole indicates overall flatness; the observations of visible matter give you a picture which can't be reconciled with that, and then the gap between them is the place where you postulate the dark matter.

RT: Yes, but again this is only one piece of evidence, there are at least three or four different lines of evidence coming from different observations that all add up to the same numbers. So it's not just one, there are many of them, all indicating the same thing.

This dark matter is puzzling, it's not visible yet. Even though we talk about 'detection', those are indirect pieces of evidence. Although there are lines of research that are being pursued now, putting big dark matter detectors deep in caves, to shield them from other influences – the strange idea of doing astronomy underground! – under kilometres of rock to shield them from influence. You put big tanks of whatever detectors you have, and just wait for the streaming dark matter particles to give you, every now and then, a signal in your detectors when they occasionally bounce of a proton. So that would be one way to visualise them, or to detect them for real – if you give the attribute 'reality' to the data from such a sophisticated apparatus.

There would be a nice analogy here, I think, with what happened in the 1930s when Wolfgang Pauli introduced the neutrino, a new particle, to solve the puzzle of the beta-decay of atoms. They didn't know how to solve this – there was missing energy, they didn't know where the energy went. So, he wrote this famous letter to his friends at the 'Radioactive Club', saying 'Dear Radioactive Friends, today I have done a terrible thing for a theoretical physicist, that is, to introduce a new particle that nobody will ever be able to see.' But sure enough, in 1954, Cowan and Reines detected it, and later on they got the Nobel prize for it, and now there are experiments which do detect neutrinos routinely. So, dark matter might be just the same.

Such experiments are big gambles on certain predictions of a certain scientific theory: like looking for the Higgs boson, which people reckon will be found, but there is no guarantee there. You've got theoretical predictions, and the important thing is that in these theoretical predictions you have the masses, that is to say, indications of where to look for these particles. These are just numbers that are not predicted by theory, they just have to be determined experimentally, so we don't know what those numbers represent.

C: Before we go on to discuss the other lines of evidence, perhaps we can suggest a counter-example to the analogy you have just mentioned, one which is arguably closer to the case in hand than the example of Pauli's postulation of neutrinos: namely, the infamous case of the planet Vulcan. 'Vulcan' was the name given by Urbain Le Verrier in 1859 to a 'hidden' planet that allegedly perturbed Mercury's orbit, and which thus 'explained' its observed deviations from the path predicted by Newtonian physics. For over half a century astronomers attempted to prove the existence of Vulcan, and there were numerous reports which claimed to have positively 'detected' the hypothetical planet. Now, as we know, despite serious efforts to prove its existence over a period of some five decades, and dozens of putative observations of the planet in transit, eventually Einstein's GR theory came along and explained the observed perturbations of Mercury as a mere by-product of the Sun's gravitational field. So here we have a case in which a 'missing mass' is postulated in order to provide an explanation of certain observed anomalies, and for a long time it is the only explanation in town. However, unlike in the case of Pauli's neutrinos, here it turns out that what was needed was not a more sophisticated means of detecting some hypothetical 'missing matter', but rather a suitable modification of the laws of gravity. Now, you have said that the postulation of 'dark matter' *might turn out to be* analogous to the case of Pauli's postulation of neutrinos. But then, by parity of logic, ought you not to also countenance the possibility that it might turn out instead to be rather more like the case of Le Verrier's 'Vulcan'?

This of course brings us back to the question raised earlier of why one should regard the postulation of dark matter as more scientifically compelling than the option of modifying the laws of gravity on galactic and intergalactic scales. In response to that you suggested that, apart from a general reluctance to attempt to modify a theory as successful as GR, there were also good empirical reasons for favouring the hypothesis of 'dark matter', some of these relating to very recent observations of galactic collisions.

Trotta – Dark Matter

The results of the observations in question were first presented back in August 2006 in a paper by Douglas Clowe *et al.* entitled 'A Direct Empirical Proof of the Existence of Dark Matter', which announced that the observations had enabled the 'direct detection of dark matter, independent of assumptions regarding the nature of the gravitational force law.'[3] A NASA press release promptly followed proclaiming that these observations constituted 'direct proof' and 'direct evidence' of the existence of dark matter[4] and the popular media was soon awash with headlines such as 'Dark Matter Observed', 'Dark Matter Witnessed After Galactic Collision', 'Galaxy Cluster Collision Proves Existence of Dark Matter', 'Scientists Offer Proof of Dark Matter' and so on. One could surely be forgiven for assuming that what had taken place here was a veritable *experimentum crucis*, indubitably proving the existence of dark matter once and for all and definitively ruling out all rival hypotheses. It was as if dark matter had suddenly been promoted in ontological status from its previously ethereal quasi-existence as hypothetical postulate to the rank of full-fledged 'substantial' reality. And yet, without wanting in any way to diminish the significance of these observations, it seems that, from what you have just said, things are not quite so assured as we might have been led to believe, that the postulation of dark matter remains something of a high-risk gamble. Is it not at least a little premature to say that dark matter is the 'only possible explanation' of the observations, as some cosmologists have been reported in the media as having

3. http://arxiv.org/abs/astro-ph/0608407

4. http://www.nasa.gov/home/hqnews/2006/aug/HQ_06297_CHANDRA_Dark_Matter.html

claimed? Apart from the consideration that the postulation of a missing 95 percent of the universe represents perhaps the most audacious flouting of Ockham's razor in the history of modern science – especially when one considers that a mere tweaking of the laws of gravity might ultimately prove up to the job, even if none of the models so far constructed have done – is there not a case for saying that the kind of explanation proffered by the postulation of dark matter amounts to an example of 'explaining the obscure by the even more obscure'? To what extent is it the case that, even now, the very terms 'dark matter' and 'dark energy' serve less as names for a satisfactory explanation and more as a placeholders for possible explanations not yet envisaged?

RT: As far as dark energy is concerned, yes, I would subscribe to the description you give of a placeholder for a more satisfactory explanation. In fact, one of the most pressing questions is to determine observationally whether dark energy lives on the right hand side or on the left hand side of Einstein equations. If it belongs to the left hand side – that's the side of the geometry of spacetime, where the structure of our gravity theory lives – then it's a manifestation of modified gravity of some sort, even if only in its mildest but actually quite disturbing incarnation, that's to say, Einstein's cosmological constant. If on the other hand it turns out that it belongs to the right hand side – that's where the matter-energy contents of the universe are written down – then it's really a new substance, and we have to think it over again in terms of a fundamental explanation of its physical origin.

But if we are talking about dark matter, then its status is very different. I mentioned the multiple, orthogonal lines of evidence we have for it. I also briefly mentioned that we have many well-motivated candidates, usually in the form of some sort of particles beyond the Standard Model of particle physics. Now we know from other sources – for example, from the fact that neutrinos have mass – that the Standard Model cannot be complete. And we also have theories waiting in the wings to replace the Standard Model, theories that make many predictions about the existence of a plethora of new, yet-unobserved particles. For instance, in supersymmetry every known Standard Model particle acquires a so-called 'superpartner' – that's a new particle with the same properties as its Standard Model partner but with a much heavier mass. This immediately doubles the number of fundamental entities in the theory, but it seems there is really no other way around it if one wants to solve certain technical problems that we do not need to discuss now. So from the point of view of simplicity and economy, such a theory hardly ticks those boxes. But it also allows one to gain a much more complete picture of the particles and their interactions. In order to test such a theory, it remains to build a huge accelerator, smash together particles with very high energy and observe the products of the collision. Because energy is mass, if the energy achieved is large enough such collisions will transform energy into massive particles, and hopefully produce some of the heavy supersymmetric particles everybody hopes to detect. Unfortunately, the masses of the particles are just free numbers in the theory; they are not predicted, so nobody knows whether we are going to find them when the LHC is turned on later this year at CERN. People make educated guesses, but there is no guarantee. The point is that the lightest of these supersymmetric particles fits the bill for a dark matter candidate. Its properties are exactly the ones you need if you had engineered it to be the dark matter of the universe – and the thing is, you have not! The neutralino (that's the name of the particle) comes straight out of supersymmetry, and all of a sudden you realise that this could be what the cosmological dark matter is made of. So here you go, you have solved two problems at once, if only you could prove that supersymmetry exists and that the neutralino is the dark matter particle. And this is exactly what people are trying to do, both at CERN and by trying to detect dark matter particles directly.

But there is one more thing to consider, namely the fact that cosmology is fundamentally different from particle physics, or from any other brand of physics, in at least two respects. The first aspect is that cosmology is an observational science, not an experimental one. We simply cannot reproduce the universe many times, tweaking the parameters of the experiment to see whether our theory is correct. The second point is that the fundamental framework within which all observations are interpreted posits that the objects we observe are subjected to the very same laws of physics we have derived in our labs on Earth. This is an extremely strong assumption, if one keeps in mind that cosmological phenomena stretch over billions of light years in space, over the entire life of the universe in time, and over tens or hundreds of orders of magnitudes in energy. One might describe this as the ultimate scientific hubris. So in view of all this, it is important to recall that the status of the 'substantial reality' of cosmological objects must be understood within the limits imposed by the above considerations.

C: We'd like to come back to this question of the uniqueness of cosmology as an observational but non-experimental science a little later, but sticking for the moment with the question of the nature of the evidence for the 'substantial reality' of dark matter, one of the most intuitively accessible fruits of this research are the images which show the predicted distribution of dark matter in the universe [see pages 100-1]. Here we see something that to the naïve eye looks very 'organic', almost like a network of capillaries. Since dark matter is not visible, how are such images obtained?

RT: These images depict what we call the 'cosmic web' – fittingly, I think. And this is a computer simulation: this is what we think you should be able to see if you could see the dark matter distribution in the universe – those filamentary structures represent the dark matter distribution within the universe. But it's computer-simulated: what you do is to take the initial universe, which was homogeneous, but not perfectly homogeneous – you had small initial fluctuations in density within it which were the seeds, that we still see today in the CMBR, and from which eventually those structures formed – you take this universe, put it into a supercomputer. Then you switch on gravity and you let gravity do its work. So regions that are

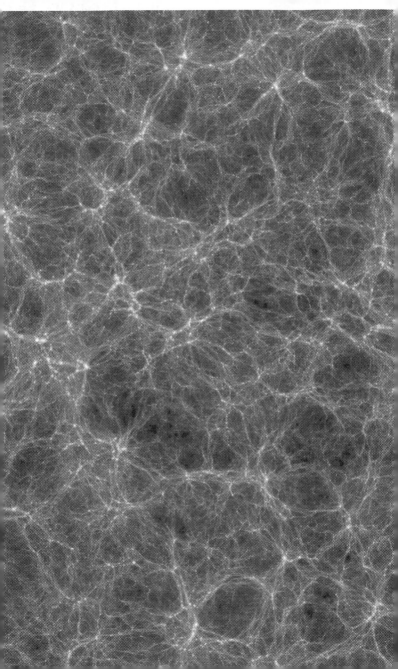

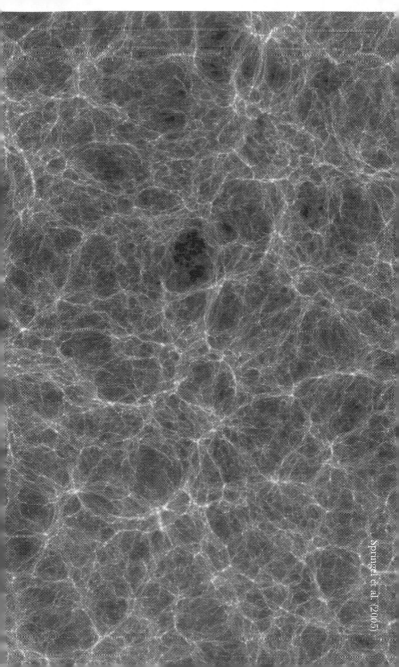
Springel et al. (2005)

dense will accrete matter from around them. Regions that are overdense would in time become critical overdense regions and this filamentary pattern appears during time.

So that's just a simulation. From the data we observe from gravitational lensing we are also able to extract some statistical properties of these filaments: we can quantify the filamentary structure itself, whether it's very filamentary or more sparse, more dense, and we can compare the numbers that we get out of the simulations with the observations. And this is the great game, to produce very many simulated universes with different values of parameters, to fit them to our observations, and to try to figure out which are the ones we actually observe in our universe.

C: Earlier you linked the 'puzzling' nature of dark matter with the fact that it is 'not yet visible', and indeed one of the ways in which the abstract mathematical sense given to 'matter' in contemporary physics is reconciled with our intuitive sense of materiality is through these kinds of images. There can be no doubt that images purporting to represent dark matter boast an all-important sense of immediacy which speaks to an interested general public. But is this engagement of the imagination also of significance for scientists themselves, providing a sort of milestone and an opportunity to 'zoom out' of the technical details of the research process?

RT: Yes, I think that's a good point, in the sense that until a few years ago scientists – especially cosmologists – we didn't have those images to look at, we hardly had any of the data we have now. So in that respect having these images is a way of anchoring ourselves to the reality of those objects. Although images that you can really look at and just understand by looking at them are very rare. Most of them have to be interpreted through statistical analysis, distilling the statistical content of the image into spectra or probability distributions or whatever. Having the 'real object' – with whatever qualifications you want to give to the term 'real' here – having the real object in front of your eyes is a way of anchoring yourself to the object so as to understand it. Although, as I say, the images, as fantastic as they are for reaching out to the public, have little informative content for scientists. They must be heavily processed, they must be analysed, they must be cross-correlated, and most of those procedures do not happen in an image space; they happen in a mathematical space, a statistical space, spaces that are highly idealized and so, in a sense, also highly immaterial. So the images are just the starting point for a much more complex process that goes on behind the scenes. It's rarely just the image that gives you the answer you're looking for; it's the content of the image that's distilled through a heavily mathematical process, and that's what's interesting for the scientist. But the images are great as the first point of contact to try to convey what we get out of the image to the general public, in a more understandable way, a way which is less arid.

C: Is there a danger that they may serve to conceal – or so to speak, shortcut – uncertainties within the theoretical model? For instance, if you have an image purporting to show 'the distribution of dark matter', you're in a sense already guilty of reifying dark matter.

RT: Yes, but professional scientists, when they look at these images, are supposed to remember this. Sometimes the shortcut is taken consciously in order to make the image more 'saleable' to the public, in order to promote the field more effectively. But it's a thin line you have to tread. For example, what's described as the imaging of dark matter is actually the imaging of gravitational potentials, which has been recovered through a set of statistical techniques, transformed through false-colour images purporting to show dark matter. So yes, it is a shortcut that's consciously taken sometimes in order to make the content more directly accessible. But we should never forget that, in taking these shortcuts, we bypass our interpretation of the data we have gathered, which is done through the optic of a particular theory, and a particular narrative as to how these data have been gathered and what they mean. The point is that the very interpretation of the physical reality of the objects we observe is dependent on an underlying theory which explains them in the first place; so they're not objects we can relate to in an immediate way.

C: The essential theory-dependence or 'theory-ladenness' of observation is of course something very well-established in the philosophy of science, and it's something which has given rise to no end of philosophical debate – regarding, for example, instrumentalist versus realist interpretations of scientific statements. The very idea that knowledge is a matter of obtaining a faithful 'copy' of a reality-in-itself, as something knowable without theoretical mediation, is one which has lost favour in the philosophical tradition since Kant. We'd like to touch on some of these questions later, but for the moment, sticking to the point of view of a 'naïve realism', one might feel almost 'cheated' to learn that so much necessary theoretical and instrumental mediation is involved in gaining access to these objects. From the lay-person's point of view the 'substantial reality' of a thing is precisely something that *ought to be* accessed in an 'immediate' way, without the kinds of theoretical contrivance you have described. Is there a sense in which all this necessary mediation amounts to a diminution of the reality itself, or is it rather the case that science has first to 'constitute' that reality in some sense – to 'bring it into being' almost – in order to determine it?

RT: I wouldn't call it a diminution, I would call it an *enhancement* of reality. Perhaps an artificial enhancement to a certain extent – mediated by the theories and instrumental apparati we use – but a necessary one, for the simple reason that we simply do not have immediate access to the reality of those objects. I would even be tempted to say that the true, the most informative reality of those objects, often is *only* revealed *after* these very complex processes, and often only in a statistical sense, which is very impalpable, giving us only access to certain relations, probability distributions and so on, whose very interpretation, once again, rests on what our understanding of probability fundamentally is, rests on many assumptions on the way the world is *supposed* to behave even on a statistical level – even for

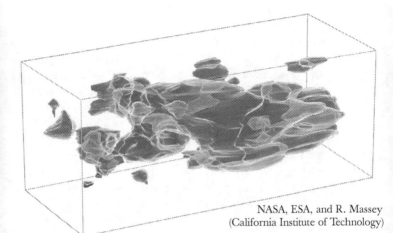

NASA, ESA, and R. Massey
(California Institute of Technology)

objects for which we don't have a statistical realisation, such as the universe itself. So in conclusion I would say that this is an enhancement of reality that necessarily takes place in order to bring into the open underlying patterns and regularities that are not visible to the 'naked eye'.

C: Coming back, then, to the images which purport to in some sense 'represent' dark matter, apart from the computer simulations – the 'cosmic web' images we've just been talking about – Hubble have very recently released 3-D images [see above] which were headlined in the media as 'The First 3-D Images of Dark Matter'. How do these differ from the 'cosmic web' in terms of how they are produced?

RT: Well, they are supposed to be real observations showing exactly the same patterns which, as we've just said, are computer simulations. But as I said before, they are not direct observations of dark matter, since dark matter is, obviously, invisible. They are obtained by using the gravitational properties of dark matter, the gravitational distortion that dark matter is supposed to bring about, by using background galaxies as sources of light. Let me describe this in a little more detail. The light coming from background galaxies goes through a field of clumpy dark matter and gets distorted, the shapes of galaxies get distorted – this is what we call 'gravitational lensing' – in a special way depending on where the clumps of dark matter lie, just as a real lens distorts the image which sits behind it; a bending of light – but not really a bending since light travels always in a straight line in spacetime, but since spacetime itself is bent by the mass concentration, we experience this as a distortion. You see now already that in order even to formulate the observation we have to have this general-relativistic theory of spacetime, so you see how the significance of even our raw data is heavily dependent on our underlying world model.

This relates back to what we were saying about the 'enhancing' aspects. There are pictures of visually impressive distortions of background galaxies that you can pick out 'by eye'; you can really see background galaxies being distorted in what we call 'Einstein rings' around the clumpy object – this is called 'strong gravitational lensing'. But that's not how the technique used to reconstruct the Hubble 3D images works. This technique is called 'weak gravitational lensing' and it works by observing tiny distortions of background galaxies, distortions in the shape of the galaxies. So if you had galaxies that were perfectly round as sources in the background and you observed them and saw their shape being distorted by 1 percent, or perhaps just a fraction of a percent, then you would be able to map exactly – by telling how the distortion behaves across the sky – the intervening dark matter distribution. Now, the thing is, we don't even have regular galaxies in the background. Instead we have galaxies that come in all different shapes and sizes, and so we are measuring distortions of shapes that we don't even know in the first place, because we don't have access to the undistorted shapes. That's where the enhancing techniques come in, because in order to get access to coherent distortions of galaxy shapes, you've got to make a statistical average. So, making the assumption that all galaxies are randomly oriented, with random shapes, if there were no coherent distortion, if you make an average, you ought to obtain zero. But since there is intervening dark matter – and that's where the enhancing techniques come in – you do these correlations, these statistical observations, and you find coherent patterns of distortions that do not average away because they are not intrinsic to the galaxies but are imprinted on them through the dark matter lens distortion. And, again, that's not something you could pick up by eye.

C: Another line of evidence is indicated by your work on acoustic oscillations of the early universe which are 'frozen' into the fabric of matter – a sort of primordial 'sound-fossil'.

RT: Yes, these acoustic oscillations are, in a way, a natural fossil. The relevance of the sound waves of the early universe in general for cosmological parameters is that it's all relatively simple to calculate, because the universe was fairly young, and these density fluctuations which eventually grew to galaxies were still very small – actually one part in a hundred thousand. So they were so small that we can calculate them with very high accuracy, and we can follow their evolution up to the point where the CMBR was released, very accurately. And so from this we can confidently infer several properties of the universe at the time, for instance how much dark matter there was, how much visible matter there was, what were the characteristics of the seeds, how the seeds were sprinkled with scale, whether there were more seeds on small scales, on large scales, or whether they were uniformly sprinkled on all scales and so on. These sorts of things can be inferred from sound waves in the CMBR, because we know the physics very well. And so it's a nice spot between the very high-energy physics of the very beginning, which we don't fully understand, and the messy, non-linear physics of gravitational collapse and evolutionary structure that we do understand, but which gets difficult to follow because it gets very complicated, as you can see from the filamentary structures you obtain through the computer simulations we discussed.

C: How do you go about reading these 'recordings' of the Big Bang?

RT: We saw that the CMBR is very homogeneous because of its cosmological origin. But now we have very sensitive detectors, telescopes and satellites that measure this background radiation to a very high degree of accuracy. And if you look carefully enough, you will see that this CMBR is not perfectly homogeneous; it has temperature differences in it. So if you look with your telescope in this direction, we see a slightly colder spot, if we look in that direction we see a slightly hotter spot. We can build a map [see below] of the sky, showing the temperature distribution of the background radiation. In order to measure the differences between the hot and cold spots with your telescope you need a sensitivity that's equivalent to the sensitivity you'd need with an optical telescope to see a mouse walking on the moon from the earth. So it's very tough. The guys who first did it in 1992 got the Nobel prize in 2006. These fluctuations you see in this map are the sound waves from the early universe, that's exactly

NASA/WMAP Science Team

what they are. When you throw a pebble in a pond you've got waves that go out in all directions; if you throw many pebbles in a pond you get a nice superposition of waves. In our case the pebbles were quantum fluctuations in the early universe, and they got frozen in at the moment this image was produced, and this is what we see – we really image them with our telescopes.

C: Calling them 'sound waves' is not just a figurative way of speaking, then?

RT: No, it's a technical definition: they're compression waves. The universe at this point was a plasma, that's a hot gas of electrons and protons, separated by the temperature, because the temperature was so high. So those were really acoustic waves, just like the waves in the air now as I speak, only they were travelling in the primordial plasma. And we can see them, as we can see in this map: it's real, it's been predicted, and we find this fantastic agreement with our models.

We usually talk about the CMBR being the uniform radiation coming to us from the Big Bang. When we talk about the temperature differences or anisotropies, we're talking about the very same radiation, but now looked at through a much more powerful telescope, so that you can highlight the temperature differences. It's one and the same thing, but you need a more powerful telescope to see the sound waves in it. I'm working more on the theoretical side of it, but people here also build such instruments. I'm interested in finding out how we can use those instruments to learn more about the conditions of the universe back then, or the conditions of the universe in the far future.

C: Let's return to the cosmological narrative, and to the 'seeds' you already mentioned briefly. For the first 300,000 years after the Big Bang, the universe is thought to have been remarkably homogeneous, surprisingly 'smooth'. The gravitational clustering which, it is supposed, ultimately structured this featureless continuum, was driven somehow by the properties of dark matter, via tiny fluctuations imprinted upon matter during the initial expansion.

Here dark matter seems to be invoked to answer a most traditional philosophical question: Why is the universe 'uneven' at all? Why does it consist of great voids and small concentrations of matter? Why is there something rather than nothing – or pure homogeneity, or chaos? The probing of anisotropy practiced by cosmologists rather recalls the original philosophical materialist, Lucretius, who, refusing divine intervention, posited an originary *clinamen* or 'swerve' which disturbed the atoms in freefall and led to the creation of nature. And unless some principle such as the *clinamen* intervenes, this heterogeneity, or what we could call the high information content of the universe, seems quite at odds with the received image of physical laws as linear and predictable. Are we to understand that some fundamentally nondeterministic processes must intervene at those crucial early stages to introduce these 'blueprints for differentiation'?

RT: Some fundamentally nondeterministic process, that's quite right, in fact. We just discussed the fact that these seeds are the ones that give rise to clusters, to galaxies, and eventually to all inhomogeneities in the universe. It's also the same seeds that we can observe in the CMBR from when the universe was very very young, 300,000 years after the Big Bang. And the ultimate origin of those seeds, we believe, lies in the very first fractions of a millisecond – actually 10^{-32} seconds after the Big Bang – during the period of very fast expansion which is called 'cosmological inflation', which takes the universe from a very small size up to cosmological scales. And at this point, since you are going so far back in time, the universe was compressed almost into a point, as it were. The overall size of the universe was so small that the microphysics governed by quantum mechanics [QM] was important. So you would have quantum fluctuations at the level of the whole universe, that then were stretched out to cosmological scales, and that's what the seeds were. Now, remember that all the evolution afterwards, the gravitational evolution of these seeds, is completely deterministic – we have the equations for gravity, we can follow them on the computer. But the 'seeding' of these fluctuations belongs to QM with its element of unpredictability, probability. The fundamental nature of it is quantum-mechanical, and so any understanding of this fluctuation is probably to be found in our understanding of what quantum-mechanical probability is.

C: This is where the intersection between fundamental physics and astrophysics comes in.

RT: Yes, it's where you close the circle: from the infinitely large scales of cosmology, you meet the infinitely small scales of particle physics, and quantum theory.

C: And presumably it's precisely here that the question of how to bring together GR with QM becomes a crucial and urgent one. To what extent does an adequate understanding of what happened in these first fractions of a millisecond after the Big Bang await the unification of these two foundational theories of modern physics in a successful quantum theory of gravity, whether that ultimately comes about in the form of some version of string theory, M-theory, loop quantum gravity, or something else altogether?

RT: Yes, that's absolutely fundamental, because all those big questions come together in the very first fraction of a millisecond, where all the interesting physics we don't yet know about happens. When, at the origin of the universe, we reach the highest possible energy scale, which is the Planck energy scale, at that point our theories essentially break down. That's the point where GR breaks down and we need to quantize spacetime itself. Remember, spacetime in our current vision of GR, is a sort of classical 'rubber–band' as it were, an arena in which quantum-mechanics take place. But when you get to this sort of energy scale, these types of miniscule length scales, it might be possible that fundamentally the quantization of spacetime itself begins to play a role. In other words spacetime stops being just an arena in which all the interactions of QM take place, but becomes a player in the quantum mechanical game, and nobody yet knows the rules of this quantum game.

C: GR and QM both break down – now, do they each break down independently in the sense that they no longer work at these extreme energy scales, so it's just a fuzzy area; or, do they break down because that's where they come together and you don't yet have a proper theory of how they can be combined?

RT: GR breaks down by itself because when you take the universe to size zero then – if you go analytically to zero in the equations describing the metric of spacetime – the zeros 'blow up' the equations, you end up with divisions by zero and our equations stop working. And the other problem is that no-one knows how QM and gravity work together because no-one is able to quantize gravity, for many different technical reasons. So yes, each breaks down on its own, and they break down together.

C: So that's a fuzzy area that's awaiting a successful theory of quantum gravity. Does it work that way, that you need a successful theory of quantum gravity in order to understand these very earliest fractions of a millisecond, these ten-millionths of a second after the Big Bang, or can cosmology itself help to solve the problem of the relation between QM and GR?

RT: Well, let me say that the fact that we don't have a successful quantum theory of gravity doesn't stop people from playing with some bold ideas. For instance, there is a scenario, called 'ekpyrotic universe', where the universe is supposed to be cyclic, that's to say it undergoes an infinite succession of expansions and contractions. So if you go back in time close to the moment of the Big Bang, when the universe is compressed at this incredibly high energy in this extremely small size, there might be some fuzzy physics, perhaps coming from extra dimensions, that makes it 'bounce back', rather than collapse to a point. Time does not start with the Big Bang, but rather you can describe the previous universes, as it were, before the Big Bang, by invoking some previously unknown phenomenon that actually prevents the Big Bang singularity, as we call it, from happening and gives you a bounce instead. So people do work on this kind of model at the level of their phenomenology, that's to say their effective description, but those are models that fundamentally are not strongly motivated at the moment. But people have these models in mind. So yes, it awaits resolution, but people are not *waiting* for it to happen.

C: The parameter z also plays a major role in constructing the cosmological 'narrative' of the universe. You are able to tell a story about what was happening at different stages of the history of the cosmos – *e.g.* 'the universe at $z = 20$'.

RT: This cosmological parameter z refers to redshift, and it has a very simple physical interpretation: it tells you that, for instance, if you're looking at the patch of the universe at $z = 20$, this is the state of the universe as it was when the size of the universe was twenty times smaller than it is today. This redshift is therefore not some abstract quantity, it's something we actually measure, by looking at the spectrum of whatever object we're observing. So if you look at a galaxy, the galaxy will contain certain elements, for instance hydrogen, iron, whatever. And these elements will emit light at particular wavelengths, particular colours: the 'signature' of the element. Hydrogen will have a particular line at a certain wavelength, iron will have a more complex signature consisting of a more elaborate pattern of lines. So we can determine, first of all, which elements are present in distant galaxies, because every element has got this set of colours which is particular to it, which comes from the quantum-mechanical structure of the atom. And by observing those lines, we can tell that on the Sun there is hydrogen, because we observe the hydrogen lines, and in the Andromeda galaxy there is hydrogen because we observe the very same lines. But the important thing is that the light of these spectroscopic signatures gets stretched while *en route* from distant galaxies to us, because of the expansion of the universe. So if the light gets stretched, that means that the wavelength of the light gets longer, and the light gets redder. In other words, we observe the same set of lines from a distant galaxy that we would observe from a local galaxy, but that set of lines is shifted towards the red end of the spectrum – what we call a 'redshift'. So by measuring the amount of redshift, we can measure how much of a stretch there has been between us and that galaxy. We can measure the redshift and we know whether this object is far away or nearby. It's uniformly shifted toward the red end of the spectrum.

Of course, as I mentioned before, there is an assumption which underlies everything here, and which is very strong, actually, especially from an ontological perspective. We assume all along – and we couldn't do without it – that the laws of physics are the same here, on Andromeda, and at the very beginning of time, which is a very major assumption. But there is little we can do if we don't make this very strong assumption.

C: Historically speaking, one might even say that it was just this very strong assumption of the uniformity of nature on the largest scales, of the universal applicability of the laws of physics, that inaugurated modern science itself. Copernicus' overcoming of the Aristotelian tradition of 'saving the appearances' by asserting the truth (rather than the mere empirical adequacy) of his cosmological system ultimately paved the way for Newton's synthesis of celestial and terrestrial mechanics via his law of universal gravitation. Of course we now know that, while the Newtonian laws of motion and gravity hold to an extremely good degree of approximation for almost all phenomena ordinarily encountered (*i.e.* for the everyday macroscopic world in which gravitational fields are relatively weak and objects move relatively slowly compared to the speed of light), they represent at best an approximate special case of the still more general laws of Einstein's GR, in which the notion of gravitational force acting instantaneously at a distance is replaced by that of the curvature of spacetime itself. But here, unlike the world described by Newtonian mechanics, which is more or less entirely consonant with the 'manifest image' of the world we derive from ordinary experience, the universe as described by relativity theory is, like that of quantum physics, deeply counter-intuitive. This is perhaps above all the case with regard to our commonsensical notions of space and time, to which the Minkowskian-Einsteinian notion of a four-dimensional spacetime continuum appears to bear little if any resemblance. The very idea that the beginning of the universe with the Big Bang was not an event which took place *in* space and time, but was rather the very coming into being of spacetime itself, is one which most people have a great deal of trouble coming to terms with. More difficult still is the related notion that there is no such thing as the 'objective present' – that there can no more be an objective division of the world into past, present and future than there can be an objective division of a region of space into east and west, or here and there. And at the submicroscopic levels where we enter into the utterly baffling world of quantum probabilities, things become a good deal stranger still. Here not just some but *all* of our habitual notions of space and time appear to break down completely, to become entirely meaningless.

All this gives rise to a number of questions relating to the very meaning of cosmological statements regarding time. For example, regarding the redshift observations which you have just been telling us about – by measuring the relative distances of observable galaxies in this way, you are also peering back into time, and determining things about the universe billions of years ago, when it was considerably smaller than it is today. These measurements, as you have indicated, are also crucial in estimating the age of the observable universe, which cosmologists have now dated rather precisely to 13.7 billion years. Such statements seem to be readily comprehensible and their meaning unproblematic. To what extent is this an illusion fostered by the isomorphism of such statements with everyday statements involving time? Must we not in some sense suspend our intuitive, commonsensical (and implicitly anthropomorphic) notions of time in order to properly comprehend statements about time in cosmology and in physics more generally?

RT: Well, as I was describing, the physically observable quantity is the redshift of the objects. It then turns out that the correspondence between redshift and cosmological time – when you do this mathematically through the equations of GR – depends on what the matter-energy content of the universe is. In other words, it depends on the relative amount of dark matter, dark energy, visible matter, radiation and so on. And so time becomes a function of the very properties we are trying to reconstruct.

C: Time evolves along with the universe.

RT: Yes, perhaps you could say that the link between the observable properties of the universe and its history as parameterized by cosmological time, goes through the very same properties of the universe, that is to say, its mass-energy density and its cosmic energy budget, which is interesting, because time becomes a function of them. At its heart this goes down to the fact that GR is a theory that links geometry on one hand, and the matter-energy content on the other. So we have matter which tells spacetime how to bend, and the bending of spacetime tells matter how to move. So we've got this inextricable mix of spacetime and matter-energy.

C: But if that is the case and if, according to GR, space and time are not to be regarded as anything like an absolute and universal stage against the background of which cosmic events play themselves out, but rather as flexible and dynamic actors – an integral part of the cast, as it were – in the cosmic drama itself, how is it that cosmologists are nevertheless able to define a concept of time that is applicable to the universe as a whole? Doesn't the passage of time depend on the speed of motion of the observer, and on the gravitational field in which the observer happens to be immersed?

RT: Well, in general, time *does* depend on the observer and the status of motion of the observer – different observers will observe different times – that's a generally acknowledged result of the theory of relativity, of course. But when you describe this evolving spacetime arena for the universe as a whole, then you introduce a sort of global co-ordinate system which you parameterise in terms of coordinates of time and space, x, y and z, and so the time you attach to this – which is the time that gets quoted as the age of the universe, and that I called above 'cosmological time' – would be the time that is measured by what we call a 'co-moving observer'. That is to say, a hypothetical observer that is swept along with the expansion of the universe, which we all are to a certain extent – our galaxy is swept along by the expansion of the universe. So that is what this time refers to: not just *any* observer, but an ideal observer that is postulated to be a co-moving observer, being swept along by the expansion of the universe.

C: But would the construction of this global spacetime co-ordinate system – this universal clock, so to speak – still be possible if the 'cosmic fossils' we have been discussing, such as redshift and the CMBR, revealed a non-uniform, non-homogeneous universe on the largest scales, rather than the surprisingly uniform, isotropic one which they appear to indicate? In a passage of his book *The Fabric of the Cosmos* which it seems appropriate to cite here, Brian Greene suggests that this background radiation not only 'gives astronomers what tyrannosaurus bones give paleontologists: a window into earlier epochs that is crucial to reconstructing what happened in the distant past', but that it is the *uniformity* of that radiation which is crucial in enabling cosmologists to define a concept of time applicable to the universe as a whole. The uniformity of the radiation is 'a fossilized testament to the uniformity of both the laws of physics and the details of the environment across the cosmos', and it is this homogeneity which, suggests Greene, makes it possible to meaningfully speak of a 'universal synchrony': 'if the universe did not have symmetry in space – if, for example, the background radiation were thoroughly haphazard, having wildly different temperatures in different regions – time in a cosmological sense would have little meaning.'[5]

RT: Yes, in fact the CMBR itself could be used by our co-moving observer to define a cosmic clock, obtained by measuring the uniform temperature of the microwave radiation and monitoring it as it cools down with the cosmic expansion. But even in the extreme case where you had a cosmological expansion that proceeded differentially in different directions, a so-called 'anisotropic universe', instead of describing the expansion with just one number – redshift – then you would have one number for each direction. You could then possibly conceive of having different dimensions evolving differently with time. What is absolutely crucial, however, about the homogeneity of the CMBR that we observe, is that this informs us about the extreme uniformity of the conditions of the universe at the epoch when the CMBR was formed. The overall temperature of the CMBR is the same everywhere across the sky, even when we compare remote locations, points so far away from each other that light would not have had the time to travel between them by the time the CMBR was formed. So how is it that such distant points all have the same temperature today, if no causal mechanism could possibly have connected them? The answer is, again, 'inflation', the extremely short period of faster-than-light expansion of the universe that we encountered earlier when we discussed the mechanism that spread the quantum-mechanical seeds on cosmological scales. During

5. Brian Greene, *The Fabric of the Cosmos* (London: Penguin Books, 2004), 227-8.

inflation, the size of the universe grew exponentially, and patches originally close-by were stretched out to cosmological distances. This would explain why we observe them to have the same temperature today: they were once in causal contact and were then separated by the inflationary expansion. So the expansion of the universe during inflation can happen faster than the speed of light without violating the basic tenet of GR, since in this case it is spacetime itself that is stretching faster than light, not a particle or other object within it that is moving faster than light. I should also add that the fundamental mechanism that drives and powers inflation has not yet been established, even though there is no shortage of speculative ideas, some of them linked to dark energy, for example.

C: Another issue regarding time we might just mention briefly is the problem of the so-called 'arrow of time'. Do cosmologists take it for granted that time has a definite *direction*?

RT: Yes, because causality is ingrained in the very structure of GR. It's unavoidable because GR comes out from two assumptions, two axioms: one of which is the constancy of the speed of light, the other being the causal structure of space-time. So yes, it's built in.

C: But is *asymmetrical* causality is built into GR? Are the equations themselves not time-reversal symmetric?

RT: Yes, they are on a microscopic level, but the global structure of spacetime is such that you distinguish between timelike and spacelike intervals, and timelike intervals are intervals between spacetime points between which there can be a causal flow of information, whereas spacelike intervals are intervals where there cannot be such a causal connection. And because of the finitude of the speed of light – which again, is built-in to GR – the two domains are disconnected: you can't make a timelike interval into a spacelike interval. So in other words, there are spacetime points that cannot be causally connected, the ones separated by spacelike intervals, because for instance, two events that are simultaneous for a given observer will not be for another observer. So by going from one observer to another you would be able to change the order of events, which would clearly result in paradoxes if the two events were causally connected. For example, you would be able to find an observer that would see the effect precede the cause. So this causality is built into GR in a hardwired way.

But let me just come back to what you said about our intuitive ideas of space and time breaking down and becoming meaningless. And my reaction is – why shouldn't they? After all, our intuitive perception of reality is an *immediate* perception of reality that has developed from our brains and our experience of the world shaped by evolution, and clearly evolution knows nothing of quantum reality, nor does it know anything about the vast expanse of time and space of cosmology. And so, it's not astonishing that those notions become counter-intuitive since we are actually extending our capability of making statements about realities way beyond the scales which our brains were designed to interact with. And so it's not an astonishing thing.

Let me give an example, the example of mathematical symmetries, which I think is very fitting in this context. We all know what a spatial symmetry is – a sphere is spherically symmetric because however we turn it in 3-D space it looks the same, so that's a spherical symmetry. So we know what a spherical symmetry is like in space, and can associate a mathematical description with this symmetry. For instance the mathematical group that describes this symmetry in space is called SO(3). But now it turns out that we can equally well define more abstract symmetries that apply to subatomic particles, symmetries that pertain to the postulated internal state of those particles – isospin, for instance. So those are just transformation groups that do not transform, do not move things around in real space; they move things around in an abstract mathematical space that we have defined to have certain properties. But then those symmetries – which have nothing to do with real symmetries, but which take their origin from our observations of real three-dimensional symmetries in the world that we *can* perceive – those symmetries turn out to play a fundamental role in describing the state of those particles, the possible energy levels that those particles can take, for example. So these principles of symmetry play an absolutely fundamental role in all of physics. I think this is a case where we start from the immediate experience of the world, where we have a symmetric configuration of things, and then we take the very same tool, put it in a completely abstract mathematical space that *a priori* has nothing to do with any domain of reality, physical or otherwise. We apply it in this other context and end up with predictions about phenomena that were not observed before and, again, can *only* be observed through these 'enhancing' powers that we discussed before, and actually turn out to be true. This is an incredible application of extending, reaching out, from the time and length scales, and also conceptual scales, of our immediate experience, into domains that are definitely beyond the realm of our immediate perception.

C: The comment about the deeply puzzling, counter-intuitive notions of space and time in fundamental physics was of course not to say – 'How astonishing, how can it be?!' – much less to make some objection to them on the grounds that they don't conform to our ordinary or com-monsensical notions. But, when it gets translated into ordinary language, when we're talking about space and time on universal scales, we can't help but assimilate what we're being told to what we know intuitively, and the question is whether our intuitive concepts are adequate to even begin to comprehend what's being said in physics.

RT: But again, I think it's another example of the phenomenon we were discussing before, when were talking about weak lensing – images that we take almost for granted, making dark matter 'visible'; yet if you are equipped with knowledge of how the evidence is collected, and how those images are produced, you understand that you cannot quite interpret them in such an immediate way. And statements about the age of the universe, I think it's the same kind of 'filter' that ought to be applied to them.

C: What is perhaps most remarkable about this whole discussion from the perspective of contemporary philosophy is that the 'big questions' about the universe as a whole which philosophers themselves have long-since regarded as constitutively beyond the limits of human reason, have now quite suddenly – that is, over the past fifty years or so – reappeared, though this time not as subjects of *a priori* speculation, but rather as concrete objects of scientific, cosmological research.

Your particular field of research is theoretical cosmology – the scientific study of the large-scale structure, properties and evolution of the universe as a whole. But apart from its scope – as we have seen, taking in both the inscrutably small and unfathomably large scales of the universe – how does theoretical cosmology differ significantly from other scientific fields?

RT: Well, as I said before, I think it's important to highlight that cosmology is very different from any other physical science in one fundamental respect: namely, that we can't perform experiments. We can only perform observations of the universe, which are intrinsically limited by many factors.

C: The distinction being that with experiments you can control parameters?

RT: And that you can reproduce your data at will. If you're not satisfied after a hundred trials you can do a hundred more, and gather more data, whilst for the universe we are intrinsically limited by the fact that we have only one universe, and we cannot create the universe a second time, as it were. And that's a fundamental distinction, one that's very important to understanding the nature of the cosmological enterprise. We can only make observations, look for correlations among observations, and make inferences using probability theory. So that's where probability theory comes into the story. For instance, if I have a theory that predicts that blue galaxies are more massive, I cannot simply grow a massive galaxy in the lab and observe if it's blue. But what I *can* do is to go out, observe as many galaxies as I can with a telescope, and then ask of my data whether I do observe such a correlation, that is, whether the more massive galaxies in my sample tend to be the blue ones. But that's a statistical connection between observed properties.

So that's a fundamental aspect, and it's limited in non-trivial ways. You might think our work is limited by the need for a certain budget to build a telescope of a certain size, for instance. But that only holds up to a certain point. For instance, for the CMBR, we have an effect that is called 'cosmic variance', which means, in other words, that we cannot get to these fluctuations as precisely as we would like, even by building bigger and better telescopes. There is an intrinsic limit to the ultimate statistical precision we can obtain, set by the fact that we have only one universe to observe. We can't travel to a very distant galaxy and observe the differences from another perspective, we're stuck here. And so this sets a limit on the amount of information you can ever collect, process, and analyse about the universe.

C: With regard to these intrinsic limitations upon, or conditions of, cosmological research, isn't this also in part where so-called 'anthropic reasoning' comes in – because the very fact of these, as you say, non-trivial limits, is something which has to be explicitly taken into account and, as it were, factored into the results of one's research? Of course, taking into account and 'correcting for' the 'subjective biases' of one's observations is part and parcel of all empirical science worthy of the name. However, in the case of cosmology in particular, there's something more fundamental at stake, isn't there, which follows from the apparently trivial and platitudinous fact that we cannot observe in an environment that does not support our existence? In other words, apart from the specific kinds of limitations you've just mentioned, there is also the basic fact that our evidence about the universe is restricted by the conditions necessary for our presence as observers.

RT: Yes, this is the so-called 'Weak Anthropic Principle' [WAP]. The way to understand this properly, I think, is not as if we are saying that human beings, or humankind, has a special role as observers *per se*. Rather, the question you could ask is: What does the fact that there are observers such as ourselves, tell us about the global properties of the universe as a whole – if anything at all? Obviously, we have to live in a very special place in the universe in order for us to be here at all. It's not just an average, randomly-picked place in the universe; we have to have the right conditions for life to be here and to be able to ask the question in the first place. So I think the only reasonable way to approach this is to start from the observation that we exist, and then try to consistently take into account the fact that all of our observations are implicitly conditional on the fact that we must be here to make them, and then carry on from there, in terms of probability statements; all the probability statements we make – such as, is our universe probable or not – we have to take into account this piece of information.

C: Part of the difficulty with the use of probability in theoretical cosmology is that it's difficult to understand how the 'frequentist' paradigm, the idea that a probability relates to a number of possible cases, could make sense. The frequentist paradigm is not only related to the repeatability of scientific experimentation but also in its origins, to gambling, to being able to play the same game over and over.

RT: Yes, absolutely. Although, from the point of view of the history of science, the Bayesian framework was born first, with Laplace, who applied it to problems in celestial mechanics, but was then superseded by what became the orthodoxy in the early decades of the twentieth century, by the work of people like [Sir Ronald Aylmer] Fisher. The frequentist approach to probability may be natural in the case of particle physics, because you have a certain number of particles, you count how many of them you have, and you count relative outcomes. But the Bayesian way of understanding probability is arguably a way which is more natural, in the sense that it's probably connected with the way that a naturally-selected mind works. Let me give you an example. If I ask, what is the probability that if I cross the road now I will be run over by a car, I am asking a question of an experiment, and I am naturally making a Bayesian inference as to what are my chances of crossing safely or not in that particular situation – I certainly don't want to repeat the experiment a hundred times and see how many times I get run over! So, in nature, actually, you want to be able to assess probabilities, chances, in terms of situations that are intrinsically unique, that cannot and will not be repeated. Now, the universe is clearly one of those cases. We have one universe – or, if it *is* repeated we certainly have no access to the repetitions, to other organisations or different laws of physics in the multiverse. And so we have one sample to work with. And we should stick to that, by understanding probability statements not as an outcome of frequencies, but rather as a state of knowledge. In other words, probability is in the eye of the beholder, in a sense. Probability is my state of knowledge conditional upon all the information and prior beliefs.

C: The problem of the applicability of concepts such as probability and chance to the universe as a whole has a long history. In his *Dialogues Concerning Natural Religion* Hume argued that, since the cosmos only happens once, we cannot hope to gain any knowledge of any regularities in how it is created. One can question the very propriety of attributing 'probabilities' to these initial or overall conditions of the world at all. Attributions of probability, it has been argued, depend upon observed relative frequencies in the world from which probabilities are inferred. To talk about the probability of a universe is, for this point of view, incoherent.[6] In a recent paper co-authored by Glenn Starkman entitled 'What's the Trouble With Anthropic Reasoning?', you raise precisely this issue, and suggest that some of these difficulties might be addressed by taking what you call a 'fully Bayesian approach to the problem' which, as you were just saying, would understand the prior as 'an expression of our state of knowledge'.[7] Could you, in simple terms, explain how Bayesian methods, and this notion of probability as a state of knowledge rather than as a relative frequency of outcomes, can work for a singular-case scenario such as the cosmological one?

RT: Yes, there has been a misunderstanding here, histori-cally speaking, in that there has been this notion of probability as frequency, and that an event which happens only once cannot be deemed either probable or improbable – it just happens. But the connection between frequency of outcomes and probability is a limited one, which doesn't necessarily cover much ground, and in particular not the ground we're interested in covering, which is events that

---

6. These formulations of the objection are taken from C. Callender, 'Measure, Explanations and the Past: Should 'Special' Initial Conditions be Explained?', *British Journal of the Philosophy of Science* 55, 2004: 204 and L. Sklar, *Physics and Chance* (Cambridge: Cambridge University Press, 1993), 313, respectively.

7. Roberto Trotta and Glenn D. Starkman, 'What's the trouble with Anthropic Reasoning?', *AIP Conference Proceedings* Vol. 878 (2006), 323-329.

are by definition non-replicable. I gave the example just now of walking across the road. As I've said, most situations in which we are interested in making predictions about the outcomes of future actions are intrinsically unrepeatable. Let's take the most basic probability example, that of tossing a coin – one of the paradigmatic examples. If asked to assess whether the coin is fair, most of us would think of tossing this coin perhaps a hundred times and seeing whether there are, say, fifty heads and fifty tails, or sixty and forty, and then based on that, we ask what is the probability of getting heads or tails, and if that's 50 percent, we deem the coin to be 'fair'. And so, when we do these kinds of tests, paradigmatic tests, we are setting out to establish, as it were, a physical property of the coin – that the coin is either fair or not, meaning that it's either well-balanced or not. A die can be loaded or not, for instance. But, if you think about it for a second you'll realise that there's no such thing as a *physical property of the coin* that determines the outcome of heads or tails. In fact, if I was skilled enough and made my 'random' throw with sufficient finesse and precision, regardless of whether the coin was 'intrinsically fair' or not, I could get it landing heads 100 percent of the time. In other words, when I'm doing random tosses of the coin, the *randomness* is the key ingredient. The randomness of the toss means that my skill in tossing the coin is not good enough in order to determine in advance what will be the final outcome. But in principle, if I could determine the initial conditions of the toss with a high enough precision, I would be able to predict exactly, or to achieve any particular sequence I wanted, by having a better knowledge of the initial conditions of the problem – since, for non-chaotic, classical systems at least, the physics is completely deterministic. So by tossing a coin, we're not testing it for fairness, we're not measuring a physical property of the coin. Rather, we're making a statement about our state of knowledge of the randomness of the toss. In other words, we're making a statement *about our knowledge of the initial conditions of the problem.*

So, how does this fit into the discussion of probability? Well, probability as a measure of *frequency* is one possibility: I define a probability intrinsic to the coin as a physical property of the coin, as the number of tosses divided by the number of tails of my series. But in the light of what I've just said, it's perhaps more useful to regard this not as a measurement of a physical property – since this property doesn't exist, as shown by the fact that I can completely change the outcome without changing physically the coin, just by changing my state of knowledge about the system I'm investigating … So it's perhaps more interesting to look at probability as expressing not an *intrinsic property of the objects* of study that has to do with their behaviour over long sequences of repetition, but rather to see that it has to do with *our state of knowledge of the object* based on our previous interaction with the object, the previous data. In this way, I can iteratively update my state of knowledge as new data come along. Based on previous knowledge – what we call the 'priors' – we can update it through new observations and get to a more informed state of knowledge.

Now, to go back to the universe, clearly we have no access to a repetition of the universe. But what we *do* have is access to information about the particular realisation we live in, and so by using this Bayesian technology, as it were, we can make statements not about the probability of an outcome of an infinite series of universes which is only posited *ad hoc* – which is ontologically debatable, in my opinion – but we can make statements about our state of knowledge of the particularisation that we happen to observe, which gets more and more informed and refined as we gather more and more information. Of course, all I've said here about probability holds at classical level – physical systems as deterministic. When we go over to the quantum level where probability is an intrinsic feature of the system, then the discussion has to take this into account, which opens up a completely new can of worms.

C: What you've said about Bayesian techniques certainly seems to problematise Quentin Meillassoux's recent critique of probabilistic arguments as applied to the universe itself, given that this critique appears to limit itself to narrowly 'frequentist' construals of probability.[8] But Meillassoux also takes issue with applications of anthropic reasoning which begin by envisaging a multitude of logically possible worlds – worlds in which the physical constants differ from those of the universe which we actually observe – and which then, having calculated that the probability of universes which permit the conditions necessary for life is astonishingly low, go on to infer that some hidden necessity must be at work which uniquely determines the constants of the observable universe.[9]

8. See present volume 64-7, and Q. Meillassoux, *Après la finitude* (Paris: Seuil, 2006), Ch. 4.

9. See present volume 77-8.

Meillassoux's argument is pitched at a purely *a priori* philosophical level, but the problem of the so-called 'fine-tuning' of the physical constants of the observable universe is a rather precisely-defined problem for cosmology, one which would seem to cry out for an explanation. While one will agree with Meillassoux that these 'fine-tuning coincidences' in no way license the reintroduction of teleological explanations such as one finds in the so-called 'strong' versions of the Anthropic Principle [AP], there is nevertheless a very real question here, is there not?

RT: Yes, indeed, from the point of view of cosmology and theoretical physics, the issue of fine-tuning you refer to is precisely the question that string theory has set out to answer – and so far has *failed* to answer. Which is to say, the hope of string theory – which is a theory that hopes to explain in heavily mathematical fundamental terms all of the structure of the particles and interactions in the universe – the hope was that it would turn out that there was a single mathematically consistent and logically possible realization of the theory, one which would account for all phenomena, structures, symmetries, particles, inter-actions, and so on. It didn't turn out to be the case, however. We now know that string theory has many different possible 'realisations', different corners of string theory space that are all equivalent to each other in some way, but none of which is unique. So it doesn't seem that the promise of string theory of being *the* final theory of physics – in terms of being unique and explaining all the phenomena – will be realised.

C: The hope was that it would explain those twenty or so free parameters of the Standard Model – the values of the constants which have to be, so to speak, 'written in by hand' – that are always invoked in discussions about fine-tuning?

RT: Yes, the hope was to explain in a unique and fundamental way all the parameters, and all the symmetries as well. But now, this hasn't turned out to be the case, and so we're stuck in a position where string theory doesn't make a unique prediction, as one had hoped, since there are multiple realisations of string theory which give you what is called the 'landscape' of solutions, which is a multidimensional mathematical object. It's called a 'landscape' because it's configured in terms of 'mountains' and 'valleys', and it turns out that at the bottom of each valley there is what's called a 'vacuum state'. Now, each of these vacuum states at the bottom of every valley represents one possible outcome for the universe. All this, so far, is of course mathematical theory, and so the question is to know which of these valleys in the landscape *our* universe occupies. But the number of possibilities for these logically possible universes, which Meillassoux mentions in a philosophical context, possibilities which are actually realised in this mathematical theory, the number of these possible universes is huge – it's something like 10^{500} – a huge, huge number. So again we have to resort to statistical techniques in order to analyse this landscape of possibilities.

The question then is, given this 10^{500} universes, our universe corresponding to the realization has been singled out in reality – how do we go from these potential universes to the actual, realised universe that we observe? This is where AP comes in, in saying that we have to count how many of these valleys are habitable. And this will restrict enormously the number of viable possibilities. Of course, we could not happen to live in one of the valleys which do not support life, say because the constants of nature there are such that life is not possible. And so you see modern physics seems to flesh out, as it were, in a very mathematically hard way, in the form of the landscape of string theory, precisely this idea of logically possible universes mentioned by Meillassoux. And now AP comes in as a possible solution, to try to explain the contingency of *our* particular realisation. Whether it's successful or not remains to be seen.

I personally have this criticism of this landscape of string theory: first of all, it's all dependent on the assumption that the heavily mathematical theory that describes this landscape is correct in some sense. And secondly, it introduces this plethora of universes, or alternative realisations, that are non-observable in principle. It introduces lots of possibilities that remain in the domain of the potential, just in order to explain how it comes about that we appear to inhabit a particularly fine-tuned realisation. But the moment you open up the space of infinite different universes you cannot observe, I think you are falling on the other side of this thin line dividing scientific enquiry from pure speculation, which cannot be scientifically tested. Which is fine – I don't want to give you the impression that I'm against these kinds of specula-tions. I'm only against them when you claim that you are able to do quantitative tests on things which, meaningfully, cannot be tested.

C: Indeed, in the paper mentioned earlier you dismissed the multiverse scenario precisely because, firstly, it seems not to be very economical, in terms of Ockham's razor; and secondly, because, as you have just said, it's not testable. Now, to take up the second point, it's obviously not 'testable' in any straightforward positivistic or verificationist sense; yet we know that a lot of things in modern physics are not testable in *that* sense. Is it not perhaps conceivable, however, that a number of quite different theories, coming from different domains of physics, perhaps as solutions to quite disparate problems, might ultimately all seem to point in the same direction – that is, in the direction of the multiverse scenario? In other words, one might reject the idea that fine-tuning *alone* is strong enough evidence to postulate a multiverse, but what if it turned out that there were other, independent reasons, to favour it? One thinks, for example, of Everett's 'many-worlds' interpretation of QM, or the very fact, as you were just saying, that string theory seems to admit of a multitude of 'solutions', or possible realisations. Is it not conceivable that a number of such theories, or interpretations of theories, might ultimately amount to a sort of evidence – indirect evidence, granted, but mutually corroborative – for some version of the multiverse idea?

But if not, what are the remaining alternatives? Do we just say that the values of these free parameters are 'brute facts' that we simply have to accept without any further explanation? But to say that – to say, in effect, 'The universe had to be *some* way, so why not *this?*' – that seems to be against the spirit of science itself …

RT: Yes, absolutely. But you see I think the problem here is that with string theory and the landscape, and this accumulation of extra layers postulated to explain physical reality, what we are doing in effect is moving away from trying to find out what are the laws of the physical universe; we are effectively crossing the boundary into trying to determine *meta*-laws governing the laws we have discovered in the first place. So if you think of these constants – one can say this is merely a brute fact, that that's just the way the universe is, but as you say, we're not content with that, we want to push forward and dig out another explanation. And one hope would be that it was possible to use this very powerful principle that we've used very successfully in the last couple of hundred years, which is the principle of symmetries. As I discussed before, these symmetries do not have to be tied up with real world symmetries – they might be the most abstract symmetries that live in a mathematical space. If those symmetries were in place, one would perhaps be able to explain these constants, because only a specific set of symmetries would allow for those particular values. For example, if dark energy is a manifestation of a cosmological constant, than the value of this constant is a very small number, and yet it's non-zero. If it were zero, everybody would be happy because – even though on the real line of numbers zero has a dimension or length of none, of zero – in fact zero is an extremely special place, so if something is zero in physics there's a symmetry which requires, which demands it to be zero. But if something is non-zero but extremely small – say 124 orders of magnitude below what you'd expect it to be – this is an astonishing fact that cries out for explanation. It could just be a brute fact and we might have to accept it as such and that's the best we can do. But, what people really are trying to look for, is to uncover the fundamental structure that will explain the smallness of this number when compared to the known energy scales in physics. So we are looking into discovering the laws or the mechanisms that possibly underlie and explain those numerical values. But even if we were to discover those laws in the form of a Grand Unified Theory or whatever – and we are not there yet – the question would remain: What is the meta-law that singles out *that* specific set of symmetries in the first place?

C: There's the risk of an infinite regress.

RT: Yes, exactly. That's what I'm trying to say. So, we're not giving up yet, but I can already peel off this layer and see where we're going.

C: The fact that you might end up with an infinite regress isn't a reason to stop.

RT: No, absolutely not …

C: There's a regulative ideal in play, such that you keep pushing on …

RT: Yes, absolutely. But you were asking whether it was possible that this explanation for fine-tuning would be testable or whether there would be enough cumulative indirect evidence. Again, you can always push the game one layer down, and find yourself asking deeper and deeper questions, and this is an infinite regression that is difficult to break, whose solution is not in sight, especially after string theory didn't offer such a way out.

C: In this respect Meillassoux introduces his distinction between chance and contingency as a sort of shortcut, or regress-stopper – he says, in effect, that you *can't* go back another level since there's an absolute, radical contingency which can't be submitted to any law whatsoever …[10]

RT: Yes, whilst cosmologists have, at least in principle, these meta-laws governing even the contingency of our universe.

C: We said that your own rejection of the multiverse proposal rests firstly upon the impossibility of experimental confirmation, and secondly upon its apparent flouting of Ockham's razor. Again, sticking to the first point for the moment, what if it turned out that something like string theory *did* ultimately manage to consistently account for the phenomena on all scales – in such a case, would experimental confirmation still be important?

---

10. See present volume, 76.

RT: Certainly, yes, I would say so. I described before how our work involves a kind of cycle of data-gathering, modelling within a theoretical framework, and observational confirmation. The trouble in this loop comes when you get to a certain point where theories are constructed in such a way as to avoid experimental confirmation or falsification altogether. So when you get to the point where you need to postulate a possibly infinite number of unobservable parallel universes in order to explain why the constants of nature are the ones that we now observe – this, I think, crosses the boundary of scientific, verifiable theories; because for such theories, experimental or observational input is *designed* to be impossible.

C: And this brings us to your second objection, that such theories needlessly postulate entities. But isn't it possible that in the future you will be faced with the alternative of accepting theories which account very well for phenomena, but which cannot be experimentally confirmed, on the one hand, and experimentally-confirmed theories which permit a relatively inferior mastery of the phenomena, on the other? In other words, is there a disparity between the potential reach of speculative theories can have, and their grounding on experimental evidence?

RT: Yes, and dark matter is an instance of this. Some of this disparity is closed, or will be closed, by improvements in experimental instruments; so, we'll build bigger, better detectors, and we'll get there eventually – even though one has to bear constantly in mind the limitations to our knowledge that are peculiar to cosmology and that I was mentioning before. But the problem is where this theoretical reach is exercised in a domain where experimental proof or disproof cannot happen *in principle*. At this point I think you are losing all the power of theory, and from a scientific point of view you give in to pure speculation, which has no testable consequence and therefore is outside the proper realm of anything we could call scientific investigation. And I think the multiverse idea is an example of this, since even if these parallel universes were real in some sense, they are constructed to be undetectable because they are outside the reach of any particle, any possible experiment you could possibly do, and so you have to question what type of reality you could attribute to this theory, if any.

C: But hasn't the progress of modern science been precisely this movement towards extremely counter-intuitive ways of thinking? Most of us find even the most basic statements of modern physics counter-intuitive. They seem to be talking about a world entirely alien to that in which we live every day.

RT: Does the progress of science show us that we are going inevitably towards a realm where our intuition doesn't apply? I think there are a few things to mention here. One is what has been termed the 'unreasonable effectiveness of mathematics'[11] – why does mathematics describe the world

---

11. Eugene Wigner, 'The Unreasonable Effectiveness of Mathematics in the Natural Sciences' in *Communications in Pure and Applied Mathematics* Vol. 13, No. 1 (New York: John Wiley and Sons, Inc., 1960).

in the first place? It can be argued that mathematics is ultimately just a product of the mind, which is arguably a manifestation of our brain structure, which, in turn, as a biological entity, must be a product of evolutionary forces that have shaped our cognitive behaviour in terms of responses to the world. But then this wouldn't explain why we're able to grasp things like QM or GR, of which we have no experience at all. I'm not sure whether there is an explanation for the fact that there are things of which we don't have any immediate experience – QM, something which is completely counterintuitive, weirder than you could possibly think – but which are accounted for by our mathematical constructs. This for me is the biggest puzzle of all – why should mathematics have anything to do with physical reality, and why should physical reality conform to this very abstract product of our minds? I don't have an answer for this question, but I think it is something that tends to be swept under the carpet, in operational terms.

C: It's perhaps precisely here that the convergence of physics and philosophy – their shared space of problems, so to speak – becomes most visible. Indeed, the very questions you have just posed – 'Why should mathematics have anything to do with physical reality?' and 'Why should physical reality conform to this very abstract product of our minds?' – are precisely the problems which Kant set out to definitively resolve in his *Critique of Pure Reason* and *Prolegomena to Any Future Metaphysics.* Kant's solution, of course, is comprised within what he called his 'Copernican experiment' in philosophy, which basically states that the reason why physical reality conforms to our mathematical concepts is that these concepts provide the 'synthetic *a priori* conditions* of natural science itself. In other words, empirical reality conforms to our concepts because these concepts are not derived *from* experience, but exist rather *for the sake of* experience: that is to say, they make experience, and the objects of experience (and for Kant this meant, first and foremost, the objects of natural science) *possible*. This was perhaps a compelling solution in terms of the mathematics and natural science of Kant's own day – that is, Euclidean geometry and Newtonian mechanics – which, as we were saying earlier, are more or less entirely isomorphic with the middle-sized world of our everyday experience. But as you have just remarked, when it comes to twentieth century physics – to QM and GR – one finds no such isomorphism, and so the problem becomes far more difficult.

This is perhaps an appropriate place to touch upon some questions we were hoping to broach regarding a certain parallel we had noticed between the use of so-called 'anthropic reasoning' in cosmology – which has already come up in our discussion several times – and certain aspects of the Kantian legacy in contemporary philosophy. Brandon Carter, who first introduced the term 'Anthropic Principle' in 1974,[12] later had some cause for regret that he had not called it something else – the 'Cognizability Principle' or some such – given the somewhat inevitable misunderstanding that it entails some of kind of anthropocentrism or 'anti-Copernicanism', whereas the real point has to do with possible 'observational selection effects'

12. B. Carter, 'Large number coincidences and the anthropic principle in cosmology' in (ed.) M. S. Longair, *Confrontation of Cosmological Theories with Observational Data* (Dordrecht: D. Reidel, 1977), 291-8.

entailed by 'observership' in general, not *anthropos*, or *homo sapiens* in particular. Carter's original point was that it is a mistake to infer from the fact that we do not occupy a privileged *central* position in the universe the conclusion that our situation cannot be 'special' *in any sense whatsoever*. The problem with what he called 'exaggerated sub-servience to the "Copernican principle"' is the risk that, from the presumption of our *non-specialness* we might infer that we are *average*, and from this that we are *representative*, and hence *neutral*. In striving to avoid anthropocentrism in this way we would, paradoxically, be reintroducing it in another form, because we would fail to take into account the specific limitations on our knowledge entailed by the fact of the very special physical conditions which must be in place if we are to exist as observers – and be the specific kind of observers we are – in the first place.

In this regard WAP invites comparison with Kant's 'Copernican experiment' in philosophy. Kant faulted the metaphysical tradition which came before him precisely for failing to take into account the fact of the essential limits of our modes of cognition – that is, of the conditions which must be in place for cognition to be possible in the first place – and thus for assuming that the (epistemological) conditions of human knowledge were also the (ontological) conditions of things in themselves. In the most simple and general terms, Kant's point was that one cannot know a thing in abstraction from the very conditions of cognition itself. Because previous metaphysics had not undertaken a properly 'critical' investigation of the epistemological conditions of its own inquiries, it had inevitably proceeded 'dogmatically' by assuming that its own conditioned vantage-point on things amounted to an unconditioned access to things as they are in themselves. Thus, as with WAP, rather than attempting to illegitimately infer meta-physically dubious anthropocentric conclusions from trivial or truistic premises, one might argue that Kant too was attempting to precisely *avoid* the anthropocentrism which follows from failing to take into account the non-trivial limitations upon and conditions of the possibility of cognition itself.

But however one interprets Kant on these matters, it has often been claimed that his 'Copernican turn' in philosophy, as a matter of historical fact, inaugurated a way of doing philosophy which, far from complementing the natural sciences by providing second-order epistemological critiques of their first-order claims, in fact runs counter to the 'Copernican' spirit of modern science itself by effectively placing man (or the knowing subject) back at the centre from which Copernicus had dethroned him. Meillassoux's *After Finitude* presents a particularly forceful example of such a cricitism.[13] According to Meillassoux, the mainstream of philosophy since Kant cannot but fail to make sense of the literal import of cosmological and other scientific statements about the universe so long as it remains within the paradigm of what he calls 'correlation-ism' – this being the name he gives to the long-prevailing consensus regarding the supposed absurdity of the idea of 'things-in-themselves' (i.e. the idea of obtaining knowledge of things as they are regardless of human experience), along with a positive doctrine which states that all possible objects must be understood strictly in terms of their

---

13. *Op. cit.* For a critical appraisal, see R. Brassier, present volume, 15-54.

correlation with either possible experience, subjective consciousness, intentional acts, language, conceptual schemes, or theories. A strong 'correlationist' position on dark matter would not merely claim (like WAP) that our cosmological models are necessarily conditional upon certain cosmological parameters which permit the empirical advent of life and of consciousness, thus putting us on our guard against neglecting these factors in our reasoning. It would affirm the much stronger thesis that in principle the very existence of dark matter is conditional upon our cognition of it, that astrophysical objects can only be said to *exist* by virtue of the conditions of our cognition – whether these conditions are intersubjective linguistic networks or the historical corpus of mathematical learning. In sum, dark matter exists, according to the correlationist, only 'for us' but not 'in itself'.

Now, this seems particularly difficult to accept in the field of cosmology where, as Meillassoux points out, 'experimental science is capable of producing statements concerning events anterior to the appearance of life and of consciousness.'[14] How, within the 'correlationist' framework – which is happy to accept scientific statements only along with the caveat that they are true only 'for us' – can we understand the meaning of a statement which purports to provide us with knowledge of entities and events which existed billions of years *before* there was any 'us' to cognize them?

The question is fundamental: does scientific objectivity allow us to in some sense 'get out of ourselves', to transcend the conditions of our experience and to achieve

14. Meillassoux, *op. cit.*, 24.

genuine cognition of the universe in itself? WAP appears to be optimistic here, suggesting that, precisely by taking into account possible observational selection effects and other biases intrinsic to our existence as observers, this is precisely what can be achieved. What we might call the 'Correlationist Principle', on the other hand, forecloses the question immediately, in accord with its assumption that everything is necessarily conditional upon the conditions of our cognition.

Now, these questions are obviously somewhat philosophically involved, and perhaps belong to epistemology rather than science proper. But one might think that, if anywhere in modern science they become urgent and uncircumventible, it is here, in the domain of cosmology. Similar questions have, of course, been central to the problem of the correct metaphysical interpretation of quantum physics for almost a century. Do you think that your own work, and modern cosmology in general, might ultimately be able to contribute something towards resolving these long-standing disputes? To what extent are such problems real and live ones for the working physicist or cosmologist? If a 'naïve realism' is no longer a real option, both because of what modern science has discovered and the sheer tide of philosophical arguments against it, what are the remaining alternatives?

RT: Well, first of all, I would certainly subscribe to the idea that the knowledge we gain of these objects which preceded the possibility of us experiencing them comes out of something like a time-shift – it's like time-travel. Because we have to remember that as we look back in time by observing distant objects we are witnessing different stages in the evolution of the universe. However, when we look at a distant galaxy we don't, of course, obtain knowledge of how the universe is 'now', as we observe it – indeed the whole concept of simultaneity is rather counter-intuitive in relativity, as we discussed. Rather, we have knowledge of the universe as it was when the light first left it. So now, when we look back to the very beginning of the universe, in a way we are looking at a point of the universe which may be billions of light years away, but since the Big Bang happened everywhere in the universe, and since we assume that the universe is isotropic – that there is no special place in the universe – then we are also looking at the universe as it was 'here', in a sense, in our location, only timeshifted.

But you asked whether scientific objectivity – perhaps supplemented by AP, purporting to correct for subjective bias – whether it allows us to have a genuine cognition of the world in itself. In science we can certainly have this sort of counter-intuitive narrative of disembodied entities, that we like ourselves to compare with. However, the selection effects expressed by AP remind us that such disembodied observers are an artifact of our cognitive process, and that quite on the contrary we have to carefully consider the physically and biologically necessary conditions for our presence. But we have to bear in mind that in order for AP to work, we have first of all to postulate, to apply this selection effect to a collection of samples, be it a class of objects in terms of realisations of the universe, different parts of the multiverse, multiple inflationary patches, whatever. And after that you need to define a reference class of observers – and this is the criticism I make in the paper you mentioned earlier. You have to define what counts as an observer in order to establish what is the probability of our being in such and such a universe. We have to define very precisely what it means for us to be observers: what is the reference class of observers we belong to – cockroaches, for instance – do they count as observers or not? That's a very fundamental point.

I think this is relevant to the question of the relation between AP and the 'Correlationist Principle' in the sense that, in order to achieve logical consistency when considering a reference class of observers, we must require consistency between the outcomes of inferences made by different members of the same reference class of observers. And this, I think, is very relevant with regard to correlationism. In other words, in order for probabilistic inference to work, we have to require that different observers, say us and some alien species on Andromeda – if we postulate that they use the same logic, that the rules of logic are valid throughout the universe, which is again one of the main postulates – we have to require that different observers in the same class of reference will necessarily achieve a consistent inference by making the same observations. And so I think that debunks, in a way, the Correlationist Principle. Because if this is true – AP supplemented by the requirement of logical consistency between observers in the same reference class – if this is true, then necessarily we don't have this freedom anymore for different observers in the same reference class to experience the world in a different way. In other words, the arche-fossil[15] has got to

15. See R. Brassier, present volume, 15-6.

be an entity of its own that can't be processed at will by interaction with different observers of the same reference class – *if* AP is to work at all.

So in other words, I think what you have represented very nicely in your question is two different ends of the spectrum of possible cognitive experiences: correcting for subjective bias through a careful use of AP, on the one hand, and introducing a new way of subjectively experiencing the world in the correlationist approach. I suspect that the two of them can't live together. I would claim that for AP to work in a consistent way – if we accept logical consistency as one basic rule of inference, for instance, which it's hard to do without – then it requires consistency among observers in the same reference class, however defined. If this is the case then it means that the entities upon which we condition in our application of AP as a selection effect – those entities must have some common, intrinsic properties of their own, properties which every observer in the reference class of observers reasoning consistently has got to agree upon.

C: This introduces the problem of relativism, of alternative conceptual schemes. But correlationism need not necessarily entail relativism, since even if all observations agreed, and even agreed *necessarily* – as in Kant's case, where the transcendental conditions are *a priori* (that is, universal and necessary) – the correlationist would still insist that intersubjective consensus is an insufficient basis upon which to claim that such observations reveal properties of things *as they are in themselves*. In fact, the correlationist would claim that it is precisely this consensus amongst observers in the same reference class which makes the objectivity of objects possible, thus collapsing the ontological problematic into a matter of intersubjective agreement or heuristic pragmatism,[16] which is precisely what the critique of correlationism seeks to avoid.

To put it as starkly as possible, the fundamental question here is whether there is any prospect of obtaining knowledge of things as they are in themselves – regardless of there being actual or possible observers – or whether it is something constitutive about cognition that it will always be a matter, not of 'nature in itself', but only of 'nature as exposed to our method of questioning' (Heisenberg)?[17] Kant's metaphor was one of reason as a judge, 'constraining nature to give answers to questions of reason's own determining',[18] and perhaps in your account of the methods and objects of theoretical cosmology you have already implicitly ratified this metaphor, whilst making it clear that it is nevertheless by no means a question of a simplistic 'correlationism'.

Another way of approaching the issue is in terms of the problem of the theory-dependency of observation which we touched upon earlier. You said that all the necessary theoretical and instrumental mediation required to access

16. See Meillassoux's critique of Goodman, present volume, 56-9.

17. 'In classical physics science started from the belief – or should we say from the illusion? – that we could describe the world or at least parts of the world without any reference to ourselves [...] [But] we have to remember that what we observe is not nature in itself but nature as exposed to our method of questioning.' W. Heisenberg, *Physics and Philosophy: The Revolution in Modern Science* (NY: Harper & Row, 1962), 43, 46. See also Kristian Camilleri's 'Heisenberg and the Transformation of Kantian Philosophy' in *International Journal of the Philosophy of Science* Vol. 19, No. 3, 2005: 271-287.

cosmological objects amounted not to a diminution but to an 'enhancement' of reality – almost as if there is a sense that one is 'producing' the reality. Does scientific knowledge, as you understand its process, fit more closely with the classical philosophical idea of knowledge as a kind of 'copying' or 'representing' of an already fully-determinate reality, or is there a sense in which the objects of physics have to be 'constituted' via the theoretical and technical 'mediating processes' you were describing earlier?

RT: Let me give you an example which I think illustrates how a reality comes into being through the scrutinizing power of the scientific methodology. Leaving cosmology for a while and turning to quantum physics – another field which is often on or across the boundary of interpretation and reality – if you take for example a *two-dimensional electron gas*, which is something that has been realized only in the last few years, thanks to various developments in sub-microscopic technology. This two-dimensional electron gas has a set of nice properties that we can investigate: we can

18. 'When Galileo caused balls, the weights of which he had himself previously determined, to roll down an inclined plane; when Toricelli made the air carry a weight which he had calculated beforehand to be equal to that of a definite volume of water [...] a light broke upon all students of nature. They learned that reason has insight only into that which it produces after a plan of its own, and that it must not allow itself to be kept, as it were, in nature's leading-strings, but must itself show the way with principles of judgment based upon fixed laws, constraining nature to give answer to questions of reason's own determining. [...] Reason, holding in one hand its principles, according to which alone concordant appearances can be admitted as equivalent to laws, and in the other hand the experiment which it has devised in conformity with these principles, must approach nature in order to be taught by it. It must not, however, do so in the character of a pupil who listens to everything the teacher has to say, but of an appointed judge who compels the witnesses to answer questions which he has himself formulated.' I. Kant, *Critique of Pure Reason* (trans. N. K. Smith, Basingstoke: Macmillan Press, 1929 [1789]), B xii-xiii.

put it into magnetic fields and see how it behaves, see quantised energy levels, and different types of effects which, in a way, are the expression of a potentiality which is in nature or in the laws of nature that we've discovered. But in a way it's a purely technological object – it was potentially in the structure of nature, but one might surmise that it has never been created before in the history of the universe, because it's a very particular object that needs to be very carefully engineered in order for those electrons to bind up in a certain type of state and then express or substantiate those abstract potential properties that our theories describe they have, and then go there, measure it and see what is real. So in a sense this is not just a step ahead of the process of setting up an experiment and making a verification; this is more about *creating a particular state of nature*, actualising potential properties of an object in order to display them in such a way that we can verify them. So in this sense we have achieved in some domains a level where we have a description of nature in terms of its fundamental properties, and we can engineer physical systems, and push them across boundaries that arguably have never been crossed in natural systems because of the very particular set-up that this requires, and so design and engineer new natural conditions that are actually artificial – new artificial natural conditions – which actualise the potentiality of our theory. And here you are at the boundary where you can ask of this system: well, that's a natural system because its actual properties are governed by laws which are natural laws, of course, but those particular properties that you are looking for, their actualisation is only possible in a highly artificial, highly engineered environment that we have now created.

C: A longstanding philosophical problem is how to separate out what belongs to the human input to reality and what belongs to reality itself. In the context of physics generally, and more specifically in the context of the kind of example you've just given, is that in principle even intelligible, this process of 'factoring-out'?

RT: No, I don't think that we can draw a clear boundary between the two. This is an example where we have a little liberally gone across the boundary both ways, and there's no way you can draw a line, but it's just a suggestion to say that there are systems that sit beyond the Galilean distinction of the impartial observer who sets up the experiment and then simply lets it go ahead on its own. We know that the observer plays a crucial role in quantum mechanical observations, and the whole paradigm of setting up an experiment and letting nature run its course in an impartial neutral way, I think it belongs to the past, since our decisions of which properties to observe and which to ignore, for example, will directly influence the system. So there are limitations to the Copernican Principle of the separation between observer and nature. I think science is going in this direction. In one way we are getting more and more sophisticated observations of reality, and at the same time those same observations, to an extent that is difficult to define, determine which reality one can observe in the first place, at both extremes of the spectrum – the microscopic world of QM, of course, and cosmology.

And the other thing that has to be said here is, if you peel away all the layers of the onion, for me it comes down to the issue of consciousness. Why consciousness? We have this 'correlationist' idea that the world wouldn't be there if there was no observer to observe it, but what do we mean by 'observer'? It's a problem that goes back all the way to the root of QM, Schrödinger's cat: What makes the wave function collapse, what makes the cat go from a position of living *and* dead to either living *or* dead? And again it's a fundamental problem for which there is no agreed explanation. It's more about the interpretation we give to the quantum theory. In and of itself, QM works perfectly well, it's only the interpretation as to the reality of the wave function that is disputed. Let me briefly summarise the interpretations. Firstly there's what is called the 'Copenhagen interpretation', which says that the wave function collapses into one of two states when the observer observes it. Now at this point we can question whether the observer is a machine, an electron or photon that hits the object we observe – so the universe would be observing itself all the time; or whether there is space, as people such as Roger Penrose would argue, for a special role for con- sciousness: consciousness would play the role of the fundamental observer that would make the wave-function of the universe collapse, like in quantum cosmology: in quantum cosmology you have the wave function of the whole universe.

C: But then you're introducing a strange gap into causality: a special agent.

RT: But that gap is in the equations, that's exactly the point: the equations of QM are deterministic. We've got the Schrödinger equation, and we've got initial or boundary conditions. And then the equations will evolve through time this mysterious wave-function, whose square gives you the probability of events happening. And when there is an observation the wave-function collapses from a superposition of different events to just the event that is observed. And so, the point is, everything is deterministic up to the point where the collapse happens, and we don't know what makes the collapse happen, and we cannot give deterministic predictions for the collapse, only probabilities. That's why the deterministic picture breaks down, we can only make probabilistic predictions about what happens: in the case of the cat, in the case of the seeds for the quantum fluctuations, and in the case of the universe. And there are different views. The Copenhagen interpretation will tell you that it is the observation that makes the wave-function collapse, and the alternative will die out, mysteriously. Then there is the 'many-worlds' interpretation, which tells you that at the moment an observation is made, the observer splits into multiple copies, each one of them observing at the same time different events, all possible events that can happen *do* happen, and that our particular reality is but one branch of this unimaginably vast tree. And to a certain extent there are testable predictions that have been done, that have excluded certain interpretations – the hidden variables interpretation, which was put forward by Einstein, has been partially excluded by tests of the so-called 'Bell inequalities'. But this remains very much a contentious issue, I think, and so we cannot really make up our minds as to what makes a wave-function collapse here and there, much less what makes the wave-function of the whole universe collapse, if anything at all.

But you see I think the whole point is that we try to make a narrative out of the scientific framework we're working in, so we tend to talk about cosmological time in pretty much the same way as if we were talking about our subjective time as we know it, we talk about the collapse of the wave-function without really knowing whether this object is just a model of reality or whether it has anything to do with the fundamental reality of the object, the object of the scientific enterprise. The fundamental reality of the 'nature' we're trying to investigate in particle physics and cosmology, I think, comes out from a hundred years of mathematical explanation as one or two things. One is a set of mathematical symmetries, which live in an abstract mathematical space and which give reality its structure. So for instance, conservation of impulse – as we know, if you throw a ball and there's no friction it will keep on going forever – comes from translational symmetry. Conservation of angular momentum comes from rotational symmetry. And then at the deeper level, you can say that conservation of mass, conservation of energy, come from other types of symmetry that are ingrained in the mathematical structure that we ascribe to reality. Now, when we try to uncover this structure through observations, the question arises: even if we were able, with supersymmetry or string theory, to uncover the fundamental structure of nature, the question would be, what principle put this structure in place in the first place? And the hope of string theory, for example, was that you'd find a mathematical theory which could only be consistently formulated within a certain structure: there was no other structure within which it could be formulated. And that would answer the question. But it didn't turn out that way: as we discussed, string theory has failed to yield that kind of paradigm, and Gödel's theorem, perhaps, puts a fundamental limit on how far such a programme can be carried out.

C: Yes, we note that you finish one of your public lectures[19] by juxtaposing a quote from Einstein where he asks 'whether God had a choice in creating the universe' with one from Gödel: 'If an axiomatic system can be proven to be consistent and complete from within itself, then it is inconsistent. It is impossible to find an all-encompassing axiomatic system which is able to prove all mathematical truths.'

RT: Gödel comes in precisely at this level of speculation, when you're trying to push your mathematical tools to the very extreme, to say, will I ever be able to formulate the structure of physical reality in terms of a set of mathematical symmetries that will describe reality in some sense, and then demonstrate, by requiring mathematical consistency, that this is the only possible set? The correlative Einstein quote I use is: 'what I'm interested in understanding is whether God had a choice in creating the universe' – *i.e.*, in imposing this set of symmetries. And Gödel's theorem, apparently sets a limit to this programme, tells us that there

19. See http://www-astro.physics.ox.ac.uk/~rxt/html/public.htm#course

is no way every axiomatic consistent set of rules – mathematics – can be complete: for every such system there will always be a statement that is true, but cannot be proven from inside. So this seems to put outside the grasp of any such tool such a fundamental question, it seems to me.

C: Thus leaving room for something to have 'planted' the seeds, so to speak …?

RT: It's a possibility. The fascinating thing is that everybody can make up his or her own mind on this. Leaving the door open for a designer – I don't know about that. But in trying to get out of intelligent design, if the solution is invoking an infinite set of universes that only exist in our mind, then I don't know whether this is any kind of solution. It doesn't seem to be a fundamental explanation in the sense in which we have always understood fundamental explanations before in physics.

If 'correlationism' insists that we can only posit objects as objects of possible experience, it seems to me that if we think of this idea of the multiverse – broadly speaking, this idea of 'pocket universes' everywhere, in some higher-dimensional space, with different laws of physics – it seems to be that by resorting to this kind of extreme complexification of reality, science has gone full-circle and is actually positing a series of objects which are definitely, by construction, outside the domain, not only of our experience, but of *any* possible experience. So, rather than reconciling philosophy with science, it seems to me that if you go down this route of the multiverse, you would be going full-circle and bringing science in line with philosophy, rather than vice-versa.

C: In that science would become extremely speculative?

RT: More than that, I think, it would really embrace the idea that in order to explain the one universe we observe, you need to postulate a series of unobservable universes devoid of any possible experience – so it seems to me that it's ironical, paradoxical, that certain ways of thinking of this problem will lead you to such a 'solution'.

C: Yet one might argue that the 'many-worlds' interpretation of QM, for example, while doubtless ontologically profligate, does at least possess the very real virtue of providing an interpretation which is both fully consistent with the equations and which avoids the idealistic, dualistic and vitalistic consequences of other influential interpretations. Leading proponents of the Copenhagen interpretation, on the other hand, have been prone to espouse an idealism so radical it would 'make even Berkeley blush' – one thinks, for example, of Wheeler's notion of a 'participatory universe' according to which 'the observer is as essential to the creation of the universe as the universe is to the creation of the observer.'[20] Similarly, the postulation of a 'multiverse' or 'ensemble universe' as an answer to the fine-tuning problem, AP being introduced in

20. J. A. Wheeler, 'Genesis and Observership' in R. Butts and J. Hintikka (eds.), *Foundational Problems in the Special Sciences* (Dordrecht: D. Reidel, 1977), 27.

order to explain the apparent 'coincidences' in terms of an observational selection effect, seems in many ways more compelling than a teleological interpretation which would make life and observership a necessary outcome of uniquely specified laws.

So with regard to what you have just said about the impossibility of separating out reality in-itself and our theoretical donation, or nature and the observer, would you put the point as a purely epistemological or method-ological one – that it's simply too messy in practice – or would you say there's some legitimacy in this idea of a 'par-ticipatory universe', that observership is in some sense necessarily interwoven with the very fabric of the universe?

RT: Again, you'll find the whole spectrum of views on this, from the idea of the participatory universe, or the whole universe as a huge living being, to the most rationalist, scientistic point of view which says that the brain is just a very complex computing machine, consciousness just an emergent phenomenon. So you'll find a lot of different points of view. If I were to give an 'average position' of scientists I know, to position them on this scale, I would put most of them on the rationalistic, positivistic side of it. But having said that, clearly if one wants to be rational and consistent throughout, this implies restricting one's point of view regarding the possibilities of human experience to experiences that are open to any other physical system – you have to abide by the laws of nature without room for any other phenomena that might go beyond them. So far, consciousness is the one phenomenon that seems to be peculiar to humans, and whether this will ever be explainable in the same way we can explain the working of, say, a diesel engine, is a very open debate.

C: You've said a couple of times that, when it comes to the ultimate ontological interpretation of science, 'everyone can make up their own minds' – almost as if it's simply a matter of personal preference. Is this not a huge problem? In a way one might be disappointed, after all the great progress of science, in particular over the last century, to be told that science itself is unable to instruct us regarding its own ontological interpretation. It seems as if you're saying that one can 'cherry-pick' whatever interpretation one wishes, that science itself doesn't place any constraints upon the kinds of metaphysics one might be able to extract from it. But one might have hoped that science would have offered us clues – indeed, more than just clues – to these questions about the ultimate nature of reality.

RT: I think it's too much to hope from or to ask of science, to put the onus of making this decision, passing this judgement, on science itself.

C: But if not science, then who?

RT: I think the methodology of science itself finds its expression and its field of applicability within a domain that is ever-growing but that is delimited by the way science explicates itself in a reflective way. So the main way you can apply science is defined by its methodology; but the context in which you place this methodology and this narrative cannot be analysed by the same methods. In other words you need a bigger arena in which to place science, and I think it's ill-conceived to try and ask of science to determine those answers – they should come as an input from the outside, as a different discourse.

C: But we *do* look to science to guide us in these questions, and if science is itself not capable of providing these guidelines for its own ultimate interpretation, or if the question of its ontological or metaphysical interpretation is something extraneous to science itself, then it seems as if science itself will never be able to do what it is its explicit aim to do, which is to tell us what the structure of reality is.

RT: I disagree that this is the goal of science – to tell us about the structure of reality itself. I think we can only describe it as a logically-consistent narrative of the structures of our models, models that conform to the observed inputs of the world, and in those terms the most we can ask of it is for it to be *consistent*. In fact that's the way we expand its domain of applicability. But we ask only for a consistent narrative of the world – I think it's hopeless to ask of science to give us a 'true reflection of reality'. The only thing we can ask from science is to provide us with a logically-consistent, experimentally observable, predictive narrative of a model of reality. Apart from that, in order to interpret this model, to delimit its applicability, we need another form of discourse which necessarily sits beyond the methodology of science itself.

C: A philosophy of science?

RT: Yes. Because science itself, in its becoming, is mindless.

C: So it would seem, from all that you've said, that cosmology works precisely on the boundary between this 'becoming of science' and philosophy.

RT: Yes, because it's by no means a sharp cut-off point: there is a foggy region where you don't really know what you're doing.

C: And presumably that is the most exciting region to be working in?

RT: Yes, it's a region where you don't know where the boundaries are. It's very exciting to be able to give a small contribution towards clearing this fog, and mapping this region. But I don't think it's clear. There might be an actual gap somewhere, only we don't know where it is. So we keep pushing forward.

On Vicarious Causation

Graham Harman

This article gives the outlines of a realist metaphysics, despite the continuing unpopularity of both realism and metaphysics in the continental tradition. Instead of the dull realism of mindless atoms and billiard balls that is usually invoked to spoil all the fun in philosophy, I will defend a weird realism. *This model features a world packed full of ghostly real objects signaling to each other from inscrutable depths, unable to touch one another fully. There is an obvious link here with the tradition known as occasionalism, the first to suggest that direct interaction between entities is impossible. There is another clear link with the related sceptical tradition, which also envisions objects as lying side-by-side without direct connection, though here the objects in question are human perceptions rather than independent real things. Yet this article abandons the solution of a lone magical super-entity responsible for all relations (whether God for Malebranche and his Iraqi forerunners, or the human mind for sceptics, empiricists, and idealists), in favor of a vicarious causation deployed locally in every portion of the cosmos. While its strangeness may lead to puzzlement more than resistance, vicarious causation is not some autistic moonbeam entering the window of an asylum. Instead, it is both the launching pad for a rigorous post-Heideggerian philosophy, and a fitting revival of the venerable problem of communication between substances.*

The phrase 'vicarious causation' consists of two parts, both of them cutting against the grain of present-day philosophy.[1] Causality has rarely been a genuine topic of inquiry since the seventeenth century. The supposed great debate over causation between sceptics and transcendental philosophers is at best a yes-or-no dispute as to whether causal necessity exists, and in practice is just an argument over whether it can be known. What has been lacking is active discussion of the very nature of causality. This is now taken to be obvious: one object exerts force over another and makes it change physical position or some of its features. No one sees any way to speak about the interaction of fire and cotton, since philosophy remains preoccupied with the sole relational gap between humans and the world – even if only to deny such a gap. Inanimate relations have been abandoned to laboratory research, where their metaphysical character is openly dismissed. To revive causation in philosophy means to reject the dominance of Kant's Copernican Revolution and its single lonely rift between people and everything else. Although I will claim that real objects do exist beyond human sensual access to them, this should not be confused with Kant's distinction between phenomena and noumena. Whereas Kant's distinction is something endured by humans alone, I hold that one billiard ball hides from another no less than the ball-in-itself hides from humans. When a hailstorm smashes vineyards or sends waves through a pond, these relations are just as worthy of philosophy as the unceasing dispute over the chasm or non-chasm between being and thought. Neither Kant, nor Hegel, nor their more

---

1. The term was first introduced in my book *Guerrilla Metaphysics: Phenomenology and the Carpentry of Things* (Chicago: Open Court, 2005).

up-to-date cousins have anything to say about the collision of balls-in-themselves. In the past century, the doctrine of Parmenides that being and thought are the same has been implied by Husserl, stated explicitly by Heidegger, and restated quite emphatically by Badiou. But this equation of being and thought must be rejected, since it leaves us stranded in a human–world coupling that merely reenacts the breakthroughs of yesteryear. To revive the problem of causation means to break free of the epistemological deadlock and reawaken the metaphysical question of what relation means. Along with causation there is also the 'vicarious' part of the phrase, which indicates that relations never directly encounter the autonomous reality of their components. After thousands of years, 'substance' is still the best name for such reality. The widespread resistance to substance is nothing more than revulsion at certain inadequate models of substance, and such models can be replaced. Along with substance, the term 'objects' will be used to refer to autonomous realities of any kind, with the added advantage that this term also makes room for the temporary and artificial objects too often excluded from the ranks of substance.

Since this article rejects any privilege of human access to the world, and puts the affairs of human consciousness on exactly the same footing as the duel between canaries, microbes, earthquakes, atoms, and tar, it may sound like a defense of scientific naturalism that reduces everything to physical events. But the term 'vicarious' is designed to oppose all forms of naturalism, by indicating that we still have no idea how physical relations (or any other kind) are possible in the first place. For as I will contend, objects hide from one another endlessly, and inflict their mutual blows only through some vicar or intermediary. For several centuries, philosophy has been on the defensive against the natural sciences, and now occupies a point of lower social prestige and, surprisingly, narrower subject matter. A brief glance at history shows that this was not always the case. To resume the offensive, we need only reverse the long-standing trends of renouncing all speculation on objects and volunteering for curfew in an ever-tinier ghetto of solely human realities: language, texts, political power. Vicarious causation frees us from such imprisonment by returning us to the heart of the inanimate world, whether natural or artificial. The uniqueness of philosophy is secured, not by walling off a zone of precious human reality that science cannot touch, but by dealing with the same world as the various sciences but in a different manner. In classical terms, we must speculate once more on causation while forbidding its reduction to efficient causation. Vicarious causation, of which science so far knows nothing, is closer to what is called formal cause. To say that formal cause operates vicariously means that forms do not touch one another directly, but somehow melt, fuse, and decompress in a shared common space from which all are partly absent. My claim is that two entities influence one another only by meeting on the interior of a third, where they exist side-by-side until something happens that allows them to interact. In this sense, the theory of vicarious causation is a theory of the molten inner core of objects – a sort of plate tectonics of ontology.

1. TWO KINDS OF OBJECTS

While the phenomenological movement of Husserl and Heidegger did too little to overcome the idealism of the previous cluster of great philosophers, they and their descendants often show a novel concern with specific, concrete entities. Mailboxes, hammers, cigarettes, and silk garments are at home in phenomenology in a way that was never true for the earlier classic figures of German thought. Even if Husserl and Heidegger remain too attached to human being as the centerpiece of philosophy, both silently raise objects to the starring role, each in a different manner. While Husserl bases his system on intentional or ideal objects (which I will rechristen sensual objects), Heidegger restores real objects to philosophy through his famous tool-analysis. It is seldom realized that these two types of objects are both different and complementary. The interplay between real and sensual objects, if taken seriously, provides ontology with a radical new theme.

In the tool-analysis of Heidegger, which fascinates his opponents no less than his allies, we find perhaps the most enduring insight of twentieth century philosophy. Our primary relationship with objects lies not in perceiving or theorizing about them, but simply in relying on them for some ulterior purpose. This first step is useful enough, but misses the essence of Heidegger's breakthrough, which even he never quite grasps. If we remain at this stage, it might seem that Heidegger merely claims that all theory is grounded in practice, that we need to have an everyday relationship with leopards or acids before staring at them or developing a science of them. But notice that even our practical relation to these objects fails to grasp them fully.

The tribesman who dwells with the godlike leopard, or the prisoner who writes secret messages in lemon juice, are no closer to the dark reality of these objects than the theorist who gazes at them. If perception and theory both objectify entities, reducing them to one-sided caricatures of their thundering depths, the same is true of practical manipulation. We distort when we see, and distort when we use. Nor is the sin of caricature a merely human vice. Dogs do not make contact with the full reality of bones, and neither do locusts with cornstalks, viruses with cells, rocks with windows, nor planets with moons. It is not human consciousness that distorts the reality of things, but relationality *per se*. Heidegger's tool-analysis unwittingly gives us the deepest possible account of the classical rift between substance and relation. When something is 'present-at-hand,' this simply means it is registered through some sort of relation: whether perceptual, theoretical, practical, or purely causal. To be 'ready-to-hand' does not mean to be useful in the narrow sense, but to withdraw into subterranean depths that other objects rely on despite never fully probing or sounding them.[2] When objects fail us, we experience a negation of their accessible contours and become aware that the object exceeds all that we grasp of it. This predicament gives rise to the theme of vicarious causation. For if objects withdraw from relations, we may wonder how they make contact at all. Heidegger's tool-analysis opens the gates on a strange new realism in which entities flicker vaguely from the ocean floor: unable to make contact, yet somehow managing to do so anyway.

2. For a detailed interpretation of Heidegger's tool-analysis, see my first book *Tool-Being: Heidegger and the Metaphysics of Objects*. (Chicago: Open Court, 2002.)

A different sort of object is the basis for Husserl's philosophy. Despite complicated efforts to save Husserl from charges of idealism, he does confine philosophy to a space of purest ideality. Phenomenology cannot speak of how one object breaks or burns another, since this would deliver the world to the power of scientific explanation, which employs nothing but naturalistic theories. For Husserl, the only rigorous method is to describe how the world is given to consciousness prior to all such theories. Philosophy becomes the study of phenomena, not real objects. But phenomena are objects nonetheless: in a new, ideal sense. For what we experience in perception is not disembodied qualities, as the empiricists hold; instead, we encounter a world broken up into chunks. Trees, mailboxes, airplanes, and skeletons lie spread before us, each of them inducing specific moods and sparkling with various subordinate qualities. Since we are speaking solely of the phenomenal realm, it does not matter if these things are hallucinations; even delusions perform the genuine labor of organizing our perception into discrete zones. Note already that sensual objects have a different fate from real ones. Whereas real zebras and lighthouses withdraw from direct access, their sensual counterparts do not withdraw in the least. For here is a zebra before me. Admittedly, I can view it from an infinite variety of angles and distances, in sadness and exultation, at sunset or amidst driving rain, and none of these moments exhaust all possible perceptions of it. Nonetheless, the zebra is already there for me as a whole in all its partial profiles; I see right through them and look to it as a unified object. Although some specific visual or conceptual profile of the zebra is needed for us to experience it, the unified sensual zebra lies at a deeper level of perception than these transient, mutable images. Each sensual profile is encrusted onto the unified zebra-object like a patina of brine. Whereas real objects withdraw, sensual objects lie directly before us, frosted over with a swirling, superfluous outer shell. But this difference seems to give sensual objects the opposite causal status of real ones. Given that real objects never touch directly, their causal relations can only be vicarious. But sensual objects, far from being withdrawn, exist side by side in the same perceptual space from the outset, since we encounter numerous phenomena simultaneously. This presents the contrary problem to vicarious causation: namely, why do all the phenomena not instantly fuse together into a single lump? There must be some unknown principle of blockage between them. If real objects require vicarious causation, sensual objects endure a buffered causation in which their interactions are partly dammed or stunted.

The situation is perplexing, but the general path of this article is already clear. Real objects withdraw into obscure cavernous underworlds, deprived of causal links. Sensual objects, by contrast, are so inclined to interact with their neighbors that we wonder why they fail to do so at every instant. In other words, the only place in the cosmos where interactions occur is the sensual, phenomenal realm. Against philosophies that regard the surface as formal or sterile and grant causal power only to shadowy depths, we must defend the opposite view: discrete, autonomous form lies only in the depths, while dramatic power and interaction float along the surface. All relationships are

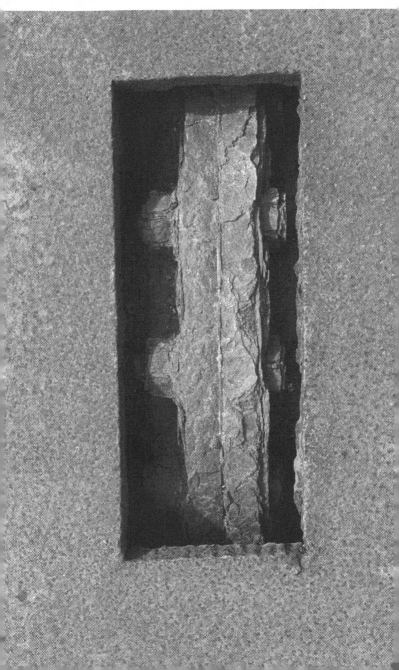

superficial. For this reason, we must discover how real objects poke through into the phenomenal realm, the only place where one relates to another. The various eruptions of real objects into sensuality lie side by side, buffered from immediate interaction. Something must happen on the sensual plane to allow them to make contact, just as corrosive chemicals lie side by side in a bomb – separated by a thin film eaten away over time, or ruptured by distant signals.

2. A JIGSAW PUZZLE

It is well known that Husserl emphasizes the intentionality of consciousness. We are always conscious of something, always focused on a particular house, pine tree, beach ball, or star, and indeed on many such objects at once. It is not widely known that Husserl also stumbles across the fateful paradox that intentionality is both one and two. For in a first sense, my encounter with a pine tree is a unified relation; we can speak of the encounter as a whole, and this whole resists exhaustive description. But in another sense, I clearly do not fuse with the tree in a single massive lump; it remains distinct from me in the perception. This gives the strange result that in my intention of the tree, we both inhabit the interior of the total intentional relation. This seemingly dry observation by Husserl has not sparked much interest in his readers. Even so, if combined with Heidegger's insight into the withdrawal of real objects behind all relations, it provides all the pieces of a new philosophy.

To repeat, the pine tree and I are separate objects residing on the interior of a third: the intention as a whole.

181

But there is a fascinating asymmetry between the members of this trio. We cannot fail to notice that of the two objects living in the core of the third, I am a real object but the pine tree merely a sensual one. The I sincerely absorbed in the things it perceives is not the I as seen by others, but rather the real I, since my life actually consists at this moment in being occupied by these phenomena, not in being a sensual object for the gaze of others or even for myself. By contrast, the real pine tree does not inhabit the intention, since the real tree (assuming there is such a thing) lies outside any relation to it, withdrawing into depths never entered by outsiders. Finally, the intention as a whole must be classed as a real object rather than a sensual one: for even if my intention of the tree is the most depraved hallucination, the intention itself is in fact underway, quite apart from whether it relates to anything outside. To summarize, we have a real intention whose core is inhabited by a real me and a sensual pine tree. In addition, there is also a withdrawn real tree (or something that we mistake for one) lying outside the intention, but able to affect it along avenues still unknown. Finally, the sensual tree never appears in the form of a naked essence, but is always encrusted with various sorts of noise. Elsewhere I have called it 'black noise', to emphasize that it is highly structured, not the sort of formless chaos suggested by the 'white noise' of television and radio.[3] Black noise initially seems to come in three varieties. First, the sensual tree has pivotal or essential qualities that must always belong to it under penalty of the intentional agent no longer considering it the same thing. Second, the tree has

---

3. *Guerrilla Metaphysics*, 183 ff.

accidental features shimmering along its surface from moment to moment, not affecting our identification of it as one and the same. Finally, the pine tree stands in relation to countless peripheral objects that inhabit the same intention (neighboring trees, mountains, deer, rabbits, clouds of mist).

We should also note five distinct sorts of relations between all these objects:

1. CONTAINMENT. The intention as a whole contains both the real me and the sensual tree.

2. CONTIGUITY. The various sensual objects in an intention lie side by side, not affecting one another. Only sometimes do they fuse or mix. Within certain limits, any sensual object's neighbors can be shuffled and varied without damaging the identity of that object, as when drifting mists do not interfere with my focus on the tree.

3. SINCERITY. At this very moment I am absorbed or fascinated by the sensual tree, even if my attitude toward it is utterly cynical and manipulative. I do not contain the sensual tree, because this is the role of the unified intention that provides the theater of my sincerity without being identical to it. And I am not merely contiguous with the tree, because it does in fact touch me in such a way as to fill up my life. I expend my energy in taking the tree seriously, whereas the sensual tree cannot return the favor, since it is nothing real.

4. CONNECTION. The intention as a whole must arise from a real connection of real objects, albeit an indirect connection. After all, the other possible combinations yield entirely different results. Two sensual objects merely sit side by side. And my sincere absorption with trees or windmills is merely the interior of the intention, not the unified intention itself. Hence, a real object itself is born from the connection of other real objects, through unknown vicarious means.

5. No RELATION AT ALL. This is the usual state of things, as denied only by fanatical holists, those extremists who pass out mirrors like candy to every object that stumbles down the street. Real objects are incapable of direct contact, and indeed many have no effect on one another at all. Even the law of universal gravitation only applies among a narrow class of physical objects, and even then concerns a limited portion of their reality. And in a different case, the sensual tree has no relation to me at all, even though I am sincerely absorbed by it. The oxygen I breathe comes from the real tree, not from my perception of it. The sensual tree is a phantasm surviving only at the core of some intention, and takes up no independent relations even with its contiguous phantoms. They are only related vicariously, through me, insofar as I am sincerely absorbed with both.

The objects populating the world always stand to each other in one of these five relations. In *Guerrilla Metaphysics*, I suggested that causation is always vicarious, asymmetrical, and buffered. 'Vicarious' means that objects confront one another only by proxy, through sensual profiles found only on the interior of some other entity. 'Asymmetrical' means that the initial confrontation always unfolds between a real object and a sensual one. And 'buffered' means that I do not fuse into the tree, nor the tree into its sensual neighbors, since all are held at bay through

184

unknown firewalls sustaining the privacy of each. From the asymmetrical and buffered inner life of an object, vicarious connections arise occasionally (in both senses of the term), giving birth to new objects with their own interior spaces. There is a constant meeting of asymmetrical partners on the interior of some unified object: a real one meeting the sensual vicar or deputy of another. Causation itself occurs when these obstacles are somehow broken or suspended. In seventeenth-century terms, the side-by-side proximity of real and sensual objects is merely the occasion for a connection between a real object inside the intention and another real object lying outside it. In this way, shafts or freight tunnels are constructed between objects that otherwise remain quarantined in private vacuums.

We now have five kinds of objects (real intention, real I, real tree, sensual tree, sensual noise) and five different types of relations (containment, contiguity, sincerity, connection, and none). Furthermore, we also have three adjectives for what unfolds inside an object (vicarious, asymmetrical, buffered) and three different kinds of noise surrounding a sensual object (qualities, accidents, relations). While this may not be an exhaustive census of reality, and may eventually need polishing or expansion, it offers a good initial model whose very strictness will help smoke out those elements it might have overlooked. What remains to be seen is how these elements interact, how one type of relation transforms into another, how new real objects paradoxically arise from the interaction between real objects and sensual ones, and even how sensual objects manage to couple and uncouple like spectral rail cars. These sorts of problems are the subject matter of object-oriented philosophy: the inevitable mutant offspring of Husserl's intentional objects and Heidegger's real ones. In turn, these are only the present-day heirs of Hume's contiguous impressions and ideas (Husserl) and the disconnected objects of Malebranche and his Ash'arite predecessors (Heidegger).

The problem of philosophy now resembles a jigsaw puzzle. We have detected the pieces as carefully as possible, and none seem to be blatantly missing. We also have a picture of what the ultimate solution should look like: the world as we know it, with its various objects and interactions. Unlike jigsaw puzzles, this one unfolds in at least three dimensions, ceaselessly changing from moment to moment. But like such puzzles, instead of mimicking the original image, it is riddled with fissures and strategic overlaps that place everything in a new light. Like five-year-olds faced with a massive thousand-piece puzzle, our greatest danger lies in becoming discouraged. But whereas frustrated children angrily throw their pieces to the floor and change activities, we remain trapped in our puzzle from the start, since it is the very enigma of our world. Philosophers can escape it only through insanity, or with the aid of rope or a revolver.

3. ONTOLOGY AND METAPHYSICS

Beginners in philosophy often ask the exact difference between ontology and metaphysics. In fact there is no consistent distinction, since each philosopher redefines these terms to suit individual purposes. For Heidegger, ontology is the account of how being is revealed to

humans, while metaphysics remains a term of insult for philosophies that explain all beings in terms of some privileged entity. For Levinas, ontology belongs to the global war between beings, while metaphysics speaks of the infinite otherness that lies beyond such conflict. For my own part, I have generally used these terms interchangeably for a realist position opposed to all human-centered philosophies; at times such flexibility remains useful, as in the opening section of this article. Yet I would also like to propose a more exact difference between them, one not unrelated to their classical distinction. Henceforth, let 'ontology' refer to a description of the basic structural features shared by all objects, and let 'metaphysics' signify the discussion of the fundamental traits of specific types of entities. In this sense, the aforementioned puzzle-pieces belong solely to ontology, since no object is exempt from their rule. These include the basic opposition between real and sensual objects, the five types of relation between them, and the bondage of sensual objects to their various qualities, accidents, and relations. Time and space also belong to ontology, since even eternal and non-spatial objects elude only the narrowly physical spatio-temporal realm, and by no means escape time and space in a broader sense. The question of universals also seems to be a global theme belonging to ontology as a whole, and there may be others. As for metaphysics, which walls off and analyzes the internal organs of any specific kind of entity, the most obvious possible topics include human being, language, artworks, and even God. Any type of object distinct from others, however hazy the boundaries may be, can become the subject of a metaphysics. There could be a metaphysics of artworks, the psyche, and language, and even of restaurants, mammals, planets, teahouses, and sports leagues. Insofar as philosophy clearly differs from activities such as singing and gambling, there could also be a metaphysics of philosophy itself, unlocking the crucial features of this discipline, whatever its numerous variations and degenerate sophistical forms.

The distinction between ontology and metaphysics is proposed here for a specific reason. Along with real objects, we have also described sensual objects, which exist only on the interior of some intentional whole. Yet intentionality is regarded by almost everyone as a narrowly human feature. If this depiction were correct, sensual objects would be confined to a metaphysics of human perception, with no place in an ontology designed to address plastic and sand dunes no less than humans. This confinement of sensuality to the human kingdom must be refused. Intentionality is not a special human property at all, but an ontological feature of objects in general. For our purposes, intentionality means sincerity. My life is absorbed at any moment with a limited range of thoughts and perceptions. While it is tempting to confuse such absorption with 'conscious awareness,' we need to focus on the most rudimentary meaning of sincerity: contact between a real object and a sensual one. For instance, I may be sincerely absorbed in contemplating glass marbles arranged on the surface of a table. This is my sincerity at the moment, since I forego other possibilities of greater and lesser import to witness this austere, Zen-like spectacle. But note that the glass marbles themselves are sincerely absorbed in sitting on the table, rather than melting in a furnace or hurtling through a mineshaft. (Though they may not be 'marbles' for anyone but humans or playful kittens, we need a nickname for the united object that we draw into our games.) The question for us is not the panpsychist query of whether these marbles have some sort of rudimentary thinking and feeling capacities, but whether they as real objects encounter the table-surface as a sensual one.

The answer is yes. We must ignore the usual connotations of sensuality and fix our gaze on a more primitive layer of the cosmos. It is clear that the marbles must stand somewhere in reality, in contact with certain other entities that stabilize them briefly in one state or another. The entities they confront cannot be real objects, since these withdraw from contact. Nor can the marbles run up against free-floating sensual qualities, for in the sensual realm qualities are always attached to objects. Only one alternative remains: the marbles are sincerely absorbed with sensual objects. This indirect argument becomes more persuasive if we examine the landscape inhabited by the marbles, which turns out to share the basic structural features of human intentionality. First, notice that these marbles are perfectly capable of distinguishing between the table and the contiguous relational environment, even if not in the panpsychist sense of a primitive judging ability. At present the marbles sit on the table, but are otherwise surrounded by air; hence, this air is contiguous with the tabletop in the life of each marble. But if we now carefully frame the marbles with bookends or melted wax, the table itself remains the same intentional object, unaffected by our eccentric manipulations. Second, the marble confronts the tabletop quite apart from its accidental coldness and slickness, though it probably registers these features in some way as well. If we heat the tabletop, or render its surface sticky or granulated by pouring different materials nearby, the table as an intentional object still remains the same. The final question is whether the marbles can make a distinction between the table and its more essential qualities, such as its hardness, levelness, solidity, and lack of perforation. Even humans can only make this distinction between objects and their qualities in very special cases; since I will soon describe these cases under the heading of 'allure', we should wait to ask whether glass marbles are able to follow suit. What is already evident is that all real objects inhabit a landscape of sensual ones, a playground whose fluctuations enable new real connections to arise. Some of these fluctuations are a mere domestic drama, while others provoke new relations with the outside. But whatever is special about human cognition belongs at a more complicated level of philosophy than these sensual objects, though it must be expressible in terms of them.

Elsewhere I have used the phrase 'every relation is itself an object', and still regard this statement as true. But since this article has redefined relations to include containment, sincerity, and contiguity, the slogan must be reworded as follows: 'every connection is itself an object.' The intentional act's containment of me does not make the two of us into a new object, and neither (for the most part) do two or three nearby perceptions of cars make a unified object. But two vicariously linked real objects do form a new object, since they generate a new internal space. When two objects give rise to a new one through vicarious connection, they create a new unified whole that is not only inexhaustible from the outside, but also filled on the inside with a real object sincerely absorbed with sensual ones. And just as every connection is an object, every object is the result of a connection. The history of this connection remains inscribed in its heart, where its components are locked in a sort of kaleidoscopic duel. But connections occur only between two real objects, not any other combination. This entails that my relation to the sensual pine tree is not itself an object, but simply a face-off between two objects of utterly different kinds. Hence, although intentionality seems to be a relation between me and the sensual pine tree, this is merely its interior. The intention itself results only from the unexplained vicarious fusion of me with the real pine tree, or with whatever engenders my deluded belief that I perceive one.

To repeat, my relation with the sensual pine tree is not a full-blown connection, but only a sincerity. This sincerity can indeed be converted into an object, as happens in the analysis of our own intentions or someone else's. When I analyze my relation to the sensual tree, I have converted that relation into an object for the first time. It has become a real object insofar as its exact nature recedes from view, inexhaustible no matter how many analyses I perform. We now face a merely sensual apparition of the original sincere relation, which withdraws from analysis just as hammers withdraw from handling. A second, more tedious observer might now decide to perform an analysis of my analysis, thereby converting it into an object whose nature can never be grasped, and so on to infinity. But note that this is not an infinite regress: all of these objects are not contained infinitely in the situation from the outset, but are sequentially produced *ad nauseum* by an increasingly twisted and pedantic series of analysts. Back in stage one, even my relation to the sensual pine tree is not a real object, but simply a sincere relation of two distinct elements inside a larger one. Unified objects can be molded at will from that clay-like interior. This already shows a way for sincere relations to be converted into real connections. Whether it is the only such way, and whether this method belongs to humans alone, is still unclear.

Another point is in order before passing to the final section. To say that every object is located on the sensual molten core of another object undermines some of the key assumptions of Heidegger. For him, human being partially transcends other beings, rising to glimpse them against a background of nothingness. But the interior of an object leaves no room for transcendence or even distance: a horse seen in a valley several miles away still touches me directly insofar as I witness it. Distance lies not in the sphere of perception, where everything brushes me directly with greater or lesser intensity, but only between the mutually exclusive real objects that lie beyond perception. We do not step beyond anything, but are more like moles tunneling through wind, water, and ideas no less than through speech-acts, texts, anxiety, wonder, and dirt. We do not transcend the world, but only descend or burrow towards its numberless underground cavities – each a sort of kaleidoscope where sensual objects spread their colours and their wings. There is neither finitude nor negativity in the heart of objects. And each case of human mortality is just one tragic event among trillions of others, including the deaths of house pets, insects, stars, civilizations, and poorly managed shops or universities. The Heidegger-Blanchot death cult must be expelled from ontology, and perhaps even from metaphysics.

4. ALLURE AND CAUSATION

Some may find it disturbing to think of the world as made up of vacuum-sealed objects, each with a sparkling phenomenal interior invaded only now and then by neighboring objects. A more likely problem, however, is indifference. There seems to be no need for such a weird vision of reality, since it is easy enough to think of the world as made of brute pieces of inescapable solid matter: 'primary qualities' supporting a series of more dashing, volatile human projections. In my view, however, Heidegger has rendered this picture of the world obsolete. Though his tool-analysis aims to describe only the withdrawal of objects behind explicit human awareness, practical activity is equally unable to exhaust the depth of objects, and even causal relations fail to let them encounter one another in full.[4] Finally, even sheer physical presence in space is a concept shaken to the core by the tool-analysis: after all, to occupy a spatial position is to take up relations, and however objects might occupy space, their reality is something deeper. The world is neither a grey matrix of objective elements, nor raw material for a sexy human drama projected onto gravel and sludge. Instead, it is filled with points of reality woven together only loosely: an

4. The idea that physical relations also have an intentional structure is a minority view, but by no means my own invention. See for instance George Molnar's fascinating *Powers: A Study in Metaphysics* (Oxford: Oxford University Press, 2003) 60 ff.

archipelago of oracles or bombs that explode from concealment only to generate new sequestered temples. The language here is metaphorical because it must be. While analytic philosophy takes pride in never suggesting more than it explicitly states, this procedure does no justice to a world where objects are always more than they literally state. Those who care only to generate arguments almost never generate objects. New objects, however, are the sole and sacred fruit of writers, thinkers, politicians, travellers, lovers, and inventors.

Along with the distinction between real and sensual objects, there were five possible kinds of relations between them: containment, contiguity, sincerity, connection, and none. Our goal is to shed some light on the origin of connection, the one relation of the five that seems most troubling for a theory of ghostly, receding objects. A connection simply exists or fails to exist; it is a purely binary question. Furthermore, connection must be vicarious, since one purely naked object always recedes from another. An object simply exists, and this existence can never fully be mirrored in the heart of another. What we seek is some fertile soil of relation from which connections surge up into existence: a type of relation able to serve as the engine of change in the cosmos. 'Connection' itself cannot provide the solution, since this is precisely what we are trying to explain; if two objects are connected, then the labour we wish to observe is already complete. The option 'no relation at all' also fails to help, since if things are unrelated then they will remain so, as long as the intermediary we seek is lacking. 'Containment' is of no assistance either. Here too we have a merely binary question: either the sensual pine tree and I are together inside a given intention, or we are not. Finally, 'contiguity' does not give us what we need: at best, the shifting play of sensual objects redistributes the boundaries between them, but cannot lead to real changes outside their molten internal homeland. The only remaining option is 'sincerity.' This must be the site of change in the world. A real object resides in the core of an intention, pressed up against numerous sensual ones. Somehow, it pierces their colored mists and connects with a real object already in the vicinity but buffered from direct contact. If light can be shed on this mechanism, the nature of the other four types of relation may be clarified as well.

It all comes down to the dynamics of sincerity, whether of a human or any other real object. Sincerity contends with sensual objects that are defined by their qualities and shrouded with peripheral accidents and relations. What we seek is the manner in which sincere relation with a sensual object is transformed into direct connection with a real one. The coupling and uncoupling of real and sensual objects is now our central theme. We know that a sensual object is detachable from its accidents and relations. The interesting question is whether it can also be detached from its qualities, which seem to belong to it more intimately. By qualities I mean the essential qualities, without which we would regard an object as no longer the same thing. Remember, there is no hand-wringing crisis of objectivity here, since we are speaking of qualities that belong not to the essence of a real object, but only to the sensual things that command our attention – a realm where we ourselves are the highest judge in the land. Now, it might be

imagined that we could liberate the qualities of the marbles by overtly discovering and listing all the crucial features that the marbles cannot do without. This was the great hope of Husserl's method of eidetic variation. But the effect of this procedure is superficial, and does not grasp the sensual marbles in their essence. Notice that even as our analysis of these objects proceeds, we continue to take them seriously as units, even if we brilliantly slice them into thousands of separate features. Even in the case of a sensual object, the essential qualities cannot be stated or analyzed without becoming something like accidents: free-floating traits artificially detached from the sensual object as a whole. Our sincerity is not really concerned with such a list of detached features, as Husserl realizes when he grants privilege to unified sensual objects over their myriad facets. The unity of such objects even indicates that there is just one quality at issue: this marble-essence, this pine-essence. The unified quality of the thing is not noise at all, but is the sensual object itself. Concerning Aristotle's question as to whether a thing is identical with its essence, the answer for sensual objects is yes. Although qualities were described as a form of noise earlier in this article, this is true only insofar as they veer off toward the status of accidents, when broken free and itemized separately. But the existence of a unified quality of things means that the sensual realm is already home to a certain 'I know not what' that makes the marble a steady focus of my attention. Unlike the followers of Locke, we do not say *je ne sais quoi* in a spirit of gentle mockery, but as a true statement about sensual objects. The sensual thing itself has a unified and basically ineffable effect on us, one that cannot be reduced to any list of traits. But if such listing of traits does not sever a thing from its quality, there may be another way for this to happen. We have also seen that vicarious causation – the enchanted unicorn we seek – requires contact with the essential qualities of a thing without contact with the thing as a whole. In this way, discovery of how the sensual object splits from its quality may be a stepping-stone toward discovering an analogous event among real objects.

The separation between a sensual object and its quality can be termed 'allure.'[5] This term pinpoints the bewitching emotional effect that often accompanies this event for humans, and also suggests the related term 'allusion,' since allure merely alludes to the object without making its inner life directly present. In the sensual realm, we encounter objects encrusted with noisy accidents and relations. We may also be explicitly aware of some of their essential qualities, though any such list merely transforms the qualities into something accident-like, and fails to give us the unified bond that makes the sensual thing a single thing. Instead, we need an experience in which the sensual object is severed from its joint unified quality, since this will point for the first time to a real object lying beneath the single quality on the surface. For humans, metaphor is one such experience. When the poet writes 'my heart is a furnace,' the sensual object known as a heart captures vaguely defined furnace-qualities and draws them haltingly into its orbit. The inability of the heart to fuse easily with furnace-traits (in contrast with literal statements such as 'my heart is the strongest muscle in my body') achieves

5. See also *Guerrilla Metaphysics*, 142-4.

allusion to a ghostly heart-object lying beneath the overly familiar sensual heart of everyday acquaintance. Notice that the inverse metaphor is entirely asymmetrical to the first: 'the furnace is a heart' draws cardiac traits into the orbit of a sensual furnace, which is freed from bondage to its usual features and evoked as a sort of hidden furnace-soul, one whose *animus* now powers rhythmic beating and circulation. Humour does something similar: we can follow Bergson's *On Laughter* and note the tension between a comic dupe and the traits he no longer freely adapts to changing circumstances. These qualities are now exposed as a discrete visible shell beneath which the agent haplessly fails to control them. There are countless examples of allure. In instances of beauty, an object is not the sum total of beautiful colors and proportions on its surface, but a kind of soul animating the features from within, leading to vertigo or even hypnosis in the witness. When Heidegger's hammer fails, a concealed hammer-object seems to loom from the darkness, at a distance from its previously familiar traits. In language, names call out to objects deeper than any of their features; in love, the beloved entity has a certain magic hovering beneath the contours and flaws of its accessible surface. The list of possibilities is so vast that they deserve to be categorized in some encyclopedic work of aesthetics. Until now, aesthetics has generally served as the impoverished dancing-girl of philosophy – admired for her charms, but no gentleman would marry her. Yet given the apparently overwhelming scope of allure, aesthetics may deserve a rather vast role in ontology.

Different sensual objects within the same intention are described as contiguous; they do not melt together, but are treated by the intentional agent as distinct, and this agent is the final court of appeal in the sensual realm. This pertains to what has been termed the relations of sensual objects. But accidents are a different case. The surface of a sensual object does not merely lie side-by-side with it. Even though we look straight through these accidents to stay fixed on the underlying sensual thing, the accidents are not viewed as separate from that thing, but are encrusted onto it. This frosting-over with peripheral qualities comes about in an interesting way. Recall that the sensual tree as a whole is made up of just one quality (the one from which it is severed in allure). But notice that this unified tree-apparition still has parts. If we start taking away branches and leaves, there will come a point at which we no longer regard it as the same tree; the tree is dependent on its parts. Yet these parts are only unified in the tree along one specific path. It never devours them completely, but employs only a limited portion of their reality. What we know as the accidents of the sensual tree are simply the remainder of its parts, the remnant not deployed in the new object. Each of these parts is complicated because it is made up of further parts, and so on to infinity. But however far we advance toward this infinity, we continue to find objects, not raw sense data. It would be wrong to think that we confront a field of colour-pixels and then mold them into objective zones. For in the first place, it is arbitrary to think that points of green are more qualitatively basic than a unified tree-quality or branch-quality; all are capable of filling up my sincerity, and all have a specific personal style. And in the second place, even a supposed pixel of green at least takes the spatial form of a dot, and hence is a complicated object in its own right. There are always largest objects in the sensual realm: namely, those that are recognized by sincerity at any moment. But one cannot find a smallest, since there will always be a leftover remainder of parts, and parts of parts, like the endless overtones of notes struck on a piano. These accidents are the only possible source of change, since they alone are the potential bridge between one sensual object and another. For there can be no changes in the sensual object itself, which is always a recognized *fait accompli*; at most, it can be eliminated and replaced by a new one. Accidents alone have the dual status of belonging and not belonging to an object, like streamers on a maypole, or jewels on a houka. Accidents are tempting hooks protruding from the sensual object, allowing it the chance to connect with others and thereby fuse two into one.

But the relation of part and whole does not occur only in the sensual realm. A real object, too, is formed of parts whose disappearance threatens its very existence.

The difference is that the parts of a sensual object are encrusted onto its surface: or rather, certain aspects of those parts are fused to create it, while the remainder of those parts emanates from its surface as noise. By contrast, the parts of a real object are contained on the interior of that object, not plastered onto its outer crust. In both cases, however, there is a vicarious cause enabling the parts to link together. This can be clarified through the historical difference between scepticism and occasionalism, which are complementary in the same manner as encrustation and connection. Hume and Malebranche face opposite versions of the same problem. Although Hume supposedly doubts the possibility of connection, note that for him a connection has actually already occurred: he is never surprised that two billiard balls lie simultaneously in his mind, but doubts only that they have independent force capable of inflicting blows on each other. In this sense, Hume actually begins with connection inside experience and merely doubts any separation outside it. Conversely, Malebranche begins by assuming the existence of separate substances, but doubts that they can occupy a shared space in such a way as to exchange their forces – leading him to posit God's power as the ultimate joint space of all entities. Like Hume, we can regard the intentional agent as the vicarious cause of otherwise separate phenomena. The tree and its mountainous backdrop are indeed distinct, yet they are unified insofar as I am sincerely absorbed with both. But more than this: when the parts of the tree fuse to yield the tree with its single fixed tree-quality, I too am the vicarious cause for the connection of these sensual objects. Even if I merely sit passively, without unduly straining eyes or mind, it is still for me that these parts have combined. Here, a real object (I myself) serves as the vicarious cause for two or more sensual ones. In the inverted case of Malebranche, we cannot accept the pistol shot of the deity as our vicarious cause, since no explanation is given of how God as a real object could touch other real objects; fear of blasphemy is the sole protection for this incomplete doctrine. Instead, just as two sensual objects are vicariously linked by a real one, two real objects must be vicariously linked by a sensual one. I make contact with another object, not through impossible contact with its interior life, but only by brushing its surface in such a manner as to bring its inner life into play. Just as only the opposite poles of magnets make contact, and just as the opposite sexes alone are fertile, it is also the case that two objects of the same type do not directly touch one another. Contiguity between sensual objects is impossible without a real intentional agent, and connection between real ones does not occur except by means of a sensual intermediary.

This entails that all contact must be asymmetrical. However deeply I burrow into the world, I never encounter anything but sensual objects, and neither do real objects ever encounter anything but my own sensual facade. The key to vicarious causation is that two objects must somehow touch without touching. In the case of the sensual realm, this happens when I the intentional agent serve as vicarious cause for the fusion of multiple sensual objects: a fusion that remains only partial, encrusted with residual accidents. But in the case of real objects, the only way to touch a real one without touching it is through allure. Only here do we escape the deadlock of merely rolling about in the perfumes of sensual things, and encounter qualities belonging to a distant signalling thing rather than a carnally present one. The only way to bring real objects into the sensual sphere is to reconfigure sensual objects in such a way that they no longer merely fuse into a new one, as parts into a whole, but rather become animated by allusion to a deeper power lying beyond: a real object. The gravitational field of a real object must somehow invade the existing sensual field. Just as I am the vicarious link between two sensual objects, the alluring tree is the vicarious link between me and the real tree. The exact dynamics of this process deserve a lengthier treatment, but something unusual has already become evident. The separation of a thing from its quality is no longer a local phenomenon of human experience, but instead is the root of all relations between real objects, including causal relations. In other words, allure belongs to ontology as a whole, not to the special metaphysics of animal perception. Relations between all real objects, including mindless chunks of dirt, occur only by means of some form of allusion. But insofar as we have identified allure with an aesthetic effect, this means that aesthetics becomes first philosophy.

Demons Get Out!

Interview with Paul Churchland[1]

From his first significant publication in 1970[2] to the forthcoming Neurophilosophy at Work[3], *Paul Churchland has established a reputation as a brilliantly iconoclastic philosopher of mind and science. Along with his wife and frequent collaborator Patricia, Churchland remains the most (in)famous proponent of 'eliminative materialism', whose canonical formulation opens a seminal paper from 1981:*

> *Eliminative materialism is the thesis that our commonsense conception of psychological phenomena constitutes a radically false theory, a theory so fundamentally defective that both the principles and the ontology of that theory will eventually be displaced, rather than smoothly reduced by, completed neuroscience.[4]*

Although this radical claim has certainly tended to provoke consternation among philosophers who have sought to integrate commonsense or 'folk' psychology into the ambit of natural science, the stakes of the eliminativist hypothesis evidently transcend the niceties of academic philosophy, with professional philosophers of mind moved to

1. This is an edited version of an interview conducted by Sophia Efstathiou, to appear in Greek in *Cogito* no. 6 (See http://www.nnet.gr/cogito.htm).

depict the promised 'elimination' in apocalyptic terms ('[it] would be, beyond comparison, the greatest intellectual catastrophe in the history of the species').5 For Churchland proposes nothing short of a cultural revolution: the reconstruction of our phenomenological self-image in light of a new scientific discourse. In the following conversation Churchland reemphasises his commitment to eliminative materialism, exploring its broad consequences for science and philosophy, and remarking upon key research outcomes and philosophical problems which have influenced its development.

COLLAPSE: Let's start where the totally ignorant person would start: according to the current entry on *Wikipedia*,6 Paul Churchland is a philosopher who believes in eliminative materialism, which says that folk psychology should be replaced. Our propositional attitudes can be reduced to neuroscientific language.

PAUL CHURCHLAND: I haven't gone to *Wikipedia* and seen my own entry [!] but somebody else told me that that's the first entry and of course it's strictly true. That paper is a paper I wrote twenty-five years ago! But it's the one that most captured people's attention and as they describe it, in two or three sentences, they are correct. I really am

2. 'The Logical Character of Action Explanations', *Philosophical Review* 79, no. 2: 214-236.

3. Cambridge University Press, 2007.

4. 'Eliminative Materialism and the Propositional Attitudes' in *Journal of Philosophy* 78, no. 2, 1981: 67-90. Reprinted in P. M. Churchland, *A Neurocomputational Perspective: The Nature of Mind and the Structure of Science* (Camb., Mass: The MIT Press, 1989), 1-22.

5. J. Fodor, *Psychosemantics*. (Camb., Mass.: The MIT Press, 1987), xii.

6. See http://en.wikipedia.org/wiki/Paul_Churchland

inclined still, after twenty-five years, to think that our conception of our own cognition will change as we learn more and more about the brain.

What I'm most suspicious of, in our common sense conception, are the so-called 'propositional attitudes' – talk about 'beliefs that p', and 'desires that p', and 'fears that p' and 'hopes that p', and 'preferring that p to that q', where we describe our mental states in sentences in some language or other. I'm suspicious of that for a number of reasons, and one of them is that we are the only creature on the planet that uses language! And I want to ask the question: How do we account for the cognition of all the other creatures – the dogs and the cats and the mice and the lobsters and eagles and the porpoises and so forth? I doubt very much that they are all talking to themselves in some inner language in the way that we think of ourselves as doing; and because our brains are so similar to theirs, I have to be skeptical about whether our cognition has that form.

Now, of course, that is how I think of *myself*, in terms of propositional attitudes! I am as much in the grip of that conception as is anybody else – and at the moment I don't know of any systematic alternative; one has not been developed yet. But I'm sceptical that propositional attitudes describe more that 2 or 3 percent of human cognition. I would guess the other 97 to 98 percent of cognition has nothing to do with language or the forms, the structures, that you find in language. So I am as sceptical about propositional attitudes as I was twenty-five years ago.

Indeed my scepticism has only grown, because I've

learnt more and more, the human race has learnt more and more, about how brains – all brains, not just human brains – how all brains represent the world. And we're learning about an alternative way of describing how brains represent the world; it has to do with population coding. We're learning something about how brains process information. And the answer seems to be that they transform one higher-dimensional vector into another. These models, which are now fifteen to twenty years old, are ever more successful at explaining how we can do interesting things such as recognize faces or recognize voices or [reaching for cup] reach for something that is in front of us.

The neurosciences are making progress, exciting progress, and they're *not* making progress because they're paying attention to 'propositional attitudes'. So, I think that in the long run science may decide that propositional attitudes are not the fundamental mode of cognition of human brains. That's why I'm inclined to think that in the long run science will eliminate them from its basic story of how brains work.

Other parts of human cognition like sensations and emotions, I don't think they'll be eliminated at all, because we are already starting to get neuronal explanations of sensations and what they are and how they work – how the brain codes for color, how the brain codes for pitch of sound, how the brain codes for tastes and smells – and also the emotions, although there it looks like biochemistry will play a larger role, rather than the activities of neurons. The different emotions look like they're connected with different kinds of neuropeptides like oxytocin or adrenalin or other chemicals like that. The brain is a chemical machine as much as it is an electrical machine. And I think those things will be successfully reduced or explained by modern science. In this sense I'm not an eliminativist at all; I'm a reductionist. But I am suspicious about the propositional attitudes still, for what I think are good reasons.

Now, I hope you will realize that the position I just outlined isn't quite as radical as the first two sentences in *Wikipedia* make it sound. I'd like to be thought a radical, but I don't want to be thought *crazy*!

C: So do you still think that folk psychology is a kind of theory?

PC: I do, and I think it will change as we learn more and more. That is the theory, the theoretical framework. The way we talk to one another will change. We already talk to one another about being adrenalized or being depressed because our dopamine levels are down. At least, some of us do. Just as we learned to look at the night sky and see it differently from how Aristotle saw it. He looked up and he saw the inside of a sphere with little jewels stuck on it that turned around us. We look up at the sky and see sort of an infinite space going off to infinity and the stars aren't moving at all, it's the earth that's turning. So this kind of major change in how we perceive or understand something has happened to the human race before, it's just that it's very close to home this time; it's going to be the way we think and talk about *ourselves* …

C: But is folk psychology similar to a physics theory, or is it more like the sort of common knowledge that we have? Let's take the example of picking up my glasses here. It might actually be that a resultant force is acting on them and describes this move. But I would just say 'I'm picking up my glasses.' Is it that kind of relationship that folk psychology might have to the more basic scientific theory? The kind that common-language claims would have to a physics theory?

PC: I think that the analogy is a good one. People talk about 'folk physics'. And the physics of Aristotle, if you go back two-thousand-some years, describe pretty much what folk physics thinks, and most people today still think in terms of folk physics. But physicists don't, and people who've learnt some physics see the world interestingly differently. And I think the same will be true of folk psychology; Anyone who learns a great deal of neuro-science – especially cognitive neuroscience, high level systems neuroscience – will understand the people around them in interestingly different ways.

And I don't think of this as being cold and machine-like, or something frightening, something from science fiction that you want to run away from! I think of it as just the reverse. If you have a much deeper understanding of how brains work, and how they function well when they do well, and how they function badly when they do badly, then we'll be able to see in other people when things are going wrong! You can *see* that someone is not being cruel, they're depressed for some reason and they're having a hard time dealing with the world; or you can *recognize* that somebody has not just gone off the deep end and is doing crazy things, but that they're bipolar; or that somebody is frontal – has a frontal deficit – they can't see the consequences of their action more than, say, twenty minutes into the future, and so they behave recklessly.

If you can see into the human mind and see what's going on then you're in a better position to act in a benign way toward that person. You can help them get out of trouble; you can help them get an antidepressant so that they can come out of their gloom; you can find new and interesting ways to pour oil upon the troubled waters; you can be a better human; a more caring human. So I'm not frightened by advances in neuronal theory; I think they will make us more humane, they will make us more caring.

C: But the point was one of replacing folk psychology altogether. It seems like you're still using those common-knowledge terms.

PC: Yes, I agree. Replacing it entirely will take a long time. And by 'a long time' I don't think it will happen in one hundred years; I think it will take a *thousand* years before it is systematically replaced. And of course I'm guessing when I say that, because most of the science lies ahead of us. We don't yet know how wrong we are in how we think about the brain. But we're learning that some of the things we thought about the brain are wrong – and there's an analogy here, from history, that I think everyone will appreciate.

Five hundred years ago we didn't know what life was, what a living thing is, what made something a living thing – and correspondingly we didn't have an idea about what it was for a life to be unhealthy. We had some idea; if you smelt bad and you rotted and fell over dead, you weren't healthy!

But our theory of what made people unhealthy ... There were theories that you were possessed by a demon, or that you had too much black bile, or too much phlegm – or any of the four humors of ancient medicine. And as we know of course, this is a *terrible* theory about health and about disease! And the sorts of things we would do based on this theory, our medical practices, were mostly *pitiful*! [laughs] If someone was possessed by a demon, you would try to drive the demon out. And you could drive a demon out in two ways: you could burn the person at the stake – well, that's not too good for the person! Or another way was you could cover them in excrement! And the demon thought this was a horrible place to be and so would fly away! Of course neither of these things worked, and maybe even medicine was uniformly ineffective.

Now, look how medicine changed our evaluation of what health is, after we came to understand what life is. We came to understand metabolism, and cell metabolism, we understood anatomy, we understood the thermodynamics of life, we understood energy flow; we came to understand that there are viruses and that there are bacteria; we came to understand what life is, including genetic defects in much greater detail than anybody had before – and with it we had a much better understanding of what the difference is between being healthy and being unhealthy.

And the difference allows us to be much more humane. We can cure people. If they have a septic infection we can give them antibiotics; we can prevent disease by giving children an inoculation against smallpox, and do all sorts of things we couldn't do before.

Okay, so that's a happy state. Let me bring you now to the case of cognition – that's the parallel to life. We don't understand very well what cognition is. The virtue of cognition is rationality: being reasonable, being moral. And we have some idea of what being rational is, what being moral is, or what being stupid and what being cruel is, but imagine how much better we will understand the virtues of cognition, when we finally understand what cognition *really* is! I think we will have a much deeper insight into mental health – cognitive health, intelligence, reasonableness, rationality – even things like scientific insight and moral insight.

So I'm not afraid of this at all, I think that it's going to set us free – it already is! We can be better now at treating certain standard kinds of mental illness than we ever could before. But we are still a long way from being perfect and, as I said, it will take a thousand years before we know everything … And probably – I take that back – we will *never* know everything! But as the centuries go by we know more and more. And I think, when we do learn more it changes the way we conceive of the world. And I don't see why our case is immune from the changes we've seen elsewhere.

We think of the heavens utterly *differently* than we did two thousand years ago – a thousand years from now, we might think of cognition utterly *differently* from how we do now. And we will simply throw away the old ways of talking and the old ways of thinking: they will survive in the history books, but even in the market and at the dinner table people will interact with one another differently from how they do now.

C: What's your opinion of Dreyfus' view of socially embedded and embodied cognition?[7]

PC: Oh, I think he's right – and it isn't just Dreyfus who's following on from Heidegger, it's other philosophers like Tim Van Gelder, John Haugeland and Andy Clarke. I think they're entirely right. And what they're discovering is something that I've discovered only belatedly – and that's how important the surrounding culture is to the kind of cognitive activity that any person engages in.

It's important because the conceptual framework you and I use wasn't generated just by us, scrambling around in the forest by ourselves. We downloaded a conceptual framework that had already been tested and tested, many times, by many prior generations. It's called the language that we speak. Languages evolved over time and books that contain wisdom evolve over time and the institutions – the police department and the hospitals and the Mayoral office and the legislature for the states and the Congress legislature, all these levels of cultural control, I'm thinking of the judiciary as well and the way the courts function –

7. See H. Dreyfus & S. Dreyfus, *Mind Over Machine* (NY: Free Press, 1986), H. Dreyfus *What Computers Can't Do: A Critique of Artificial Reason* (NY: Harper & Row, 1972) and H. Dreyfus, *What Computers Still Can't Do: A Critique of Artificial Intelligence* (Camb., Mass.: MIT Press, 1979).

all of these regulate our lives in ways that we're not always aware of. At bottom all this happens, I think, because humans invented language fifty thousand years ago – or a hundred thousand years ago, nobody knows. But it had the effect of making cognition communal, instead of individual. It also had the effect that the language we learn to speak could begin to accumulate wisdom over the years and the decades. And so the language we speak long outlives any person who is fleetingly born, speaks the language, perhaps modifies it a little bit, and then dies. That has allowed for cultural evolution. And once you can speak a language you can write it down, you can write books and legends and stories; use it to make laws to govern commerce, and to govern social behavior – it makes modern human civilization possible. So, I think language is very, very, very, *very* important; it's probably the single most important thing that ever happened to the human race. But I don't think language reflects the basic structure of animal cognition. We are animals in the end, and speaking a language is a trick the brain learnt along the way – a very very good trick. But it used different resources in order to learn that trick – and the other species didn't learn that trick. (Well, I'm not sure … maybe the dolphins, maybe the whales … maybe even birds, I often wonder what they're chattering to each other about. Is that a kind of language? For all I know it is.)

C: I'm also thinking about art, and other ways of representation and communication. How important are non-propositional ways of communicating, learning, teaching?

PC: I think they're very important. And it's interesting that pictures start appearing on cave walls round about the time that we guess that language began as well. Humans were concerned to represent things that were not present. They could do it in language, they could do it in pictures, so I suspect that those two things evolved alongside each other. There are also other representational media. Music might be a way to represent emotions or a way of representing communal activities like dancing, or chanting.

Yes, I think that those things are enormously important. And when you look at society you realize that language is not the only medium of representation. Think of the enormous importance of blueprints, of diagrams for constructing skyscrapers, diagrams for constructing a coffee-maker, diagrams for constructing an automobile, diagrams for constructing an integrated circuit, drafting and architectural drawing – these things are of incredible importance.

C: A second set of questions concern the problem of qualia. Nagel has argued against excluding the phenomenal features of experience from an account of mental phenomena and thinks that these phenomenological features – qualia, or subjective experience – are excluded from materialist reduction.

PC: He thinks they're special, and physical science will never explain them; that's right. But I think he's wrong! Just straightforward wrong! I agree with him that it is *hard* to imagine how a physical theory of the brain, neurons firing and chemicals sloshing around, could explain something like the visual sensation of red or the smell of a rose the taste of garlic, or something like that. The qualitative features of experience that are present to consciousness do indeed seem to be very very different from a complex neural activity in the brain. Of course it *seems* to be something very different. I grant him that entirely. And when you first come across the problem and someone asks how you're gonna explain this in terms of that, it *isn't* obvious – it's *far* from obvious! But I am unimpressed by this – he is *very* impressed by it. I'm unimpressed and here's why: think of the wonderful phenomenon that was light. And even primitive people thought light was what God created first: [deepens voice; gestures] 'Let there be light!' And there was light. In vain, then, would we try to explain light in terms of things that God only created afterwards. Light also seems special and utterly mysterious – especially to people before 1850, or thereabouts. There were theories that light was particles or light was waves, and philosophers like Wolfgang Von Goethe and William Blake, the English poet, thought that this was just a ridiculous idea. This couldn't *possibly* explain it!

And things only got worse when somebody suggested that light might be electromagnetic waves. An electromagnetic wave is an oscillating magnetic and electric field, at right angles to one another, moving through the ether at a very great speed. And someone might say: 'Look, I know what a magnetic field is – that's what makes compass needles wobble; and I know what an electric field is, that's what happens when you rub your comb and then you pick up little pieces of paper; But what's that got to do with *light*!? Isn't there an explanatory gap there? How can you possibly explain the wondrous features of what light is, in terms of this arcane physicalist, made-up phenomenon, electromagnetic waves?'

And yet as we all know, when you look at all the properties of electromagnetism – how fast it goes, how it's reflected by mirrors, how it's refracted when it goes through a lens, how it carries energy, how it's generated in incandescent objects – it turns out it has all of the behavioural features of light and more besides. Because the theory entailed that there should be such a thing as invisible light; ultraviolet light at wavelengths shorter than blue, and infrared light, wavelengths much longer than red. And people's initial reaction was – 'invisible light?! That's a contradiction in terms! [laughs] Light is essentially visible, and makes everything else visible!'

C: I know what you're going to say next – black yellow...![8]

PC: That's right ... ! Well, actually, I wasn't gonna go there. But here's where, in the history of science, there's a parallel case, I would suggest. And people did resist the idea that light was electromagnetic waves – they thought the idea patently absurd. It took people a long time to get used to the idea that it might be true – and there wasn't any slam dunk [slams the desk] proof at any point, that they were identical. It's just that the explanatory successes of the theory of electromagnetism got bigger, and better, and wider, and after a while, the resistance just sort of – died.

---

8. See Paul Churchland, 'Chimerical Colors: Some Novel Predictions from Cognitive Neuroscience', in Brook and Akins (eds.), *Cognition and the Brain* (Camb.: Cambridge University Press, 2005).

Churchland – Demons

This is starting to happen, I suggest, in the case of neuroscience and subjective qualia. And if we had time I would tell you again the story I've already told you about the chimerical colours. These are impossible colours analogous to invisible light, but they turn out to be there. But I agree this is just a little case. Neuroscience has a long way to go before it can equal the success of electromagnetic theory. And so the question is still, strictly speaking, open. Still, it's *possible* that subjective qualia are a reflection of a non-physical, spiritual domain. That possibility has not yet been definitively ruled out, but I would bet money on the other side, because I see the science developing and in some cases it's already offered us some explanations – about colour, for example. There is an important area of qualia, where we have systematic explanations from the Hurvich-Jameson neural networks story. Other cases, we're still waiting and hoping. But I don't see the argument that Nagel gives or that Chalmers gives or that Alex Levine gives are – it used to seem that they were decisive – qualia *couldn't be* states of the brain. But it used to seem decisive also, that light *couldn't* [thumps on desk] be electromagnetic waves – and, I'm sorry … it turns out that it could be and it *was!*

C: Would the appropriate answer perhaps be that the kind of reduction that Nagel hopes to obtain is not even obtained in natural science? He would like to have some sort of complete description of contextualized objects, but that subjective character of natural phenomena is not and doesn't *have to be* captured by natural science. It seems that natural science does a lot *without* capturing that.

221

PC: I disagree. My position is more optimistic than that. I think we *can* explain that qualitative feature – why it has the qualitative dimensions that it does. We can even predict it has new ones, and that's what we are doing – with colour for example.

If you remember, the scientist Munsell looked at the phenomenology of human colour and he saw that all possible colours – at least the ones that humans can perceive – could be located within this double cone spindle, with white at the top and black at the bottom, with all of the hues on the equator, and they would fade through pastels up to white at the top and black at the bottom and gray at the middle. This is a way of describing the range of possible subjective sensory qualia. And, one can then ask: Why do our subjective qualia organize themselves that way? Why is orange between red and yellow? Why is green between yellow and blue? Why is gray between white and black? And the new neuronal theory of color processing in the brain – this is a theory that has been established for at least twenty years, the Hurvich-Jameson theory[9] – now explains, quite adequately, why that space has the shape that it does, why the various colors that are located within it are located where they are. It gives you a systematic explanation – this was supposed to be impossible – of why the qualia are as they are, why they have the similarity relations, the dissimilarity relations, that they do.

This is real scientific explanation, by real physical stuff, of phenomenal qualia. And moreover it predicts some new

9. See L.M. Hurvich & D. Jameson, 'An Opponent-Process Theory of Color Vision', *Pyschol. Rev.* 64, 1957: 384-404.

things. Some things that commonsense didn't know about. And you go and you check these predictions to see whether they're true; the predictions come out ...

So, this is a happy case, not of finding some excuse for failing to explain a qualia, but of succeeding and explaining the qualia surprisingly well, thank you very much. I agree we haven't done it for the whole range of qualia – that will take many many years, but I'm no longer filled with despair. *They* are. But I think they're just arguing from ignorance. They are taking the limits of their imagination to be the limits of what's possible.

C: What do you think are the reasons why traditional artificial intelligence failed, and what are the prospects for artificial intelligence research today?

PC: I think it failed not because the computers that we built weren't fast enough – [hushed] the computers we built were much faster than you or I – I think it failed because the way in which classical AI tried to represent information in a computer was by way of sentences – Propositions! They were sentences in a computer language rather than in English, but they were sentence-like representations. And the computer processed the information by drawing inference-like relations between them. If you like, it was an attempt to push folk psychology onto computers. And we deliberately made these machines so that they would function as folk psychology suggests the way we live – we fill with propositional attitudes the things that the computer knows. It knows that p, that q, that r, and so

223

forth, and then you can let it figure out whether t by examining whether or not there was an inferential chain between the premises and the conclusion. Initially things worked pretty well, partly because the computers were so fast – they could do an awful lot of things very very quickly.

But it began to emerge that when you ask them to do things that humans and animals do very easily – like recognizing a face, within a third of a second, or recognizing somebody's voice as the voice of your wife or the voice of your child, or detecting the emotion in somebody's cry – is it a scream of delight, or a scream of terror? – that sort of thing is something humans and animals are very good at – and when people tried to write programs to do that, it isn't that they failed utterly. It's just that it turned out that the programs had to be *enormously* complex if they were to succeed at all. And it took the computers ten times, a hundred times as long as it took humans to do it, even though computers function a million times faster than we do – because they're conducting electricity through wires rather than conducting action potential trains down an axon. Those things ride at about the speed of a human bicycle, this is practically the speed of light. So people began to scratch their heads, thinking 'what's going on here?' And the suggestion – and here I get to the positive side – I think that's why they failed: they misrepresented what cognition is at bottom.

Other researchers started to say: 'well, let's try and take our instructions from the brain, here – how is the brain wired up?' And you have about a hundred million neurons on each retina, and they project their axons back to ten million neurons at the LGN,[10] and they project their axons to five hundred million neurons and you realize that biological brains are doing an enormous number of little computations, simple things: [hushed] ... all at the same time – *all* of these synaptic connections attached to *all* of these neurons *all* doing a little something, a very *little* something, *at the same time.*

The contrast with these machines is that they're doing a little computation too – but they're doing it – *phrrrrrrrrr* – as an enormously fast sequence. It's easier to do large numbers in parallel than it is to do them serially, or one after the other. So when people looked at the computing power of the brain, given the vast number of cells, and neurons in the brain, and the vast number of connections, it turned out that the human brain was doing more computations per second than the biggest and most powerful computer in the world. The computers were getting close, but again, they're using serial processing, so they're still behind us. So I think that the prospects for artificial intelligence are still very very good. Because I too am inclined strongly toward physicalism, given the success of the physical sciences, but I think success will come when we try to build an artificial intelligence that mimics the way the brain is wired up; then we will start to get interesting artificial intelligence.

C: So, what is connectionism?

10. Lateral geniculate nucleus: the part of the thalamus that receives visual signals from the ganglion cells of the optical nerve, and transmits processed information to the primary visual cortex.

PC: Connectionism is the view that AI should follow the lead of the brain. We should reverse engineer. We should find out how mice do it, and how cats do it, and how human brains do it, and how lobster minds do it, and how ant brains do it. And then try and do it the way they do it.

That leads to an interesting possibility by the way, which worries me a little bit. If we do build a brain, say just like yours Sophia, neuron for neuron, synaptic connections – so we produce an electronic creature, that not only thinks like you do, but has the same knowledge you do, the same emotional profile has been built, we will produce an artificial Sophia. But this Sophia will think a million times faster than the real Sophia, she would think in ten seconds, what would take you ten years.

C: [Laughs] Can you build her please?

PC: I would be afraid of a creature like that, because she would be able to think faster than any of us. Here is a case where our children may be made of metal, but we may love them as much as if they were made of flesh and blood – that is a worry I have. Artificial intelligence is possible, and if we reengineer the human brain to produce an electronic version, a parallel system that is a normal brain, it will function very much faster than normal brains do, and I would frankly be afraid of such a thing. I think we have to tiptoe very carefully here, even though I'm very optimistic about the prospects.

Now I don't think this will happen very quickly, again I think we're talking about two hundred years at least, into the future. But it's a possibility that I think we have to be aware of.

C:But we have created atomic bombs, things that are much more powerful than we are.

PC: More knowledge breeds more power. And power can always be abused, and what the human race has to do at every stage, is to grow up. When we learned to make fire! Uh! That was a dangerous advance! Suddenly you could burn a whole village, here, in half an hour. Did we give up fire? No – we just learnt to be responsible with its use. And when we made atomic bombs, it was terrifying, we could destroy an entire modern city in three seconds. But of course, I think within a hundred years most of our power will be coming from nuclear power stations – we're going back to nuclear power because oil and coal and gas have too many drawbacks. This is another case of technological advance yielding power when we must be careful that it's not abused.

C: How do you conceive of the relationship between science and the philosophy of science? You have said that you think that a philosopher of science doing epistemology is like a cognitive scientist, and so in that sense you think of yourself as a cognitive scientist. But what is at stake in the divisions philosophy of neuroscience/philosophy of science, and philosophy of science/science in general? And what is the difference between philosophy of neuroscience and of the life sciences in general, and the philosophy of, say, physics? Because it seems that the vocabulary and the artillery of neuroscience and the life sciences in general deal with things much closer to our hearts than maybe physics does. And in that sense, perhaps they are also more dangerous.

PC: I think ultimately that all of us – the philosophers and the scientists – are all doing the same thing. We're trying to understand the universe. And we're trying to understand different parts of it. And people used to think, back in the early twentieth century, and particularly in places like Oxford, that philosophy was something very different from the sciences. Sciences were doing empirical research, philosophy was doing conceptual research, or conceptual analysis, or something like that. I think *that's* a made-up story! I think philosophers are trying to explore the conceptual frontiers – but so do scientists, when they make up new theories. Philosophers are distinguished only because … [sighs] what we call a philosophical problem is a problem that's so far from scientific solution that no self-respecting scientist will touch it! And so they throw it over to philosophy and say, here, *you* worry about it! And a successful philosopher is someone who manages to bring some order or insight inside the area, sufficient order that you can then start asking empirical questions – you can start proposing experiments, and saying: 'Oh! I was wrong! You've got to modify that theory'.

It used to be, of course, that it was philosophers who did physics. The department of physics at Cambridge – that department goes back to 1200, or something like that

– is still called the Department of Natural Philosophy – philosophy of the natural world! And philosophy used to encompass astronomy, but astronomy went off on its own, back in classical Grecian times, and physics went off on its own during the Renaissance, and chemistry, which also used to be part of philosophy – remember the alchemical search for the philosopher's stone that would allow you to turn base metals into gold? They thought of that as a department of philosophy. As disciplines become more self-contained and more driven by empirical data, we don't call them philosophy any more, we call them sciences. Now, there are always some residual problems left, like the mind-body problem, or the problem of life – there's a problem that solved itself in the middle of the last century. Biology went off – it too used to be part of philosophy, just like chemistry was. All of those cases are cases of philosophical success. We finally get enough of a grip on a problem that you can start performing experiments, to test the theory and to modify it. We finally learn from experience rather than sheer speculation, mere stabbing in the dark. Philosophers are trying to do the same things that scientists are. They're just addressing some of the hardest questions, and they're engaged in stabs in the dark, and so, philosophy moves forward more slowly than the sciences do. Now, you said you had a worry. What was your worry?

C: I was thinking of cases where the language of science has been used to promote political goals. For example the use of holistic biological language by the Nazis to promote their totalitarian goals: the idea of the *Führer* as the head and the *Volk* as the body of an organism that functions in unison. Those kinds of metaphors that travel from a domain like biology – especially from life-science domains, whose vocabulary seems compelling – to the domain of politics. To what extent should philosophical work be constructive – what balance needs to be struck with a negative, critical theory?

PC: Well, yes, evil metaphors are certainly just as possible as benign metaphors. The metaphor of a master race, ruling over subjugated races, was a lousy metaphor and it was a misuse of biology. The idea that evolution was something that leads from lower to higher and that northern Europeans were the most evolved was a false conception of how evolution works. Evolution works in a radiated fashion rather than arrowing towards some goal.

I think the broad answer is that science can provide compelling metaphors for a number of things. And sometimes they are very revealing. Newton said that the moon is just like a flung stone, it moves in an elliptical arc focused on the earth – that's an illuminating scientific metaphor. And then there are other metaphors that aren't so illuminating at all, like the notion of a master race, or the notion of evolution focused on the *Führer* itself, or on blond-haired Aryans.

We have to resist the ugly metaphors. Science is as rich a source of metaphors as anything else, and we have to resist the bad ones and nurture the good ones and we have to learn how to tell the difference. And that means that we have to *test* them in systematic ways – they have to be subject to criticism. The Nazis weren't interested in having their metaphors tested in systematic ways, they were interested in using them for political purposes. Newton was interested in having his metaphor tested, and he was lucky and most of the tests turned out very well indeed thank you. So in that way we can discriminate between good metaphors and bad metaphors. Beforehand you often can't tell the difference. You have to get them in a position where you can test them.

Some of them of course will look morally ugly, even before you can test them. Maybe then you want to resist them. But I remind you of cases like the smallpox vaccine. When it was first invented, in the early 1800s, the Church thought it was a *horrible* thing, because they thought that if you were giving people vaccinations you were playing God. Whether or not you got smallpox and died was God's will, and if you were protecting your children by giving them smallpox vaccine, you were intervening in God's plans, and the Church tried to prohibit the smallpox vaccine for quite some time. But after fifteen years someone did a survey in Northern France, and the number of deaths of innocent children from smallpox fell from one hundred and forty-five thousand to four thousand in just fifteen years. Now, all of a sudden it starts to seem like: no, smallpox was not a case of being morally evil, it wasn't a case of playing God, it was a case of protecting innocent children from something that has nothing to do with them.

Now, it's never easy to see what's true and false, it's never easy to see in the long run what's right and what's wrong. One needs to keep an open mind and evaluate things as you go along.

C: Is connectionism a good source for metaphors?

PC: I think so. I think so, yes. But the research is in such an early stage, it's still at a very theoretical stage, so I can't claim any grand successes. It is a fertile metaphor because it suggests that the way, say, the visual cortex represents the world, could be more like the way your television screen represents a baseball game. If you go up at the screen and look really closely you see all those little pixels: there's two hundred thousand little pixels – some of them green, some of them red, some of them blue – and any little picture – say Dan Rather, reading the news – is a particular pattern of activation levels across all of those pixels; some of them bright, some of them dark. Well, any particular representation across the visual cortex in the brain is a particular pattern of excitation levels across one hundred million neurons – not two hundred thousand, but one hundred million! So, the resolution, if you like, of the visual cortex, is much higher than a television screen. And that's true of a monkey, that's true of a mouse – this gives you a new respect for the representational power of the brain. It may be representing – not always like a two-dimensional picture – but representing with activation levels across millions and millions of neurons. And then it transforms one representation into another – because you've got many different populations in the brain. And you can do computations over these representations.

And this is a metaphor for conceiving what's going on inside the human brain. It looks like a useful metaphor for understanding motor control, facial recognition, auditory recognition; it looks like a very promising metaphor for human research. And that's why we're pursuing it. But the proof of the pudding is in the eating. We'll see how this research programme pans out. It could very well die, just as classical AI died. After ten or fifteen years of trying, this may wither on the vine as well.

C: I guess part of keeping the metaphor tight relies on reproducing the architectural structure of the brain adequately in your model – figuring out the criterion of what's an adequate simplifying assumption, and what's just plain misrepresentation.

PC: Well, that comes out in the testing. If you can get useful idealizations, then fine. But if you end up misrepresenting what's there and the explanatory power gets feebler and feebler and the metaphor gets more and more and more strained … That's what happened with classical AI. The idea of an internal set of sentences crunching away according to logical rules – that turned out to be a poorer and poorer metaphor. We strained it and strained it and the behavior of the machines that were being programmed, the investment didn't justify the payoff. And that's why people are switching to new ways of trying to create AI, because the old ways failed. Well, these new ones may fail too! But at the moment they seem to be flourishing! So keep your fingers crossed – and come back in ten years.

C: This seems very classical-Greek: the idea of the philosopher doing the work before the scientist steps in.

PC: Yes it is very much like the classical Greeks. Aristotle was a proto-scientist, and Plato was a proto-scientist – but he was not very good [laughs]. And then if you look at Theophrastus and Strato of Alexandria who came after Aristotle at the Lyceum … Were they philosophers, were they scientists? It's a silly question! They were *both*!

C: My only worry is keeping a critical distance from the practice of science, insofar as that enables you to see the mistakes, see the confusion. So I guess both philosophy and science need to be there. And keeping the balance is the tricky thing.

PC: Yes, keeping the balance is the tricky thing. You can't have a balance until you have *both*.

COLLAPSE II

Nevertheless Empire

Clémentine Duzer & Laura Gozlan

Pestilent fumes had tainted the atmosphere of the suburbs so that little by little passers-by began to steer clear. But some remained, unafraid, while the epidemic continued to spread. Such was the case with private investigator K9: his thoughts were haunted by a woman of the worst kind.

She ran a brothel.

*

'He used to run an out-of-town osteopathic clinic, took on a few drugged patients for three large ones a week.

As you know, the epidemic was swiftly killing off the hired help. Our workers were spilling all over the lino, you understand, liquified bones softening the flesh.

It was all going from bad to worse. We were hiring younger and younger recruits, but it was no good.

We were about to shut up shop, before we had the idea: the graft.

We had some failures. Yes. Automutilation with fan blades. In short, it turned against itself.

So we eventually discovered that female parts are much more co-operative than male. Accordingly, as you will understand, the very best grafts come from domesticated animals … '

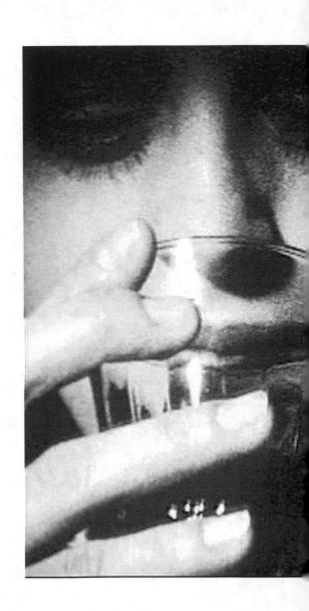

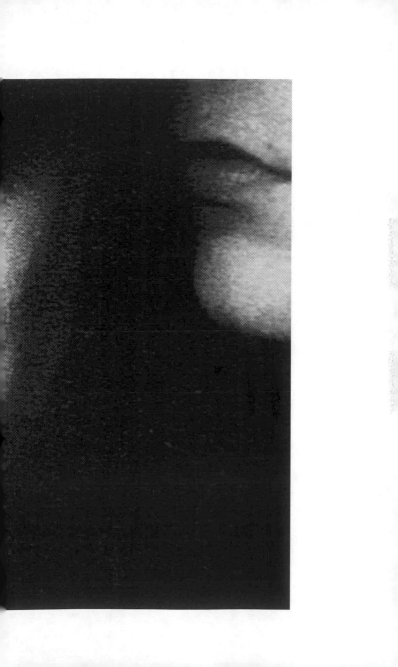

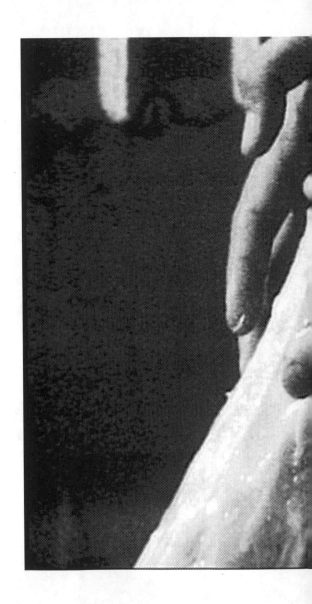

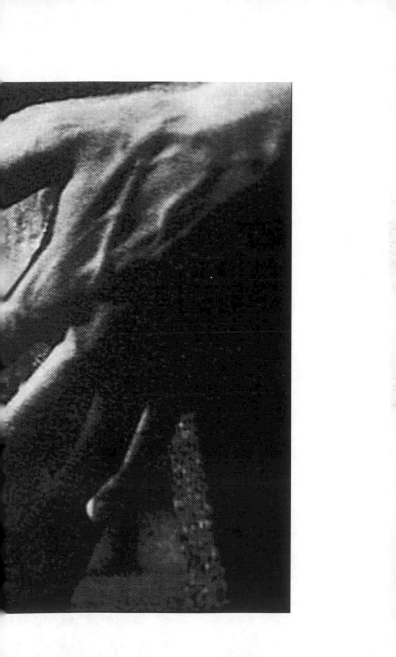

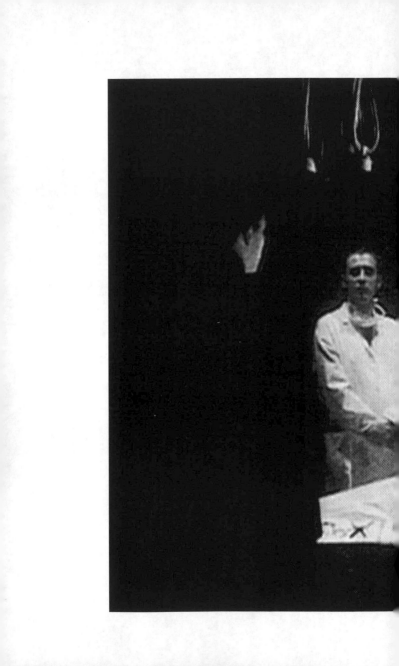

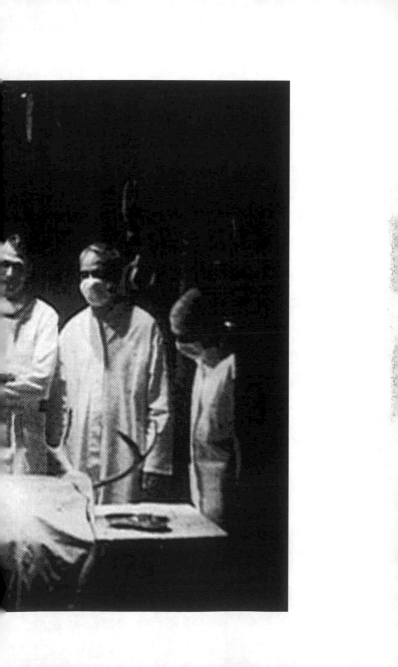

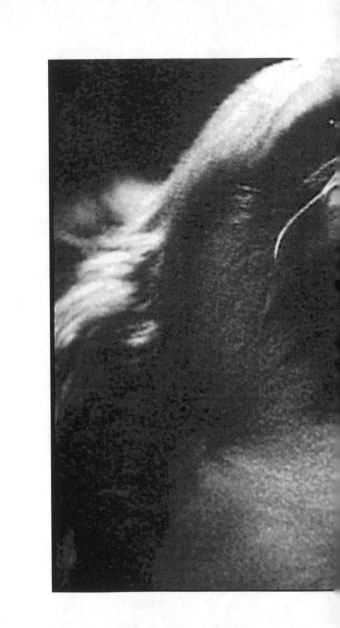

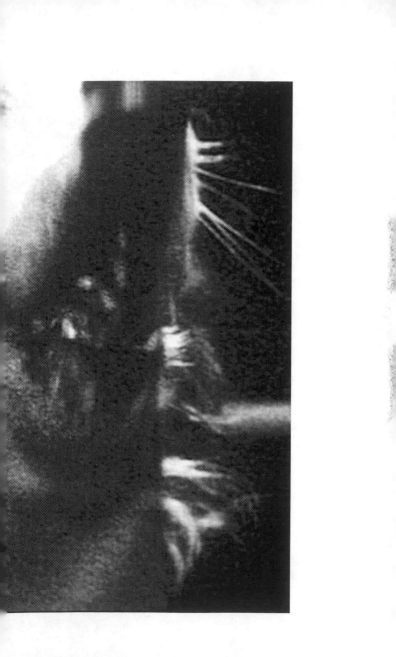

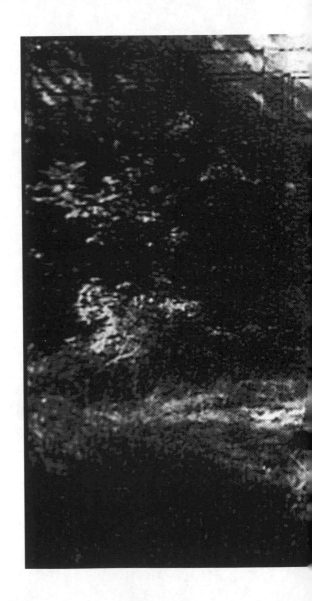

Elysian Space in the Middle East

Kristen Alvanson

ONTORIUM. *The Western graveyard is a place of consummation for the ontotheological horizon which dominates Western engagement with time and space. The site of the graveyard bridges the ontological contents of the living and the* post-mortem *protrusion of these contents, thus marking the transition from ontology to theatrical ontology. Or, in other words, here ontology is staged both as it is – or as it functions – and as the result of its own accomplishment (effect). Thus, all ontological projections of architecture flourish in the graveyard. Taking into account Heidegger's notion of 'settling'* (regelung) *which, from both objective and subjective perspectives, describes the connectedness of building, being and thinking, the graveyard, then, is a rich resource for reasoning back to the experience of the ontological encounter with space and time and the uniqueness of this experience within each culture or ontotheological formulation of Elysian Space.*

The following visual staging of Middle Eastern and Islamic graveyards illustrates their status as a focal point for elements and influences peculiar to the Middle East. It also focuses on how an Islamic graveyard proposes a space which, in its serious concreteness, principally lies outside of Western ontological or ontotheological modes of thinking, dwelling and building. The spectator's experience of a Middle Eastern graveyard is partly a radical alienation from Western thought and building, partly a disquieting discovery of the creative forces present there.

MORE THAN A VOLUME, LESS THAN A SPACE. The Western ontology of dwelling has it that *residing* (remaining) alone in a space which both separates its dweller from, and connects them to, their surrounding environment, is not in itself enough to define dwelling. Therefore, residing or occupying cannot be appropriately integrated with building and being – and for that reason, with the human. Dwelling is the inhabiting and populating of a space by an entity. This definition requires an axial factor which is sustained by an entity and its dwelling place; a factor that can be defined as 'the minimum space required for the inhabiting and populating activities of a given entity in a given place'. The basis of these activities is movement. The dwelling-place, or room, is a space in terms of its capacity to accommodate contents or allow actions. What is required for such a definition is, firstly, a volumetric instance of building that can support both an entity and its actions, or

more specifically, its movements within the space. The consequence of dwelling, then, is more than mere inhabiting; it also includes different actions provided by this 'enough' space or room which fundamentally takes shape and is built upon the minimum, that is, the minimum space. According to this ontology of dwelling, then, the human as a dweller builds its action on a limit which is that of the minimum, and which is maintained in every ontological context related to (the) *room*. Western graveyards push this ontology of dwelling to its extreme. Such an ontological orientation only makes sense when an onto-theological disposition of dwelling in its fully-fledged sense is involved; for otherwise, the application of the dwelling ontology of the living to the dead would merely signal the reduction of ontology to law. Sarcophagus and coffin as above-ground and underground volumetric spaces of room are examples of this ontology of dwelling that is manifested in Western graveyards and entombment. Similarly, the required limit for dwelling or room as 'enough' space entails not only an adequate space within each grave but also between graves, determining an orderly arrangement in the graveyard.

PROXIMITY, PRIVACY AND NEIGHBORHOOD. In Middle Eastern graveyards, graves randomly infringe or interfere with each other's affairs and private space. The openness of graves is only superficially restricted by the size of the horizontal grave slabs and their boundaries. The slabs are commonly used as markers, as opposed to vertical tombstones. Neighboring grave slabs or horizontal markers form a relatively uniform surface, a solid flatness as opposed to a volume. If the Middle Eastern graveyard exhibits a single ambition, it is that of partaking of and sharing flatness. Socializing with the dead in Middle Eastern graveyards is partly inspired by the elimination of 'room' or sufficient space of dwelling. In order to reach loved ones, a visitor has to walk over neighboring graves. Greco-Roman graveyards maintain a type of dwelling or

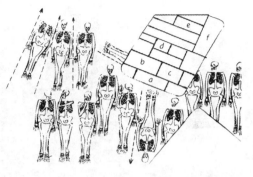

adequate space for the living and extend the dwelling space of the living to the dead via a law-abiding transition of ontology to the ontotheology of the living. The reason for Western culture's preoccupation with the roaming or walking dead can be found in the establishment of the graveyard as a residential complex, a settlement which the dead should have no reason to abandon. In Western graveyards, the space of graves can be given as a metric value, each person being allotted relatively equal space for their grave and its surrounding. In Islamic graveyards this space varies: some graves are inches away from each other, others slightly further; many are buried on top of each other, as new cemeteries are carpeted exactly atop older ones. Sometimes five layers of new cemeteries – as in the case of Iran's *Dar-o-Salam* graveyard – bear each other's tombstones, graves and their contents; only the most recent graveyard is visible, while the rest form the bedrock of the new cemetery until rain or soil change force a small part of the older graveyards to surface in an unexpected place, sometimes beneath a recent tombstone. Thus the

hadith that 'no one can build any palace or even a house other than on top of someone else's home' is exemplified in a typical Middle Eastern graveyard. The *hadith* aims at the nihilism of economy or its impending fate, because this is understood to lead to a tranquilized economy. If layers and layers of graves over each other – in addition to the literal contact of graves and their horizontal slabs – have one ontotheological message, it is the intimacy of the living with the graveyard, the dead and their own demise.

ELYSIAN OR EMPHATIC HORIZONTALITY. Western coffins or burying spaces are by their nature sarcophagi. They are governed by the fate of volume: providing room. Western graves bespeak dwelling space on two levels: one is the coffin or casket which provides its contents with room; and the other is the surface tombstone or perpendicular marker that represents a volume. The difference between Western and Middle Eastern – or specifically,

Islamic – graveyards in their approach to building originates from their difference in grasping or working with the solid as a building or architectural component. If, for the Western graveyard, dwelling is supported by solid volume, or the solid that brings space to volumetric enclosure, for the Islamic graveyard the solid subtracts dwelling from the volume. In Islamic graveyards, solidity is the privileged state of matter; unlike its role in the Western graveyard, where it creates volumes, it is replete, and has only one role: to remove room or adequate space for dwelling from the grave. The body in an Islamic burial is not placed in a coffin; coffins are used only by family and friends when carrying the deceased to the grave site. The body is placed atop a solid stone slab deep in the ground, tightly wrapped within a *kafan* or shroud sheet. 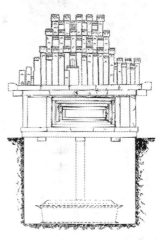 Another slab of the same size is put over the body to fully press its weight on the deceased, crushing the chest and eliminating any space or air around the body. Then dirt or soil is dumped on the slab, swallowing the body into an Elysian horizontality which is that of a filled solid without room. Finally, another slab is placed on the surface to conclude this Elysian horizontality for the living.

In general, then, graves in Islamic graveyards have no 'dwelling' potential. Heidegger ties building and dwelling to the twofold of thinking and being. Thinking is entailed by *raum* (room) or dwelling space. In the wake of the Western graveyard and its ontological dwelling-space, continuing as it does either on the ground or under the surface as in the coffin, the Western aspiration for thinking

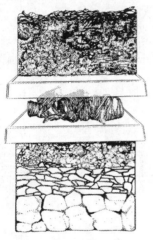

is carried on even beyond death, in the grave. The act of removing the dwelling-space in Islamic burial leaves no space for thinking. The Elysian space of Islam creates spaces which, by virtue of their resistance against the ontology of dwelling, subtract the creative force of building and being from the Western exigency of thinking.

Unlike the comforting Western spaces, the slabs of the Islamic burial exert pressure. Their emphatic horizontality rises from bottom to top, diminishing *post-mortem* relief. The two slabs under and over the body transmit the hardness and the weight of deeds in life. These weights create a crushing force which makes use of tolerance and turns it into pressure; because sin (pressure) reaps its potentiality from tolerance. When tolerance reduces, or one becomes less tolerant by various means, such as temptation or loss of hope, sin ensues by virtue of this lack of tolerance. Yet the dead have no

tolerance. If theology nourishes faith by being well-grounded and valid to the very End, the Islamic graveyard deals with a theology thatmaintains faith by purposely stopping making sense.

OVER ONE'S DEAD BODY. An Islamic graveyard encourages an uncommon socialization with the dead. The dynamics of this socialization are for the most part inspired by the building forces of the graveyard. If the dignity of the dead is nothing but the indulgence of the living, then the living too ought to be liberated from the legal codes that bind the graveyard to dwelling and traffic taboos. Firstly, everyone, regardless of religion or orientation, can be buried in an Islamic graveyard – as long as one can endure the place. In the Middle East, the graveyard is fully connected to the social body; it is located in the vicinity of social activities. The Islamic graveyard is a place of casual socialization. Fruits and snacks are brought to the graveyard to be distributed among the poor. The poor come to the graveyard to eat and return to the communal structure of society. The graveyard levels the dead as well

as the living; privatization of the space around graves rarely happens. When it does, it is to construct a shade over the horizontal slab to protect the marker from the sun. If in the West, graves represent private spaces even when they have no walls built around them, in a Middle Eastern graveyard this private space is casually broken by people walking over graves. Tens of footprints on each grave mark the evidence of this passage from restricted dwelling to collective wayfaring.

Lastly, the graveyard is trans-gender. In the Islamic graveyard, the faces of deceased women are often rubbed off from the photos which are placed on their graves.

Given the fact that historically in Islam, the face of God and holy figures must not be depicted, and vermin are faceless people, removing the faces of women amounts to verminizing the Divine, or making God and woman equal.

Islamic Exotericism:
Apocalypse in the Wake of
Refractory Impossibility

Reza Negarestani

Unlike other strains of monotheism, Islam cannot be said to include the idea of an apocalypse in the sense in which we usually understand this word. In fact, the radically external, 'impossible' (non potest) nature of Allah renders the judaeo-christian apocalypse structurally impossible (impugnable). At the same time, Islam posits an apocalypse that is neither feared, hoped for or expected, but which, in the ideal of pure submission, is inhabited by the faithful as pure impossibility. In order to comprehend what appears, in its violent irruption into western chronology, as the apocalypticism of radicalized Islam, we must understand how Allah's absolute externality has as its consequence a different conception of temporality, different mechanisms for the maintaining of faith, and an apocalypse which cannot be reduced to a chronological moment or a possibility in unification.

COLLAPSE II

THE OUTSIDE OF OUTSIDERS. The Islamic account of Genesis spirals around a non-ontological unity. Firstly, as Mollasadra (1571-1640), the Iranian philosopher, emphasizes,[1] Allah is not 'Being' (yet neither is it *nihil*); its truth can never be known, either through being or through non-being, either before or after the Apocalypse. Secondly (and in parallel with the foregoing), Man can never attain an integral unity with God – such a unity as would, in other strains of monotheism, exalt and transform Man from his former (*quondam*) state. Man can only return to Allah, not unite with him. Unity or completeness in terms of the human is only entailed by affordance,[2] a state of mutual affordability or an economical openness: the state of being open to. In Islam, however, God is constantly external to Man, and only 'unlives' through the impossible, an absolute *potestas* so ultimate that it is im-*posse*-ible for Man; Al Farabi (870-950CE) in his *chef-d'oeuvre*, *On the Principles of the Views of the Inhabitants of the Excellent State*,[3] clearly brings into conjunction the possibility of possess-ability and impossibility, to suggest an *im-possess-ability*.

1. Al Farabi, *On the Principles of the Views of the Inhabitants of the Excellent State,* trans. Seid Jafar Sajjadi (Tehran: Ministry of Culture and Islamic Affairs, 2000).

2. Polish philosopher Roman Ingarden, in his works focused on ontology – written after breaking from Husserl's phenomenology through a critique of transcendental idealism – expounds on the problem of openness and affordance, suggesting that closure (or modulated/economical openness) is a priority for open systems, and analysing niches as power projection zones and inhibitors of unwanted interactions and communications. The openness of the niche protects itself from what makes it open, by opening itself to what makes it closed. Only through such an openness can the existential moments be afforded, and modes of Being are then able to emerge. For more details on affordance, see my 'Militarization of Peace' in Mackay (ed.) *Collapse* Vol. I, 72n.11.

3. Mollasadra (Sadr al-Din al-Shirazi), *The Beginning & the End on Transcendental Philosophy (Al-Mabda wa'l- Ma'ad fi'l-Hikmat al-Muta'aliyyah)*, Vol. 2 (Tehran: Sadra Islamic Philosophy Research Institute, 2002).

Possibility must be afforded if it is to be reached, its *potenz* must be attained, possessed and sometimes even activated through a dynamic course of action in order for it to be released (X is possible for Y if and only if Y affords X *i.e.* if Y is able to reach X and authenticate its possibility; or, Y must attain the capacity to afford X as a possessable objective). But Farabi bifurcates impossibility into a 'Latent/Passive Impossibility' (an impossibility character-ized by its quiescence) and an 'Active/Unfailing Impossibility', where the former is merely a symptom of a subjective capacity or temporary lack of mutual affordance. That is to say that Latent or Passive Impossibility describes a situation where, once Y achieves the desiderata necessary to capacitate itself and afford X, the Latent Impossibility will be actuated as Possibility. Latent impossibility attests to the fact that the impossible object(-ive) (X) still remains in the horizon (boundary) of the subject in relation to which we attribute its impossibili-ty; it is necessary only that it be afforded and that it mutually afford the subject in order for it to become possible (possess-able). At the same time this makes it certain that the latently impossible object(-ive) remains bound to the logic of the boundary, of conditions and char-acteristics (having its own idiosyncrasies which must be afforded in order to be activated and become achievable for the subject Y). Thus it remains existentially perusable and intrinsically inert and transient (it is not permanently and fully impossible). And it is neither functionally nor spatially external to the subject Y; on the contrary, it (latent impossibility: X) exists just as the subject Y exists, waiting to afford X to turn it into a possible (possess-able).

Christian luminary Nicholas of Cusa (1401-1464AD) argues in *De Possest* (a neologism best understood by breaking it down to its pre-existing elements *posse est*) that 'God alone is what (He) is able to be.'[4] Nicolaus Cusanus expounds on a microcosmic proto-monadic system which is shaped around his term *Possest* (*Posse Est* or *Können-Ist*) which draws an intrinsic and interiorized line of alliance between Able-ness (being able to) or Actuation, and *Potentia* or Possibility. To exist is to be possible in the sense of *possest*; or more accurately, 'able-ness' and 'actuation' are immanent to potency and possibility. Possibility alone renders existence, just as potency alone renders able-ness. According to Cusanus, *possest* means that 'possibility itself exists' ('*posse est*'); then he concludes that because what exists, exists actually (existence is the actuation of possibility), the 'possibility to be' or the 'potentiality to be able' exists insofar as the 'possibility to be' is actual. Cusanus calls this *possest*. In other words, and from a different etymological and biblical perspective of the term *possest*, it means that the 'potentiality to be' exists as effectuation and able-ness (*posse/possibilis*).

The proposition 'God is *possest* (actualized-possibility and able-potency)' captures an omnipotent quality, to be opposed to created beings who can never completely fulfill their potentialities and can never fully reach their possibilities. This intrinsic and autonomous transition in *possest* between possibility and actualization, or potentiality and able-ness, can only be established in the presence of

4. See Nicholas of Cusa, *Metaphysical Speculations*, Volume 2, trans. Jasper Hopkins (Minneapolis: The Arthur J. Banning Press, 2000), *A Concise Introduction to the Philosophy of Nicholas of Cusa*, trans. Jasper Hopkins (Minneapolis: The Arthur J. Banning Press, 1986), and *Nicholas of Cusa: Selected Spiritual Writings*, trans. H. Lawrence Bond (New Jersey: Paulist Press, 1997).

capacity or affordability; because actualization or able-ness emerges when possibility or potentiality achieves and satisfies a certain capacity (*i.e.* in the case of chemical processes, reaching a certain gradient in potency to trigger a specific action) that leads to a certain actuation and effectuation. Designated actuation is the matter of designated affordability, or the range of capacity for a potency which must be fulfilled (afforded).

The necessity of capacity as the ground on which possibility and actuality are mapped together, or in other words, capacity as what connects possibility and actualization together, can now be examined through an apagogical argument (*reductio ad impossibile*) and in conjunction with the theological context at stake here. To this purpose, we shall assume that the connection between possibility and actualization (or potentiality and able-ness) is direct and immediate, and they operate in regard to each other without an intermediary, a *capacitas* which can contain something.

In the absence of capacity and affordability as bases which underlie both possibility and actualization, every possibility could lead to any actualization and any able-ness could be ensued by a potentiality with no required gradient or degree of quality or quantity. Or in other words, no particular ability would exist, since it is the capacity and gradient of fulfillment that lead a certain potentiality towards its able-ness. Once we assume that capacity and its subsequent affordability do not exist in the transition of possibility to actualization – ergo the *possest* of God – there would not be any boundary (limit) or compass for the actualization of a possibility, or *vice versa*.

Consequently, in the absence of capacity, the possibility of being God and actualization of that possibility – being the Divine, that is – for Man would be equal to the *possest* of God itself: so to speak, Man and God would be potentially and actually at the same level; a theological conclusion that is not only invalid for monotheism but also confutes its own grounding structure. Therefore, to this extent, the relationship between possibility and actualization, both in the actualized-possibility of God (*possest*) and possibilities of Man, is subjected to the economy of capacity and ability – in the sense of tolerance (range of modulation) – which is an economy of affordability rather than openness, environmental surround rather than radical outside. Now if capacity is latently and potentially attainable at all times (can be afforded at any time) and it constitutes the grounding nexus of possibility and actualization for both God and Man, then Man can afford the Divine all the time – which is not the same thing as 'Man being God' or 'becoming the Divine instantaneously'. God can be afforded all along. This affording of God – which is delineated as the possibility of Man being actualized as God (ultimate actualized-possibility or *possest*) and is not 'to be God itself' – incessantly maintains the position of the Divine within the range (*confinium*) of Man's affordability (either incapaciousness or capaciousness: capacity), or in other words, interior and endemic to Man's *ecologia* and existence.

Following Cusanus, in God's *possest*, actuality and possibility can correspond and conform to each other symmetrically (with an equal scale) only if the capacity between them is equal to the unit distance or the unit capacity. That is to say, *ab* is posed as the unit measure (*unus*: 1) for any other variation in actuality, possibility and capacity *i.e.* a unit in the threefold of existence. Accordingly, *possest* can be diagrammed as *ab,* which is equal to the unit capacity and the symmetric fold between actuality and possibility (see Diagram 1). To put it differently, *possest* as the complete symmetry and corresponding state of possibility and actuality (God) can only come to existence if both actuality and possibility are aligned with the Absolute or the un-conditioned (x=0); since any condition, or more concretely, any variable step (*gradum*) or status, either in possibility or actuality, is formulated as a deviation (*d*) from the unit distance or the unit capacity ($d \succ 1$). To this point, beings are perpetuated as variations, and their existences are deviations from the unit capacity (*ab*), which is immutable to variation and digression. For created beings, either actuality or possibility is characterized as the ratio of this deviation to its corresponding capacity. For instance in Diagram 1, for possibility of a created being this ratio of deviation is b_1b, *i.e.* b_1 to b_1o (similar to a cosine function: b_1/b_1o). Likewise, the existence of a created being becomes tangential to the existence of God. The existence of a created being is posited as the ratio deviation of both its actualities and possibilities (a_1, b_1) to the unit capacity (*ab*) which is *possest*

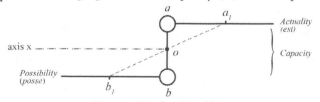

Diagram 1. The Threefold of Existence

or God itself (similar to the tangent function): $(a_1 b_1)/(ab)$.

Here the qualitative or quantitative characteristics of One and its formation as a specific *com-plexus* (or according to Cusanus, God's *complicatio*/enveloped in relation to the world's *explicatio*/developed), namely unity, should not be presented as the reductive 'indifference of the unity itself toward itself' (Hegel) by way of totalization or exclusion. Unity here serves monotheistic theology only by the virtue of its (i) positioning, (ii) the alignment it takes and (iii) the fold it plaits (as a fold-line which is itself a plait) in the threefold of existence. It is by way of these three acquired attributes (subsidiary to its unitary quality) that unity – as of God – more than being the exclusive oneness, is posited as the unit capacity, the measure (*metron*) of affordance. And affordance is the only and exclusive destination for the openness between Man and God in this territory and the ontological relevancy between possibility and actuality. Only through economical (dyslogistically economical, of course) possibilities of affordance or reciprocal affordability, can actuality be posed as the ideal realization of possibility, an end in itself, an entelechy. Unity of and through God is the fold of connection and communication made in the name of affordability and capacity (so long as one can afford). Neither unity nor its formative processes (unification) are totality or exclusion in themselves. To highlight the problematic of 'Unity as immanent totality', it can be suggested that different numeric principles can be applied to unity itself, in the same way that Kazimierz Twardowski[5] proposes that Leibniz's spiritual system is

5. Kazimierz Twardowski, *Selected Philosophical Writings (Wybrane Pisma Filozoficzne)*, (Warszawa: PWN, 1965), 200-4

subject to two different numeric principles. Consequently, Leibniz's system only includes monism of kind but not numeric monism. Unity as a process is perpetuated by two main numeric systems – of which at least one is manifold – which are applied synchronously together from both ends in the process of unification. In Christian theology, one is the numeric multitude or the participation of people (Man) in God; and the other is the numeric monism of God, which also envelopes the monism of kind. Moreover, one can embarrass the presupposed tautology ('I be that I be' [Exodus 3:14]) that is associated with One not only by the logic of exception (which again is directly extracted from oneness as counter-generalization) but also by the singularity function of One by which One separates from its unitary predeterminations. At the same time, from another direction, infinite growing processes can encapsulate the same singularity of One and develop the same 'object conception'[6] that is applied to One. If One consolidates everything under its banner by any means possible, every anomaly, unilateral development, exception, germinal multiplicity and constant driftage – that is to say, infinite perversion $(d \succ 1)$ – can also be gathered under the flag of One. This is the remobilization program (in a military sense) that is harvested from the double-dealing dynamism of heresy. If God basks in his house, let us reconstruct it according to the laws of demons.

To this end, the monotheistic theology in which the existence of beings is tangential to the unit course

6. Ed Dubinsky *et al*, 'Some Historical Issues and Paradoxes Regarding the Concept of Infinity: An APOS Analysis: Part 2', in *Educational Studies in Mathematics*, Vol. 60, No. 2 (The Netherlands: Springer, 2005), 253-266.

(*unbedingt*) of God makes sense; but only at the cost of postulating the existence of God as capacity, or more accurately, the unit capacity in the threefold of existence. The *possest* of God is transversally interposed between actuality and possibility, an imposition that not only establishes a monopoly of God, for which beings are mere excursions, but also economizes existence. God is the *metron* of affordance; Man's affordability tangentially folds over and contains God (see Diagram 1).

The affordability of God (*i.e.* God being afforded or God within the fold of Man's existence) perpetuates the Divine as domestic or in-the-house (cohabitant) in connection to Man. The Almighty's omnipotence is merely effectuated in the wake of its confinement, which includes and covers Man too; while the latter is a part, the former is only environment, the neighbouring, the one that is tethered to the part's capacity. If the Triune God is existentially possible, it is because this God cohabits the same space in which Man resides, which is functionally bound by the economical closure of affordance between the two (Man and God) and is rendered volumetrically limitless by the opposition between 'the becoming of Man' and 'the Being of God', which determine the ongoing perpetuation of affordance (see Diagram 2). The affordance or mutual affordability between God and Man is an economical openness through which overlap and 'radical communication' (indifferent to capacity) are not attainable. Here, communication and overlap can only take place in the presence of and within a third capacitor, which is situated as an intermediate state (*meso-philic*) by both sides and interposes a buffer between them capable of consociating and bringing the sides to one capacity, coordinating a domain of communication for God and Man. This capacitor is partially shared by both sides and does not preexist for them individually; it is conceived and formed by the movements of Man and God to each other (see Diagram 2). Coexisting contemporaneously and dynamically, these diametric movements whose course of action is affording, participate – in the sense of orchestration – in the coordination of a communal capacity, a *hospitium*. The hospitality of axes, here, cannot be exalted into an act of conjoining, unless through the act of lodging each party on the basis of their regulations, ineptitudes and failures toward each other and in themselves – the hospitality associated with the foundation of lazar-houses or the erection of hostels as loathsome places of dejection and parsimony. If God and Man are incapable of fusing with each other outside of their affordability, and for that reason their oneness is eternalized through a shared vessel (*vehiculum*) which renders both subordinate to each other, they never fully overlap each other; though at the same time they do overlap on a bounding level. In other words, the affordance or mutual affordability between God and Man can only lead to unity (continuity in and of One, *un-us*) when the boundary of Man is afforded (economically affirmed) by God. In the wake of Franz Brentano[7] and later, more concretely, Roderick Chisholm's theories of coincidence, which propose 'if something continuous exists as a boundary, it must be in connection with other boundaries and it must pertain to a continuum of higher

---

7. Franz Brentano, *Philosophical Investigations on Space, Time and the Continuum*, trans. Barry Smith (Sydney: Croom Helm, 1988).

dimension',[8] the continuity of God and Man in a 'shared capacity' determines and marks out not only the boundary of Man, but also of God. Unity cartographically outlines the shared and coinciding boundaries of Man and God, the afforded boundary. In unification as culminating affordance, all possibilities – including the possibility of unity and the possibility of Man's deification – are molded

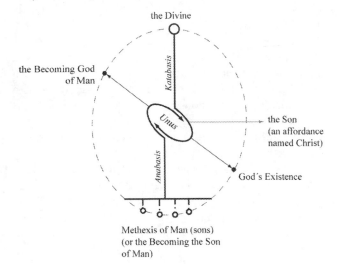

Diagram 2. Monad Mechanics

by the capacity and boundary of Man which necessitate a boundary for God as the continuity of Man's boundary in unity. The possibility of unity entails the possibility of a coincidence of boundaries in the congenial company of

8. R. Chisholm, *On Metaphysics* (Minneapolis: U. of Minnesota Press, 1989), 83-90.

Man and God.

Having ratiocinated the threefold of possibility, actualization and – *en passant* – meso-philic capacity, the investigation of Possibility and Impossibility for Man and God can be pursued by, and in conjunction with, Farabi's Islamic question of Active/Unfailing Impossibility.

For Farabi, Being and being united with God demarcate a passage that is trodden through the intersection of Latent/Passive Impossibility and Possibility (symbolised as A∩B), and whose boundaries are outlined by the 'symmetric' difference of Latent/Passive Impossibility and Possibility which is the union of both

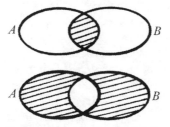

Diagram 3. Union and Symmetry in *Possest*
(After Nicolaus Cusanus' *De Possest*)

minus their intersection and can be symbolized as (A∪B)–(A∩B). Farabi refutes any manifestation of 'possibility of Being' in the existence of God, because possibility of Being is – with the same scale or *sun-metron* – symmetrically determined by the relative complements of A and B (symbolised as A–B and B–A) which maintain existence by exclusion and debarment of other parts (simultaneously full A and full B) (see Diagram 3).

COLLAPSE II

The Christian doctrine of Apocalypse and Return to God adheres to the model of Latent/Passive Impossibility; it is maintained that the Unity with God which is now impossible will eventually be afforded, and, as possible, will ensue. Affordance, or 'the openness to possess', is the *causa causans* of 'possibility (*posse*) to be able and actualized'. In the presence of affordance, possibility is assumed as the capacity (amplitude) or the containing possibility to do something. Possibility as affordability – in its economical receptivity and investment – exists prior to possibility as ontological potency. Parallel to, but entirely dissociated from, Latent Impossibility, it is the other impossibility (im-possess-ability) delineated by Farabi that designates the plane on which Allah pervades everything in Islam; it is Active or Unfailing Impossibility, which cannot be afforded under any circumstance. Hence it perpetuates and postulates itself outside of possibility and possess-ability – that is to say, potentiality for Being and being united. Farabi's Active Impossibility, which suggests itself as consistent and radical, equals radical externality. Allah's externality renders it im-possess-able; its active impossibility originates and reinforces its un-existence or im-possess-ability for all modes of existence. But at the same time this un-existence is not that of the *nihil*, since it is immanent to existence and all modes of being. Allah does not afford, but is the total openness which must be afforded, regulated, grounded and moderated in order to be transformed into modes of existence, into survival; otherwise, its active im-possess-ability would be the resolute terminus of all beings.

According to Islam, then, existence is the consequence of the prevailing impossibility of Allah, and Allah's absolute openness can only be afforded (that is, submitted to economical communication or the affordable passage from passive impossibility to possibility) but not radically communicated. Ontological modes of openness or 'openness bound to existence' cannot be absolute, since they would thereby transgress their existential necessity (first and foremost, they must survive and their openness is bound to their logic of survival). They merely afford this active impossibility and maintain their survival through its im-possess-ability, since possessing it in its entirety would be the undoing of affordance, and consequently of the survival that affordance makes possible and maintains. Absolute openness cannot be communicated, it can merely be afforded; and existence emerges out of this very lack of radical communication with the Absolute Openness (or in Islam, the impossibility or im-possess-ability of Allah) and its pathological symptom, affordability.

The revelational conclusion or the unitary apotheosis with God is defined as coming to union with God by participation, or participation in God through the Son. In this revelatory process, the aperture of man's epistemological focus in relation to the Divine must surpass his ontological isolation by means of a third capacity outside his own capacitance or the state of his capacity: an *extenta* whose boundary (or boundedness) ontologically shares and overlaps that of Man, and whose epistemic expanse (of unboundedness) intersects with the Divine. The mechanism of 'coming to Union' or unificatory disclosure of the Apocalypse (Revelation), while it is subjected to variations of either ontological or epistemological directions, constantly partakes of a fundamental revelatory process in a monadic or unitary sense: participation by the necessity of incompatible entities or parts and their ordained unity, *i.e.* difference, and adding a quality or amount (a content) to the difference to satisfy and fill it. This attributable content which takes form as *contentum* (the conjoiner) and *contentus* (the satisfier) cannot be anything. Precisely speaking, it should be – by the virtue of its satisfying function – determined and individuated by exclusion, or the logic of negativity, to locally fill and neutralize the effect but not the cause of the difference – that is to say, to be 'something specific' at last. This 'specific something' must share the contents of both the Divine and Man without transgressing their capacities or boundaries outlined by affordance, which actuates the coincidence of boundaries (*viz.* necessitating both the existence and coincidence of boundaries) between God and Man; it can be the groundwork of participation and affordance if and only if it is perpetuated by the sum exclusion of both sides – neither outside of X nor outside of Y. To this extent, this certain content reinvents the autonomy of participation in ostracism and repels the ephemerality of its existence by double-satisfaction. The Son is the ultimate *contentus* of Revelation and Unification, the double-satisfier of Platonic participation. If according to Hans Urs von Balthasar, transcendence to Christ manifests the apocalyptic consummation of History and Christ gives the world (the *exteriora* of the created world, the *interiora* of human essence and the *superiora* of heavenly order) its *Gestalt*, then both the configuration and consummation of the world (essence itself) exist only in affordance and economical participation through capacity.

Negarestani – Islamic Exotericism

We shall become Sons by participation (methexis)
(Cyril of Alexandria)
Totus Christus, Caput et Corpus

Four factors are involved in neo-Platonic and later Augustinian doctrines of *methexis* (participation): **(i)** The divine source of experience or the horizon (*horismos*: whose formation is characterized by an inner hegemonic boundary – *perata* – and an external boundlessness) of participation, which affects the spiritual senses of the human beings. Apart from this horizon there is no motivation for participation, since *methexis* presupposes the lack of an autonomy between participants, *i.e.* participants undergo *methexis* through their lack of autonomy and the hegemonic autonomy of the Divine. **(ii)** The *telos* of experience or the intention of the source, the purpose and goal for human being, which is unity with the Divine. *Methexis* presupposes myriad levels of being necessarily emanating from the Divine to unify later with the Divine as the ultimate One. **(iii)** The transformation brought about through experience which is based on the capacity/affordability between participants (*participans*) with each other, on the one hand, and the participant with the Whole or the *contentus* of participation (*participatum*), on the other. The persistent interference of capacity and affordance in participation, and in the reciprocal relation between participation and participants, imparts a self-correcting or gravitational quality to the collectivizing process of participation towards a satisfactory collectivity – thereby constraining in its collectivization dynamics – for the participants and the content of participation. This state of participation undertakes the together-ness of relationship as long as the capacity of nexus can be fulfilled; therefore, it operates as 'coming together (*com*) under a bound or an obligation (*munis*)'. This is an Obligation that can only exist as One (*unus*) because it is directed and achieved by and through capacity and affordance between entities in participation, or to be exact, by the collective affordance or the 'shared' capacity, the capacity shared by all as the sum affordability that can be fulfilled by all. For such an obligation, which can only survive and influence as a shared capacity, the plane of movement is necessarily one of convergence and concentration. Here, the participation dynamic inexorably describes a transition from *munis* (collective obligation) to *unus* (being one) in the wake of a collectivity (*com*) which perpetuates itself through affordance (see Diagram 4). This is why, in the New Testament, discussions and references to participation are mostly expressed in terms of *koinonia* (in its Platonic sense) which signifies sharing, and suggests an obsession with economic fixation, rather than *Methexis* (participation). **(iv)** The affective states that accompany the experience of participation are already modulated by the affordance between participants and the Whole, and the hegemonic autonomy of the Divine, which imposes unity with itself upon all modes of participation – *methexis*.

The Christian apotheosis promises a final unity with the God through a transcendental participation or *methexis* (or what Theodore Runyon calls Orthopathy)[9] – with the Son (as an indispensable intermediary or channel-regime of this exchangeability, the double-binding chain of the Atonement, the double-satisfier) and the other sons (men)

9. Theodore Runyon, 'The Importance of Experience for Faith', in *Aldersgate Reconsidered* (Nashville: Abingdon Press, 1990), 93-108.

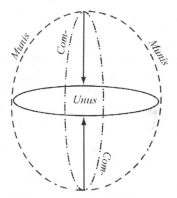

Com-: Coming together-ness of
parties from both ends

Diagram 4. Monad's Communication Dynamics

taking part in a process of concrescence (the theological
becoming grounded upon economic participation or
methexis) oriented towards unification with God. But Islam
openly rejects such a theologically relieving covenant. Man
can never be unified with Allah and Allah will never be
revealed to Man; the knowledge of Allah can be obtained
neither through the affirmative desire of *cataphasis* nor the
logic of negativity and emphatic negation of *apophasis*. In
more precise terms, in Islam, unity with the Divine is
eventuated neither on the ontological nor on the epistemological level. The son can never return to the father since
there is no son and no father; there is only Allah, external
to all beings and their surrounding outside *i.e.* the possibilities of their transgression. Because transgression is
conveyed on the plane of affordance and the dynamics of
'being open to', a tactical line of openness constrained by

the plane of logistics rather than the subjective line of command. This radical outsideness, however, is not prompted by the jealous impulsions of God, passed on to the victim(-ized) body of Man (a parasitic creed stubbornly energized and exploited by the exchangeability between *lex talionis* and victimology, their double-binding system carved on to the monopoly of God), but rather that immensity that is the undoing of Man, of all potential sons and the Father alike.

> While God was the exclusive source of the revelation to Muhammad, God himself is not the content of the revelation. Revelation in Islamic theology does not mean God disclosing himself. It is revelation from God, not revelation of God. God is remote. He is inscrutable and utterly inaccessible to human knowledge [...] Even though we are his creatures whose every breath is dependent upon him, it is not in interpersonal relationship with him that we receive guidance from him.[10]

Islamic Apocalypticism is not a contemplating process, a river (a flowing transcendence or a process of concrescence [A.N. Whitehead])[11] tending towards unification with God, as the complete state of its refinement. It is a process which seeks to ultimately and fundamentally

10. Edmund Perry, *The Gospel in Dispute: The Relation of the Christian Faith to other Missionary Religions* (New York: Doubleday, 1958), 155.

11. *Concrescence* emphasizes an economical participation through the theological doctrine of *Diaconate* which assembles a regulating all together; the itinerary of this process is continuously guaranteed by the responsibility of each entity to serve and survive for the other, becoming a passive negotiator-field to save the continuity of the self-refining flux. In such a participation (*methexis*), one cannot escape and still survive; the entities which cannot bear this dynamic but fully economical participation are automatically forced to leave the dynamic network of pseudo-flux (forced to be dumped out of the dynamic course of the flow).

'surrender' to the impossible which remains external to being (absolute surrender or pure *Islam*). Submission occurs according to the imperceptible Will (*Hoda*) of the im-*posse*-ible (Allah). Everything is preserved and maintained by a pure externality, not because of the power – ontological or epistemological sovereignty – it imposes upon being, but for the sake of externality itself – the radical outsideness that simultaneously provides the possibility of being, affordance and survival. The process of surrendering and submitting (or *Islam*) which leads Man towards God is suddenly disrupted by *Qiyamah* (*Ghiamat*) which is wrongly translated as Apocalypse. *Ghiamat* is a vast desert where Man finds that he can never reach (possess or afford) the Absolute or the Unconditioned (*unbedingt*). Here Man is totally disillusioned (one of the functions of *Ghiamat* is an awakening, in the sense, not of resurrection, but of disillusionment, *entebaah*) of everything he 'believes' himself to possess, and of existence as ontological corollary of affordance. Islamic Apocalypse occurs where (not when) Man grasps the utter externality of God to himself (an externality based on the radical outside-ness of function and an unaffordable openness of communication – rather than on a distance, which in the Islamic account of the divine is regarded as the utter glory and generosity of God to Man). Deleuze and Guattari[12] diagram the Absolute in terms of a movement qualitatively different to relative movements but necessarily associated to them. In Islamic Apocalypse all movements which give rise to the Absolute (and flow 'through' and 'as' Islam) abruptly cease to process (they cannot install Man

12. Gilles Deleuze, Félix Guattari, *A Thousand Plateaus: Capitalism and Schizophrenia*, trans. Brian Massumi (Minneapolis: University of Minnesota Press, 1987), 509.

as multiple or even One); the process of rendering a Unity by exception or subtraction fails before it is initiated. Before such an impossibility, the Deleuzian escapism to the Outside is an aesthetic movement based either on the idealism of reaching/possessing the Impossible (the active im-possess-able) or on becoming open to an absolute openness which can only be economically afforded and explored by the survivalist policy of 'being open to' and its escapist lines. This radical openness is so unrestricted that it turns all modes of openness ('being open to' in particular) and lines of escapism into a romantic struggle to tolerate it. However, every instance of toleration of this immense openness (even in the form of economical openness, escapism or 'being open to') results in a suffering which affordance and all economic regulations carry with themselves as the consequence of their restrictions and survivalist moderations. Economical openness (or escapism, which employs its dynamism on the plane of 'being open to' *i.e.* economical openness) as an instrument for moving towards Absolute Openness, operates in the form of an economic reformation of affordance and suffering. For such an economical openness relies on a movement or escape according to a subjective capacity – bound to the capacity of the Whole – which can crack at anytime, leading to a crisis of survival and toleration at different levels. This crisis or symptomatic side-effect associated with economical openness is both the result of the lack/capacity it must include in order to survive (regulation of communication) and of the radical openness which affordance cannot fully regulate and which, therefore, will eventually cut it (the subject of economical openness) open. Is escapism on the plane of 'being open' therefore a reformation of Atonement, its reinvention in another territory?

Escapism presupposes that openness all happens on the plane of 'being open to' (it excludes the radical side of openness or openness from the Outside *i.e.* 'being opened by'). The propulsive body of 'the line of flight' (Deleuze and Guattari) runs on this plane of openness to explore the Outside, or in other words, to be open to the Outside. Consequently escapism is involuntarily prone to unlimited appropriating functions and restrictions of capacity, since these maintain the openness for both the subject that escapes and the environment that affords and supports this escape – the capacity or affordance of the Whole. As the escape reaches critical levels in opposing the gravitational forces (territory, the State, organic life, *etc.*), its capacity for 'being open to' becomes a burden of tolerance and confinement (the limits of capacity) rather than a propulsive engine. To this extent, the over-tolerance for escaping becomes equal to suffering (*thlipsis megale*) for salvation. When it comes to the exigency of capacity, a scintilla of openness on the plane of 'being open to' – which is always oriented in opposition to the function of gravity but is aligned with affordance – can be likened to a tribulation whose conclusion (salvation) is not liberation from capacity but arriving at, shifting to, a reformed capacity.

In Islam, Man does not reach the Absolute, nor does the Apocalypse manifest the Absolute. Unlike other apocalyptic revelations, Islamic Apocalypse is a disruption for a transcendental process towards an Absolute which is impossible; a cessation, manifesting neither a succession nor an interlude but an utter terminus for transcendental Absolutism. Islamic Apocalypse is a momentary process for dismantling all manifestations of Absolutism, only highlighting the absolute externality of God as the Imperceptible or irreducible exteriority – 'The secret of God is eternally ungraspable by Man'; the Quran does not speak about the concealment of a secret but of the utter inaccessibility of the radical externality of God. This latter always remains secret, not in the sense of a mystery [*muein*] whose accessibility varies between the initiated and the uninitiated and according to the epistemological tools at ones disposal, but in the sense of 'being ungraspable and unthinkable forever' for everyone. According to Islamic scholars, it is the limitless generosity of this externality that, despite its radicality, makes 'being' possible for Man by posing itself as refractory impossibility. Theology in general, particularly Christian theology, is vigorously involved with the act of giving or the biblical *didômi*, and the measure of this act is determined by the emphatic limit of the act of giving in the sense of the Divine which is Revelation, or the epistemological Gift. The Gift of Revelation – by the necessity of the aforementioned affordable structure of Revelation – abstains from excess and ceases to be radical in itself and in the act of donation. The principle of gift-economy consolidates around its compensability. When a gift is afforded by the receiver of the gift, it can also – potentially and by virtue of the capacity of the receiver who has already met the expense or level of the gift – be paid back or re-gifted at least with a gift of equal or lesser value. When the gift is Revelation or the ultimate giving and Man is the receiver, the potential re-gift is proportionally equal to the possibility and the existence of God (*Esse*) itself in Revelation. The radicality of the gift originates from its exorbitance (it is outside the cycle of exchangeability), the absence of any opportunity to counterbalance or compensate it, and its externality to satisfaction, hence reducibility to a content. In Islamic theology and according to explicit Quranic verses, the ultimate gift from Allah averts satisfaction and does not satisfy Man in terms of providing what the human deems enough (*satis*). Nor can it be exchanged or compensated. Allah's gift attests to the immensity of the ultimate act of giving: the ultimate gift is essentially external to possession and possessability. If Allah's gift were to satisfy, or position itself as exchangeable, it would bring human being to extinction, an epistemological inferno and an ontological eradication; the gift then would contradict the act of giving and its giftness by becoming the act of absolute seizure or abolishment in the name of confiscation. The gift is merely the disclosure (in terms of unfolding) of Allah's externality on a radical and all-encompassing level, the affirmation of refractory impossibility and the repudiation of the possibility of an *apocalyptio* (unveiling) of a content, whether of God or of Man, which again should be differentiated from the content of the Divine in the usual understanding of Apocalypse. Disillusionment is the function and realization of such a gift. Islamic *Ghiamat* manifests enlightenment under the holocaustic luminosity of radical outside, and presents human possibility, of both ontological and epistemological potentialities, in the wake of refractory impossibility.

To this extent the monotheistic belief – *hena theon, unum deum* – does not describe a rewarding destiny in Islam; it submits the *cogito* to an externality for which belief is at the same time a plethora of uselessness and a minimally organized line necessary for attaching to the eradication of itself as it blindly pursues the eternal Unrevealable. Islamic Apocalypse is an anti-absolute politics. God is the only Unconditioned; it is neither grasped nor unveiled and thus cannot 'come into being' transcendentally; it is eternally external to Man, it is the Absolute as the desert of un-restriction (*ab-solvere*) for which Man or ontological potency is a restriction, a *modus* and a deterrent. Upon such an unfathomable externality, Man is left deserted; yet he is not abandoned, for this externality is mapped as an extra-proximity, utter and ungraspable closeness ('We are closer to him than his jugular vein' – thus the Quran). This is a panorama similar to the Survival Economy (*libban*, of Germanic origin) or what is commonly called life but is the territory of living (afforded Life or the process of affording life) and (un)Life, or life in its externality to affordability. Life is external to survival yet survival is allowed to live by means of the very 'possibility of containing' – or capacity – that Life makes accessible for it (either for the eradication of survival or in order to lure it elsewhere). What is given to Man is precisely what unlives for him. According to Islam, Man is liberated in *Ghiamat* not by joining the divine but through a disillusionment from his own being, a disillusionment made possible by the externality of God not the quiddity of this externality (*i.e.* the *Wesen* of God). *Behold the Outside, you shall not explore it*! For such an openness comes forth as a reactionary extinction by and through being, an inevitable self-destructive repercussion triggered by the affordance of capacity. But its unfathomability can be grasped; this indeed is the way that 'Return to God' is depicted in Islam. According to Islamic commentators, *Ghiamat* (the Insurgency) – which, again, is wrongly translated as Apocalypse (the moment of uncovering or revelation, *apocalyptio*) since even in *Ghiamat*, Allah is ungraspable and unrevealed to Man – promises a simultaneously brutal and glorious encounter of Man with what is radically external yet closest to him; awakening this externality for Man and awakening Man to grasp the radicality of this externality – the Unrevealable, the irreducible, full-fledged horror.

Revelation is extruded from the dynamic vector of a 'loving to know the unknown' as Augustine suggests, but not a loving of the unknown itself. In Islam, however, the Unknown itself is venerated in its full externality to the *cogito* and to love. Reverence then is influenced by an *outsiding* glory (radicality of outsideness) as an affect passing and emerging through existence, not in the sense of an advent or arrival from an outside which affords a tendency, that is to say, a constraining extension, but as a perpetual foreigner. Advent can only be registered as an event when it is fulfilled or reaches its tendency, a status where its foreignness ends (arrives at an orientation). Anything that has the quality and movement of an advent is bounded by a condition and a destination corresponding to that condition; its outside-ness is only provisional. To approach an unattainable without anticipation of reaching it and in the absence of a destination as a position to be possessed, the movement and its affect must be inherently upheld in relation to *xenos*, as a resident but ceaseless outsider (*xeno*) – insistent alien.

When the Unknown is unknown because of its radical externality, not because it is superior to human knowledge[13] – a position which can be afforded if not communicated or fully identified in itself – epistemological disciplines, in the same vein, unfold as alien tools. For such an unknown imbued with refractory impossibility, mysticism or contemplative theology proves itself to be not only otiose but a romantic project, a symptom of the loss of hope in a rigorous encounter with radical externality. If mysticism culminates in the form of an epistemological salvation or deliverance through initiation, its principles are constantly refuted by refractory impossibility, as simultaneously pusillanimous and irrelevant exploitations of ignorance on behalf of a redeeming unknown.

> 'Apocalypse' is a genre of revelatory literature with a narrative framework, in which a revelation is mediated by an otherworldly being to a human recipient, disclosing a transcendent reality which is both temporal, insofar as it envisages eschatological salvation and spatial insofar as it involves another, supernatural world.[14]

13. The latter is exemplified by the theologies of Augustine or Aquinas. ('*In finem nostrae cognitionis Deum tamquam ignotum cognoscimus*' [Thomas Aquinas, *Boetium de Trinitate*]). Following Aquinas who did not pursue the heretical trail of his remark and did not travel to the outer limits of his theology, one comes to this conclusion about the Divine as the *superiora* of knowledge: that 'God exists as ignorance'. This does not denote that God is ignorant or is ignorance in itself but that God existentially registers itself in human knowledge as Supreme Ignorance. Therefore, the true existence of God as the ultimate knowledge (immutable wisdom and knowledge in its full presence) is dependent on human knowledge or real ignorance as something capable of being transcended, if the God's true face is to be unveiled (namely, 'God as ignorance' realized as 'impeccable knowledge').

14. John J. Collins, 'Introduction: Towards the Morphology of a Genre,' in *Apocalypse: The Morphology of a Genre*, ed. John J. Collins (*Semeia* 14, 1979), 9.

Schelling's obsession with Revelation (*Philosophy of Mythology*, *Philosophy of Revelation*) which re-presents the Judaeo-Christian account of Revelation and is a pivotal *quodlibet* in non-Islamic monotheistic religions, is rendered completely obsolete in the Islamic account of Apocalypse (*Ghiamat*) and is regarded as heresy. It is described by Schelling as 'that which exists [...] only in order to see if I can get from it to the divinity'. Such a statement is based on the primal prophetic promise of Revelation, the promise that the divinity must be eventually revealed or exposed to Man through transcendence and its anabatic movements. The true glory of the lord is exposed to Man when it is revealed ['God can be known' (John 1:18; 14:7; 17:3,6)]. In Islamic Apocalypticism, such a promise is absent and is regarded as *Kufr* (apostasy). Motahari, the Iranian Islamic scholar, once suggested that the glory of Allah bursts forth at the exact moment when Man realizes that nothing of Allah can be revealed to him. According to Islam, in such a moment one encounters the utter mercifulness of God, for if God reveals itself, all modes of survival and being would be rendered impossible. If God were to reveal itself, everything would be overkilled. According to Islam, the most merciful moment (supreme glory) is the moment when Allah shows Man that despite its utter externality to all beings, they exist precisely by virtue of this externality. Allah's radical supremacy is delineated more according to its degree and radicalness of externality and openness than to its authority over being (According to Islamic literature, Allah does not need to enforce authority; authority is the consequence of this externality which maintains the survival of all beings for if Allah reveals itself, the undoing of Man will be inevitable).

On the topic of external sovereignty, Islamic scholars pose the question: if God is external and sovereign, then how can beings exist? This question is answered by recourse to an ungraspable generosity (not forgiveness) and Glory (both of which are purged of any quality) which surge up through beings as the only reason for their existence. Even the purpose of this Mercy and Glory will remain unknown, Outside: nothing of God itself will be revealed. With the consequence that applying the term Revelation (*apokalypto*) to the Islamic account of Apocalypse is highly problematic. Even on a technical level, Apocalypse, constitutive as it is of monotheism, is not designed for or capable of the particular functions that it presents in other monotheistic threads in the Last Day. *Ghiamat* (or *Qiyamah*), whilst it includes the diametric discourse of the Judgment Day and its monopoly on inevitability, as Al Faruqi points out, also adds a new and radical twist to the Apocalyptic politics common to all strands of monotheism; *Ghiamat* does not mean *apokalupsis* (involving the process of lifting the veil). Rather, it heralds *Ghiam* or rebellion, which is connected to *Sura Al-Takvir* (overthrowing). The Quran depicts *Ghiamat* – Ultimate Insurgency – as being governed not by a climax-oriented narrative, based on the consumption or depletion of the number of its possibilities, but on a series of participations, a chain of minor insurgencies (*ghiams*) which bring with them possibilities external to the capacity of the narrative.

Al Faruqi and Alameh Tabatabai both suggest that the Quran wholly withdraws from the diametric concealing/disclosing revelation of other monotheistic

Books, from the opening verse through to the end. It declares itself as an active cipher; it even shows a radical cynicism (or even hatred) for the facsimile by twisting the very foundations of monotheism as expressed in the Bible or Torah, progressively making itself unidentifiable, connecting what has already been told to anonymous (both in the sense of *an-onoma* and *a-nomos*) lines which make its contents accessible through an ulterior structure. This deviation from the familiar path culminates in the nomenclatural system usually associated with the Last Day; *Ghiamat* (Ultimate rebellion, Insurgency, Standing to respect, Awakening in the sense of disillusionment) becomes the substitute for all other names in Apocalyptic literatures which frequently suggest revelation (with *velum* at the center), resurrection or strict judgment (functioning through the dynamic scaling and measuring processes of *metron*).[15] The unity of the Advent Hope is frequently expressed by such phrases as 'the last days' and 'the end of the age'(Heb 9:26). Apocalyptic thought apparently arose within Judaism following the sixth century Babylonian exile of the Jewish people. Although the book of Daniel is the only complete example of an apocalypse in the Hebrew Bible, other passages contain ideas that are either apocalyptic or similar to apocalyptic thought – Examples

---

15. *Metron* (Greek origin), to be found etymologically encrypted in English words such as Dimension (from *dimetiri*: measure out), meter, etc. Keeping well in mind the famous doctrine of Protagoras, 'Man is the metron of everything' (*pantôn chrematôn metron anthrôpos*), *metron* can be translated as Scale, Measure, Standard, and Value. According to Sextus Empiricus *metron* expresses *criterium* (scale, measure) but Heraclitus and Sophocles saw it as certifying dominance, a domination over something. Therefore, *metron* indicates that both measure and dimension interconnect with Power, Justifying and Reasoning. The critique of *metron*, then, diagrams how dimensions (namely *metron*) bring Power into effect, mobilizing and propagating it.

would include Zechariah 9-14, Ezekiel 38-39, and Isaiah 24-27.

In Islam, and particularly in Sunni accounts of Islamic theology, examples of revelatory apocalypse and even seeing Allah in *Ghiamat* can be found (Abu Hurairah, Al Bukhari, Al Hajjaj, *et al*). However, most of these apocalyptic attributes originated from Hadiths – and hence had been subject to alteration, hadiths having being collected in different times and by different narrators. Their authenticity being thus questionable, they could not maintain a lasting presence in Islamic theology and Islamic accounts of *Ghiamat*. Not only because of their disputable origin (as in the case of Abu Hurairah for example), but also because of their contradiction of the emphatic statements in the Quran regarding *Ghiamat* and absence of revelation, in Islam apocalyptic theology (in the sense of revelation and epistemological or ontological unity with God) did not succeed in extending its influence beyond classical and early Islamic theology. In Islam, explicit reference (*nas-e sarih*) to the Quran is prior to everything and must not be transgressed. Cultivated by the Al-Azhar School's rigor and animated by such figures like Mahmood Shaltoot who inveighed against the classic theologians who advocated apocalyptic eschatology of Judeo-Christianity and worked mainly outside sectarian doctrine, the revelational doctrines were denigrated in Islamic theology.

16. *Apokrisis* or *ekkrisis*, the Anaximanderian universal pro-creationist process of separation which is a prerequisite for unification and ultimate union. The process of *Apokrisis* stratifies the universe into properly arranged layers (unlimited appropriation and regulation by lamination and stratification) which make unification as a dynamic process possible. This process of separation is prerequisite for the cosmic union/separation machinery of the ultimate unification, or in other words, the final union which functionally presupposes a series of separations and unifications leading

The externality of Allah cannot be oversimplified into a mere process of separation (*ekkrisis*).[16] Aristotelian philosophy shows us that separation always presupposes a unity through a cyclic transcendence of separations (of *chorismos*) and unions (of *to hen*) which rotates – or in more technical terms, refines itself – towards a distilled Quiteness or Unity with the Divine, a unity which is not present in Islam. Moreover, unlike other modes of monotheism, for Islam this externality is not the result of a primal moral collapse or original sin (the Revelation system of Christian redemptive history influenced primarily by Tertullian [ca.155-220]); it is intrinsic to the existence of being. Neither does this externality have anything to do with sinfulness or the concupiscent nature of Man – who in Judaeo-Christianity must be cleansed, introduced to *katharos* – since in Islam the present condition of Man is not sinful but normal; in the Islamic account, sin emerges only as a consequence of the mis-perception of this externality, as a result of latching on to the quiddity of this externality, Allah.

Islam does not construct itself on redemption and/or revelation. Redemption (the wayfarer becomes totally at one with God's way of redemption) is inseparable from its consequent hope and boredom or redeeming despair, and modes of development which are steered by the conjunctive bonds between these two. The promise of

to a purely distilled Unity (corresponding to the classic distilling mechanism). Anaximenes, however, developed the process of *ekkrisis* into the two processes of rarefaction (corresponding to separation) and condensation (corresponding to unification); we can follow these processes in the unificatory and distilling mechanism of Kerotakis (reflux condenser) which was invented and designed according to the cosmogonic traditions of alchemy and Aristotelian philosophy. On *Apokrisis*, see Theophrastus commentaries on Anaximander; also, Hippolytus' *Refutation*.

Revelation presupposes a reward for a vigorous transcendentalism through the loss of sin and the accomplishment of unity with God – or more precisely, the reformation of affordance, and the capacity of Man to turn the (latent) impossibility of the Unity with God into a possessable possibility. In Islam there is no such reward, no such promise; there is only the inexhaustible activeness of refractory impossibility or Absolute Openness, crushing affordance and the economic regulations of capacity, disillusioning Man from his repressive openness *qua* economical self- and environment-protecting communication. Externality is diagrammed by a simultaneous formidable closeness and externality of function, a concretization of 'closer to you than your jugular vein' (what a vampiristic horror!)

IN ISLAM, CHRONOLOGICS IS A HERESY.

> The individual's encounter through faith and grace with a personal God then salvation is contained precisely in the human surrender to God (*Islam* [Submission]) and that divine guidance (*huda*) which according to the Koran remains or should remain forever unaltered by time and history. Accordingly, there is no reason to conceive of revelation as something temporal or historical.[17]

Norman Brown is right to suggest that Islam is thoroughly apocalyptic but without a sense of 'Time' that could be grounded as the ordinance and understructure of the spectacles of Grand History (whether *Heilsgeschichte* or

17. Abdoldjavad Falaturi, 'Experience of Time and History in Islam,' in Annemarie Schimmel & Abdoldjavad Falaturi (eds.) *We Believe in One God* (London: Burns and Oates, 1979), 65.

Weltgeschichte). 'Only the moment is real,' Brown notes,[18] but goes no further. The moment is transient, its function is traced by its escapability, momentary variation and particle frequency, by its *gradus sine vestigio*; the moment in its entirety is an *uncogito* with a pulsatory intermittent existence, ungraspable by Man and inaccessible by mapped courses of action. All that is graspable are the moment's trajectories, its tails which complicate and diagram time according to their spatial multiplicity, rather than the chronologics of Time. Too many traces left by the ever-escaping moment result in the loss of time, 'untraceability of all narrative lines and temporal relations'[19] (= The Islamic Apocalypse, *Ghiamat*), the fall of the Kingdom – the emergence of a sinister imminence constructed not upon temporal relations or modes, but upon the loss of them. Such a constant imminence surpasses necrocratic terror: when Omega is always imminent and one cannot look backwards and ask what happened, the necrocratic fear of death – powered by anticipation of the future as well as the questioning of the distance to the Outside – is but a neutralized repression.

Time is absent in the Quran; the absence of any occurrence of the word *Zamaan* (Time: *chronos*) is one of its most noted enigmas. Instead of using the word *Zamaan*, the Quran frequently addresses events through the word *vaght*, conveying them through *vaght* and not *zamaan* towards *Ghiamat*. *Vaght* is concerned with 'Whereness'

18. N. O. Brown, *Apocalypse And/or Metamorphosis* (Berkeley: University of California Press, 1992).

19. Norman Brown writes, 'the Quran breaks decisively with that alliance between the prophetic tradition and materialistic historicism – "what actually happened" – which set in with the materialistically historical triumph of Christianity.' (*Ibid.*)

whilst also obscuring the quiddity of this whereness as spatial but unlocalizable ubiquity; it can only suggest an unchronological Now (neither permanence nor discontinuity; all entities are regarded as events through a denuded space with no chronologic dominance), a 'timeless where' through which beings are suspended but not stopped. But 'Where is Now?' The Quran never answers. 'Now' always remains anonymous; its ever-expanding Where which is essentially based on its whereness (the quality of its spatial continuity), is ceaselessly contagious. For whereness engineers terrains to remain ubiquitous and be actively divergent, a multiplicity which is a manifest epidemicity. Where is intrinsically and autonomously contagious. All manifestations of history (or even histories) are regarded as an infidelity towards this spatial and contagious Now (*vaght*) which is the most functional plane for utter submission (*Islam*) to the eternal externality of Allah, the pervading or epidemic impossibility. *Now* is the only plane on which Being can be saved from complete extinction by its illusions, which foam around its grand obsession with unity. Abdoldjawad Falaturi is possibly the first Islamic commentator who has rigorously worked on *vaght* in the Quran and on the Islamic sense of time (See his *Experience of Time and History in Islam*, and other essays).

In the sense of *Ghiamat*, is it too early or too late? Only by your 'participation' with this spatial Now (*vaght*), can you find out. We are always in a premature *Ghiamat*.

Islamic imminence escapes the doctrine of the Advent and the Christian Imminence. 'The great day of the Lord is near and hastening fast'(Zephaniah 1:14); 'O Sovereign

Lord, holy and true, how long before thou wilt judge and avenge our blood?'(Rev 6:10): such Nearness or Distance is at the heart of the Christian imminence, architectonically constructed on Waiting and Patience ('Be patient' [James 5:8-9], James admonishes believers). The affordable *esse* of the Christian God posits the Outside in terms of distance or opening-between (an openness that is situated in-between is affordance rather than openness). Distance and affordance realize movement only in the anticipation of reaching a destination, even if the destination is not accessible and only exists as an affordable event or entity. In terms of economical openness, what is afforded has already been achieved with the same scale of possibility and actuality. If distance potentiates destination, and destination actualizes distance, a movement that either travels according to the distance or according to and towards the destination would remain passive in its dynamism, because it would have already been presupposed by affordance. Such a movement, one whose course has already been afforded, does not undertake the risks of venture, instead it accepts the consequences of anticipation (immanent to distance and the afforded movement). Here opens a horizon of passivity as the inexorable glorification of patience and chronological toleration organized by the promise of Revelation, as a moral urgency of the Advent and Revelational Hope. Or, to be exact, this nearness of the Christian Imminence is articulated by the passivity of waiting and patience as the consequences of anticipation, whose endemic affliction is expectation, which in turn provokes hope and negative despair and gives rise to crises of faith (as for the first century Christians who expected the grand return of Christ: "'My master is delayed," the unfaithful servant complains'[Matt 24:48]). And it is through this prolonging of hope and persistence as to the affordability of openness (of both Man and God to each other), that faith is manipulatively maintained. To this extent, the distance (wait, patience, nearness, expectation) of Christian imminence can be *metron*ed (measured) either by Empirical or Existential Time. But Islamic imminence, spread over the epidemic Now, has no such bond to expectation, patience or waiting, and it cannot be measured since it is entirely based on furious participations (voluntary and involuntary, triggered by total openness fueled by a refractory impossibility that cracks affordance *ab intera, ab extra*) moved by the loss of the promise of the Revelation and the eternal externality of Allah.

If Islam's process of submission affirms the radical externality of Allah as a refractory impossibility, and if Islamic Apocalypse supposes the loss of time, then for Christianity, Islam expands and inflames along the same chronopolitical dimension in which the Apocalypse deploys its cremating and concluding machinery, incinerating the western sense of time, cleaving the bonds between modes of historicity and western chronologics; a plane along which chronologics shrinks to momentary particles taking viral and swarming forms to spread through this spatial Now (or irrevocable imminence). Islamic *Ghiamat* is the vertigo of moments. For Christian chronologics, Islamic chronopolitics is that 'radical disruption in the spatio-temporal relevancy of events' which is generally called the Apocalypse. If War on Terror, on its western front, is haunted not by *fin de siècle* scenarios but also by the political manifestations of the Apocalypse and emphatic finality, it is because western chronologics has engaged an opponent which only exists as a desert levelled of all idols or transcendental abominations to Allah. It is the desert that hosts, and looms as, the Apocalypse. It is a desert lurking in the disruption of chronologics, the corrosion of history and the collapse of the spatio-temporal continuity to the outside, because it is effectuated by refractory impossibility, not the other way around. This is not a question of a clash between civilizations but a radical Time-war, between chronologics and chronopolitics or what – by virtue of its dynamism, that is affected by the Outside and Impossibility – operates as Apocalypse or time-disruptive politics within other systems. Each Western tactical line in War on Terror must inevitably configure its program with reference to Islamic chronopolitics if it seeks to engage and afford the 'conflict principles' (correspondence with other war machines in space and time) which every war machine both upsets and affirms. If, on the Islamic front, the *Ghiamat*-apocalypse is always already-there and the entities of the *pax islamica* are already desert-nomads of this contagious Now, for the most part (but not entirely) it is the Western entities of War on Terror which are subjected to apocalyptic commotions and disruptions in time. While the Western chronosphere harbours a chronological cataclysm for the Islamic front, Islam's chronopolitics betrays time and the Western chronosphere altogether.

Notes on Contributors

RAY BRASSIER
Research Fellow at the Centre for Research in Modern European Philosophy at Middlesex University, UK. Translator of Alain Badiou's *Saint Paul* (California: Stanford University Press, 2003) and Editor/Translator of Badiou's *Theoretical Writings* (with Alberto Toscano, London/NY: Continuum 2004). Author of *Nihil Unbound: Enlightenment and Extinction* (Basingstoke: Palgrave Macmillan, forthcoming 2007).

QUENTIN MEILLASSOUX
A graduate in philosophy from the École Normale Superieur, Quentin Meillassoux wrote his doctoral thesis on *The Divine Inexistence: An Essay on the Virtual God*. Has been teaching philosophy at the ENS since 1997. Author of *Après la finitude: Essai sur la nécessité de la contingence* (Paris: Seuil 2006; English translation *After Finitude* [trans. R. Brassier] London: Continuum, forthcoming 2008).

ROBERTO TROTTA
Lockyer Research Fellow of the Royal Astronomical Society at the Astrophysics Department of Oxford University, Junior Research Fellow at St Anne's College, Oxford and coordinator of the Oxford Dark Sector Initiative. Publications include 'Cosmological Bayesian Model Selection' in L. Lyons & M. Unel, (eds.), *Statistical Problems in Particle Physics, Astrophysics and Cosmology*. (London: Imperial College Press, 2006), 'What's the Trouble with

Anthropic Reasoning' (with G.D. Starkman) (http://arxiv.org/abs/astro-ph/0610330), and 'Probing Dark Energy with Future Surveys' (http://arxiv.org/abs/astro-ph/0607496).

GRAHAM HARMAN

Professor of philosophy at the American University in Cairo, Egypt. Author of *Tool-Being: Heidegger and the Metaphysics of Objects* (Chicago: Open Court, 2002), *Guerrilla Metaphysics: Phenomenology and the Carpentry of Things* (Chicago: Open Court, 2005), and *Heidegger Explained: From Phenomenon to Thing* (Chicago: Open Court, forthcoming 2007).

PAUL CHURCHLAND

One of the most influential figures in contemporary philosophy of mind and neurophilosophy, Churchland is Professor at the University of California at San Diego. Amongst his publications are: *A Neurocomputational Perspective* (Camb., Mass: The MIT Press, 1989), *Matter and Consciousness* (Cambridge, Mass.: MIT Press 1998), and *Neurophilosophy at Work* (Cambridge: Cambridge University Press, forthcoming 2007).

CLÉMENTINE DUZER

Director and screenwriter, graduated in literature and film theory (EHESS, Paris). Directed the shorts *Les Travaux*, *Requiem*, and, with Laura Gozlan, *Nevertheless Empire*. For TV, co-directed *Pigalle* with Asa Mader, featuring Lou Doillon. Currently a writer and producer for Soundwalk in New York, and preparing her next film *La Demeure d'Asmodée*.

COLLAPSE II

LAURA GOZLAN
Graduated from ENSAD Art Academy, Paris. Her first short *The Soft Machine* was awarded at the Zebra Poetry Film Festival in Berlin. Co-author of *Nevertheless Empire* with Clementine Duzer, she directed her third short, *The Abduction of the Staircase*, at the National Studio Le Fresnoy, where she is currently developing a new project entitled *Quando corpus morietur*.

KRISTEN ALVANSON
An American artist living and working in the Middle East, Alvanson has been published in John Russell's anthology *Frozen Tears 3*. She is currently working on an artistic exploration of desire and a book entitled *Lessons in Schizophrenia*.

REZA NEGARESTANI
Philosopher working in Shiraz, Iran. Author of *Cyclonopedia: Complicity with Anonymous Materials* (NY: Creation Books, forthcoming 2007)

Translation of 'Potentiality and Virtuality' by Robin Mackay. Interview with Roberto Trotta conducted in Oxford by Robin Mackay and Damian Veal. Interview with Paul Churchland conducted in San Diego by Sophia Efstathiou. Accompanying images to 'On Vicarious Causation' by Robin Mackay.

Printed in the United States
by Baker & Taylor Publisher Services